ROUSSEAU AND THE PROBLEM OF HUMAN RELATIONS

Rousseau and the Problem of Human Relations

JOHN M. WARNER

The Pennsylvania State University Press | University Park, Pennsylvania

Chapter 4 is also being published as John Warner, "Men, Citizens, and the Women Who Love Them: Eros and Tragedy in Rousseau's *Emile*," *History of Political Thought* 36, no. 3 (forthcoming).

Chapter 6 was previously published as John Warner, "Bad Education: Pity, Moral Learning, and the Limits of Rousseauan Friendship," *Review of Politics* 76, no. 2 (2014): 243–66.

Library of Congress Cataloging-in-Publication Data

Warner, John M. (John Martin), 1978– , author.
 Rousseau and the problem of human relations / John M. Warner.
  pages cm
Summary: "Investigates the psychological foundations of human sociability as they are treated in the work of Jean-Jacques Rousseau. Argues that Rousseau provides a pessimistic, or tragic, teaching concerning the nature and scope of human connectedness"—Provided by publisher.
Includes bibliographical references and index.
ISBN 978-0-271-07100-8 (cloth : alk. paper)
ISBN 978-0-271-07101-5 (pbk. : alk. paper)
1. Rousseau, Jean-Jacques, 1712–1778.
2. Rousseau, Jean-Jacques, 1712–1778—Political and social views.
3. Interpersonal relations.
I. Title.

B2137.W37 2015
194—dc23
2015029441

Copyright © 2015
The Pennsylvania State University
All rights reserved
Printed in the United States of America
Published by
The Pennsylvania State University Press,
University Park, PA 16802-1003

The Pennsylvania State University Press is a member of the Association of American University Presses.

It is the policy of The Pennsylvania State University Press to use acid-free paper. Publications on uncoated stock satisfy the minimum requirements of American National Standard for Information Sciences—Permanence of Paper for Printed Library Material, ANSI z39.48–1992.

To Byron and Cindy, my parents.

CONTENTS

Acknowledgments   ix
List of Abbreviations   xii

Prologue   1

1. Rousseau's Theory of Human Relations   5
2. Social Longing and Moral Perfection   33
3. Pity and Human Weakness   60
4. Romantic Love in *Emile*   87
5. Romantic Love in *Julie*   110
6. Friendship, Virtue, and Moral Authority   136
7. The Ecology of Justice   162
8. The Sociology of Wholeness   187

Epilogue   216

Notes   229
Bibliography   232
Index   238

ACKNOWLEDGMENTS

This project began in earnest in the summer of 1997 when I, a painfully earnest undergraduate who had just discovered ideas, began reading Rousseau's *Discourse on Inequality* at a coffee shop after an especially trying shift in the kitchen at a local restaurant. My wonderful undergraduate adviser, Larry Hall, had made me aware of Rousseau's work but, as an avowed and unapologetic critic of his, had done nothing to encourage me to seek it out. But teachers truck almost exclusively in unanticipated consequences, and Dr. Hall's passionate dislike for *pauvre* Jean-Jacques had only spurred my curiosity. So, when my shift ended, I—in no mood either to go home to my parents or to go out with my coworkers—decided to browse a few titles at a bookshop. I fell upon the *Discourse on Inequality* and was compelled by the back cover's confident proclamation that it was "the most important and incisive" of Rousseau's works. Who was I to disagree with such impressive alliteration? The *Discourse* it was. I was off to search for what Dr. Hall had found so objectionable. I did not, however, succeed in finding it. In fact, I was absolutely rapt by Rousseau's reinterpretation of why people did what they did, and read the whole work that night. It goes without saying that I was utterly unable to follow the argument, and saw none of its genius—aside from a few scraps about language and some good digs at Hobbes, I understood nothing at all. But I did see that Rousseau had something new to tell me about myself, that he was challenging my self-understanding in a serious and radical way. I knew that I had to come to terms with that challenge and, indeed, with the author who had put it to me. This book is the latest and, I hope, best attempt to do that.

As Rousseau well knew, understanding oneself is a deeply and intrinsically social act, and in the course of writing this book I have been fortunate to be surrounded by astoundingly kind, generous, and intelligent people. I wish to single out my parents, Byron and Cindy, for their unwavering support. Their profound capacity for love continues to be an ongoing source of astonishment for me, and to dedicate this book to them, as I gladly do, is a most unsatisfactory token of my gratitude. I must also single out the efforts of John T. Scott, who was an exemplary adviser and remains an outstanding scholar and good friend. I can only repay him as St. Preux repays Bomston, his friend and better, which is to say that as I move forward I will always miss my time in the department at UC Davis. My friends Wes Camden, Andrea Rowntree, and Andrenna Taylor-Jones, and my siblings Joey and Anne, all lent much-needed and much-appreciated emotional support during this process and unwittingly provided me with fodder for the chapter on friendship. I am also exceedingly grateful for Andrea Dixon's love and support. They all deserve my thanks, and so much more, for their patience, humor, and unconditional love.

I also owe special thanks to a number of friends and colleagues who provided me with invaluable assistance as this project was conceived and developed. Thanks are due, first, to my editor Kendra Boileau and the staff at Penn State Press, and to Dennis Rasmussen and Joseph Reisert, who provided such generous and insightful manuscript reviews. I hope they will be pleased, or at least satisfied, when they see the changes I have made. The Jack Miller Center and the Henry Salvatori Center at Claremont-McKenna College provided me with generous assistance and wonderful community along the way, as did the political science department at UC Davis. A special note of thanks is due to my graduate school colleagues, and most especially Gail Pivetti, John Barry Ryan, Andrea Duwel, Michelle Schwarze, Chris Dawes, and Jim Zink. Their friendship was a privilege, and our community is something that I will spend the rest of my life trying to re-create. Robert Taylor and Christopher Kelly sat dutifully with John Scott on my dissertation committee and met dreadful chapter drafts with patience, insight, and generosity; Alex Kaufman supervised my master's thesis on Rousseau at the University of Georgia and provided helpful direction and feedback in that capacity. I also happily acknowledge my debt to my former teacher Larry Peterman, who was a constant source of both consolation and amusement and whom I will always remember fondly. I was especially lucky to be surrounded by a host of supportive and deeply dedicated teachers at Belmont

University, where I did my undergraduate work: Ginger Osborn, Mike Awalt, Ronnie Littlejohn, Mark Anderson, and the aforementioned Larry Hall all bore my eagerness with great patience and foresight. They also encouraged my interest in Rousseau without actually sharing it themselves, and were tireless and loving advocates for all their students while carrying crushing teaching loads. This book is hardly repayment for their efforts, but I suppose it's a start.

Finally, an earlier version of chapter 6 appeared in the *Review of Politics*, and an earlier version of chapter 4 is forthcoming in the *History of Political Thought*. I thank the publishers for their permission to reprint this material.

ABBREVIATIONS

C	*The Confessions*
CGP	*Considerations on the Government of Poland*
DI	*Discourse on Inequality*
DPE	*Discourse on Political Economy*
DSA	*Discourse on the Sciences and Arts*
E	*Emile*
ES	*Emile and Sophie*
GM	*Geneva Manuscript*
J	*La Nouvelle Heloise; or, Julie*
LD	*The Letter to D'Alembert on the Theater*
ML	*Moral Letters*
RSW	*The Reveries of the Solitary Walker*
SC	*The Social Contract*

Prologue

This is a study of human relations as they are treated in the work of Jean-Jacques Rousseau. It is animated by two very basic, but very important, questions: (1) what do we want out of our relationships? and (2) can we get what we are after? I think that if we can find good answers to these questions, we will have made some progress in understanding both ourselves and the social and political worlds we inhabit. And though I will leave to others the somewhat distasteful business of pleading for Rousseau's relevance to this or that contemporary problem, I think that his answers to these questions are well worth considering. In fact, I am increasingly persuaded that much of his considerable value as a thinker consists in the way he confronts, enriches, and problematizes these central matters: figuring out what it is we want when we turn to other people is no simple matter, and it is, in some sense, even less so after reading Rousseau. But his writings illuminate the hidden dimensions of these mysteries with an unsurpassed power and penetration, and have resonated so strongly with so many readers for so many years that it is difficult to dismiss Rousseau's analysis of social phenomena as the romantic fancy of an overheated imagination.

Given the importance of the questions guiding this book, it may be fairly wondered whether there is much left to say about them. Few authors are interrogated as frequently as

Rousseau is, and many, if perhaps not all, of the component parts of the argument presented here have been subjected to close, and repeated, scrutiny by other scholars. There are, for instance, many treatments of Rousseau's understanding of romantic love (e.g., Bloom 1993; Wingrove 2000), and many, many more on his theory of politics (too many, in fact, to cite here). There are some very fine books, and piles of articles, on *amour-propre* (e.g., Dent 1988; O'Hagan 1999; Rawls 2007; Neuhouser 2008), and even a bit of research on his conception of friendship (e.g., Reisert 2003). Yet this is, to my knowledge, the first comprehensive treatment of Rousseau's theory of human relations. That is to say, I know of no other study that presents a reasonably complete survey of the major forms of human association as they recur in Rousseau's work, along with a theory that explains both how they are connected and the extent to which they can satisfy the desires to which they give rise. This, then, is what the present volume proposes to do.

I happily grant that it was both a pleasure and a relief to find that this particular set of questions needed more attention, for after a long graduate career spent combing through vast archives of books and articles—pausing only to convince myself that there *must* be something more to say about Rousseau, and then pausing again to worry that there wasn't—it was a delight not only to find some space in the literature but also to find it precisely where I wanted it to be. The very questions I most wanted to ask of Rousseau, those that his oeuvre seemed to me to be so well-designed to illumine, had still not been put to him, or at least not in quite the way I thought appropriate. Eureka! My first real idea. Maybe I was right not to go to law school.

One other feature of the argument offered here deserves mention: its skeptical or "tragic" character. In my survey of romantic love, friendship, and the political or civil association, I shall be at pains to show how each form of association, whether considered individually or in sum, systematically fails to solve the problem of "dividedness" that I take to be located at the center of Rousseau's thought (Starobinski 1988). Rousseau's moral universe is a fragmented and unforgiving place—it is full of costly trade-offs, difficult choices, and frustrated expectations. The margin for error is razor thin, and people pay dearly for the mistakes they inevitably make. Considerations like these lead Rousseau, on my view, to conclude that social life necessarily prevents us from enjoying even a decent approximation of the unity—the feelings of oneness both within ourselves and with our environment—that we have by nature and that full satisfaction requires. This initial characterization of the argument is very broad, and perhaps too much so, but it is intended merely as a way of fixing ideas.

In emphasizing the skeptical tenor of Rousseau's social theory, I find myself both in and indebted to very distinguished company. I shall build in various ways on Judith Shklar's (1969) claim that Rousseau provides two incommensurable and unrealizable utopian visions, on Arthur Melzer's (1990, 151; 1983) belief that the coherence of Rousseau's thought cannot be comprehended unless its pessimistic and "hardheaded" character is understood, on Clifford Orwin's (1997a; 1997b) and Richard Boyd's (2004) concerns about the ethical limits of compassion, and on Scott Yenor's (2011) and Allan Bloom's (1993, 138) worries about the stability of romantic love. The "skeptical" dimension of the interpretation developed here is thus not sui generis. It is, however, far from orthodox and may be viewed as a corrective to any number of influential accounts of Rousseau that paint him, alternatively, as an illiberal Pollyanna (Talmon 1952; Nisbet 1943; Berlin 1990; Crocker 1995), a reasonable optimist looking to effect practical political reform (Rawls 2007; Cohen 2010), or a compatibilist whose domestic and political theories are interdependent aspects of a unified vision of the good life rather than separate, and incommensurable, alternatives (Strong 1994; Fermon 1997; Neuhouser 2008).

A brief word on the structure of argument may clarify its central claims. Chapter 1 is introductory: it explains the problematic at the center of the book, articulates the broad contours of Rousseau's solution to it, and more thoroughly situates my argument in the relevant literatures. Chapters 2 and 3 make up the first part of the argument proper. They are theoretical and psychological: in them I examine the psychic foundations of Rousseau's project, with the broad aim of showing both the possibility and indeed the necessity of the more ambitious social and political possibilities that Rousseau sought to establish. To this end I analyze the natural bases of human relations—sexual desire and pity—and show how they (1) enable and delimit specific forms of association like romantic love and friendship, (2) perform assignably different functions within the psychic economies of human beings, and (3) interact in such a way to help correct for each other's excesses and deficiencies. While sexual passion is the foundation for expansive moral longings, pity helps counteract the forms of antisocial anger that these longings can inspire by reminding us of our own limitations and imperfections. Likewise, we shall see that a moralized psychosexual energy constantly infuses human life with new meaning and fresh purposes, and thereby helps to offset the resignation and indifference to which an overactive sense of pity can lead. Thus our natural unity is preserved through the proper management of a dynamic *tension* between the developed forms of our social passions.

With this psychological model in tow, I go on to derive from it the specific forms of association—sexual love, friendship, and political association—that Rousseau treats in his oeuvre and to show how each of these associational forms fails to satisfy the requirements of wholeness and are therefore most properly seen as tragic. In chapter 4 my examination of human association proper begins with an analysis of *Emile* and how it discloses the tragic dynamics of sexual love. Chapter 5 pursues the same theme and shows the same dynamics at work in Rousseau's epistolary novel *La Nouvelle Heloise*. In chapter 6 I move on to consider the role of friendship in Rousseau's social theory and show it to be too anemic to satisfy our deepest social longings. The final two chapters turn to the political association and argue that Rousseau sought, through the creation of a "moral ecology," to re-create between citizen and state the same harmonious relation that obtains between natural man and his environment. They also argue that even this comprehensive reconstruction of the citizen-subject's surroundings cannot establish a stable harmony between man and his environment, for it cannot reconcile the demands of the private realm with those of the citizenship. The underlying problem in the just polity—as elsewhere—is the intransigence of natural, individuating self-love, which resists with overwhelming strength all efforts to recruit it for social and political purposes. Indeed, I take the insolubility of the problems posed by the stubborness of self-love to be perhaps the central theme of this book as a whole. Rousseau, for all his strong and persuasive criticisms of reductive modern materialism, was ultimately unable to overcome its limitations. But his ambitious failure—if it can be called a failure—is worth more to us than a modest success would have been, for his analysis of our condition both undermines our comfortable certainties while pointing to the limits of Rousseau's own critical act.

I   Rousseau's Theory of Human Relations

> Margaret greeted her lord with peculiar tenderness on the morrow. Mature as he was, she might yet be able to help him to the building of the rainbow bridge that should connect the prose in us with the passion. Without it we are meaningless fragments, half monks, half beasts, half connected arches that have never joined into a man. With it, love is born and alights on the highest curve, glowing against the grey, sober against the fire. . . . Only connect! That was the whole of her sermon. Only connect the prose and the passion, and both will be exalted, and human love will be seen at its height. Live in fragments no longer. Only connect, and the beast and the monk, robbed of the isolation that is life to either, will die.
>
> —E. M. FORSTER, *Howards End*

Humans are divided beings, and Margaret Schlegel knew it well. Every day she futilely sought to mend the cracks in her husband's brittle soul, to unite the poles that hemmed in his cramped existence, to harmonize those elements of life—reason and emotion, obligation and appetite, autonomy and attachment, self and society, "prose" and "passion"—that stubbornly resist harmonization. So long as polarities are experienced *as* polarities, so long as uncertainty and moral tension are not brought in the service of a unified purpose, human life is fated to be undefined, empty, flaccid, purposeless.

To be divided, then, is not to be confused about what to do in a moment, nor is it simply to struggle against one's desires in the quest for self-command. It is, rather, to be *truncated*. It is to lack the principles necessary for resolving internal turmoil and to have no understanding of why it would be necessary to struggle against oneself in the first place.

We can, perhaps, begin to better understand the longing for unity and where to look for its most complete satisfaction by noting that it was through her social relations that Margaret sought to "connect" the disparate parts of her personality. Her "sermon" makes the desire for reconciliation the most fundamental in the human soul, claiming that it is most fully realized not in disengaged contemplation or the continual satisfaction of vulgar bodily desire but rather in the social sentiment of "love." Indeed, for Margaret the surest sign of an integrated and thus fully human existence is the presence of a desire for meaningful social relations. In thinking thus she differs from both "the beast" and "the monk," not only because she craves reconciliation and they do not but also because she is able to enjoy meaningful social intercourse and they cannot. Both flee intimacy and seek refuge in "isolation," the latter because he hates his appetites and the former because he hates everything *but* his appetites. In so doing, however, they foreclose on the forms of self-development that are only available through social development; they truncate their own being in the quest to preserve it.

In bringing the themes of individual wholeness and social connectedness together, Forster gives fresh voice to a series of psychological and social concerns previously articulated by Jean-Jacques Rousseau. Rousseau, like Forster, held that the complex and mediated form of life ushered in by modernity had alienated man from his nature and diminished his capacity for social affection.[1] It had stifled the natural movements of sympathy, rewarded domineering selfishness, punished good faith, and crushed up in its iron gears all delicacy of feeling and elevation of soul. Intimacy had been sacrificed to regularization, fineness to mediocrity, spontaneity and sincere affection to efficiency and a superficial, mechanized politeness. The torch of progress so confidently borne by the partisans of Enlightenment had broken into a destructive wildfire that had incinerated rather than illumined the hidden springs of virtue and social feeling.

It is worth emphasizing that Rousseau's critique is not merely a condemnation of this or that form of social organization, but is, rather, a root-and-branch attack on the idea of social organization per se. It holds that the very conditions under which moral personality emerges are those under which it becomes divided against itself. Socialization itself had done profound violence to human nature by upsetting the natural harmony between desire and power, by punishing authenticity and rewarding dishonesty, by generating relationships of personal dependence and their attendant feelings of jealousy and hatred, and by introducing arbitrary forms of inequality. Love, friendship, and virtue—the consolations of sociability—are overwhelmed by the very conditions that bring them into existence. Thus civil society and its complex of destructive and alienating institutions look to be a garish facade tacked thoughtlessly up on "piles of quicksand" (*DI* 97), a constellation of alluring disappointments that bring the self into being only in order to corrupt it.[2] Insofar, then, as the divisions within the self are a necessary consequence of man's introduction into society, the social problem is insoluble and it becomes necessary to return to the forests and live with the bears.

Rousseau himself, however, dismisses this fatalistic conclusion as a deep misunderstanding of his intention for at least two reasons. First, he rejects the possibility of a return to the state of nature, strictly speaking. Human development is not retrograde; neither the individual nor the species can simply "go back" and recover the spontaneous and prediscursive unity of the state of nature. Second, even if such a return were possible it would be *undesirable*. It is important to remember Rousseau's claim that the pinnacle of human happiness was reached not in the asocial state of nature but rather in the primitive sociability of the "Golden Age," where the establishment of the nuclear family and the introduction of "conjugal and paternal love" were adequate compensations for the psychological disturbances introduced by the birth of *amour-propre* (*DI* 146–48). Consistent with this, Rousseau remarks in a different context that human being is so "elevated" and "ennobled" by the experience of settled social relations that, were abuses of social power not so likely, we should "bless . . . the moment" we exchanged the stupid animal contentment of the state of nature for the rich satisfactions and challenges of moral and social life (*SC* I.8, 56). Such remarks point toward a more constructive understanding of the social problem than the one initially sketched, for they suggest that though Rousseau believes the problem of human dividedness to have been introduced by social relations he also believes dividedness is not a *necessary* consequence of social relations. In fact, to the degree we wish to preserve our natural wholeness, the disease must become the cure; human association must heal the wounds it inflicts.

To this end, Rousseau sought to resolve the internal and external conflicts that beset us by revitalizing the associational context in which we come to understand ourselves. He did so by imbuing with new life relations grown arid, unrewarding, and exploitative. Modern political thought believed it could solve the social problem by appealing to the rational self-interest each individual had in respecting the interests and claims of others, but Rousseau argued that this appeal taught us to view one another not as beings possessed of moral dignity but rather as instruments of, or obstacles to, private desire. Modern men, grazing for a century on the antisocial fustian of Hobbes and Locke, had come to view their relations with one another in almost comically narrow terms and were increasingly eager to explain their social motivations in the reductive language of modern materialism. Rousseau viewed all this with great alarm and sought to remind readers of the deep and enduring satisfaction that might be attained through social intercourse. To this end, he wrote extensively of romance and friendship and their relationship to a good life. He painted vivid portraits of primitive peoples dancing under a tree, of lovers in the throes of a turbulent passion, of an omnipotent tutor's unceasing devotion, of friends sharing a morning in sublime silence, of citizens celebrating their solidarity in the public square, of a cuckolded husband's desperate rage.

The diversity of these images, to say nothing of the brilliant colors in which they are painted, provides a clue about the nature of Rousseau's social theory and about what he sought to accomplish through it. They point up a depth of longing and help bring into view a new and richer conception of human association that makes that depth comprehensible. Rousseau does not conceive of human relations merely as instruments of private purposes or as means to exogenously determined ends, for to do so presupposes we know what others are for us and what we want from them. He argues, to the contrary, that sociability is a cause rather than a consequence of desire—it does not merely satisfy preexisting needs but rather brings new needs into being. Social relations are therefore ends rather than means; they instantiate the very good they seek, satisfying the desires they bring into existence. To think of human association in instrumental terms is thus a mistake of the crudest and most life-denying kind, for it cannot explain the intrinsic benefits of social connectedness or the way in which the desire for such connectedness actually comes to be. In order to talk sensibly about the human good and its realization, it is necessary to understand how sociability affects both the substance and structure of human ends.

It is in light of the foregoing considerations that I put to Rousseau the following question: what may we hope for from our associations? Though such a question has clear perennial relevance and implicates a host of questions at the center of Rousseau's enterprise, it has never been directly asked of him. In quest of an answer I analyze the most prominent forms of human relations in Rousseau's oeuvre—romantic love, friendship, and civil or political connectedness—and seek to uncover the function of each in his broader project of preserving human beings in (some workable approximation of) their natural wholeness. The theme of human association provides, I think, an especially productive lens through which to view Rousseau's philosophical enterprise because it allows us to glimpse the radically critical as well as the radically redemptive elements of his social theory. He consistently portrays human relations as deeply problematic but also as deeply rewarding—as the source of our greatest disappointments and our highest joys. Insofar as getting our relationships "right" is a necessary condition for the restoration of psychic integrity, the question of what we may—indeed *must*—expect from our social life sits at the heart of Rousseau's writing.

Our focus on human relations, however, proves useful as a unifying theme for at least three additional reasons. First, it allows us to more clearly view the variety of ways the desire for recognition—what Rousseau called *amour-propre*—expresses itself. There are, of course, already a number of very fine treatments of this central passion (e.g., Dent 1988; Rawls 2007; Neuhouser 2008), but a surprisingly neglected feature of perhaps the most studied term in Rousseau's lexicon is that its demand for approval is necessarily situated in specific associational contexts. This neglect is unfortunate, for if the degree and kind of recognition we seek from others depends in large measure on the kind of relationship we have with them, then we cannot understand precisely what *amour-propre* wants until we understand the particular association in which it is embedded. Using discrete associational forms as units of analysis thus helps uncover meaningful variance that the aforementioned studies of *amour-propre* do not explore.

Second, it keeps us from following the common and, I think, somewhat misleading practice of privileging the political association over other forms of human connectedness. This kind of privileging, as I shall argue toward the end of this chapter, lacks a sound justification in Rousseau's own texts; in fact, it is driven more by the needs of interpreters than by the intentions of the author. Focusing on human relations provides greater traction in understanding where and how Rousseau's political philosophy fits into his thought as a whole by encouraging us to understand politics in terms of the broader problem of human association rather than vice versa. The approach taken here, far from attempting to bring Rousseau's teachings on love and friendship into the service of his political thought, instead views them as direct instantiations of the human good and, thus, at some remove from—and sitting in some tension with—the demands of political life.

Third, our focus on human relations helps clarify the specific function that each form of association has in the more general human quest to recover wholeness through connectedness. In so doing, it allows us to approach more productively the all-important question of realizability: to what extent *can* we actually achieve through our relations the wholeness we so crave? On this score, I argue that each associational type suffers from specific kinds of limitations that make that realization all but impossible. Rousseau writes about human relationships not only to show how they give rise to new and interesting psychic possibilities but also to show how such possibilities are ultimately frustrated. His final teaching on the question of human connectedness thus has a tragic character: even under the best possible circumstances, social relations—in whatever form—ultimately fail to satisfy the desires to which they give rise. Though consolations, even meaningful ones, do emerge from the process of socialization, the salient and even defining characteristic of man's life in society is his congenital weakness.

The arguments I shall make concerning both the relationship of the political association to its domestic counterparts and the pessimistic character of Rousseau's social theory owe much to Judith Shklar's pioneering *Men and Citizens* (1969), which powerfully evokes the pessimistic or tragic dimensions of Rousseau's thinking. Yet Shklar's portrayal itself relies on a somewhat reductive understanding of Rousseau's social vision, one that neglects the aspirational or perfectionistic drives that Rousseau finds in human nature and emphasizes, instead, the role of pity in order to highlight man's status as a victim. I, on the other hand, shall seek to understand Rousseau's pessimism about human relations in light of his ambitious and possibility-enhancing account of human desire—for to the degree that Rousseau is especially concerned to depict the sort of suffering that occurs when our highest and best aspirations are frustrated, we must move beyond Shklar's oversimple accounts of human desire and moral motivation and look more carefully at the expansive impulses that so intransigently resist satisfaction.

| The Integrative Impulse: Wholeness and Connectedness

Rousseau is on some level an unlikely subject for a study of human association. As a man, he was hardly a model of generosity or kindly social feeling, and even those who defended him conceded that he was irascible, unpredictable, and difficult. Accordingly, his social life was marked by acrimonious conflicts with figures as influential as Voltaire and as affable as David Hume (Zaretsky and Scott 2009). As a philosopher, he is commonly and not unreasonably seen as an apostle of solitude and a champion of individual freedom, but not as a theorist of human relations. His theoretical works exalt emotional independence and self-sufficiency, deny that human beings are naturally social, and insist the defining characteristic of good collective life is the absence of personal dependence. His autobiographical works tell the story of a social outcast who ultimately had to abandon society in order to recapture his natural goodness. What could such a seemingly unsocial person and individualistic philosopher possibly tell us about human connectedness?

Without denying Rousseau's personal peculiarities or his philosophical emphasis on themes of solitude and individual freedom, I submit not only that he has a theory of human relations but also that it deserves our serious attention and that its articulation was among his most important philosophical intentions. Indeed, it has such importance for Rousseau that we find him singing the glories of human connectedness not only in his political and novelistic works but also in the place where we might least expect to him to do so—an autobiographical work called *The Reveries of the Solitary Walker*. Written at the end of Rousseau's life and seemingly intended to reveal the happiness he found *outside* society, the *Reveries* wistfully evokes the shade of a now-absent social affection. Even when engaged in reverie—the most private of acts—Rousseau's mind inevitably turned toward his associational life, so much so, in fact, that the work's first and the final walks frame the entire text in terms of social relationships. He begins the *Reveries* by claiming his decision to quit society was not his own but rather was forced on him by others: "The most sociable and the most loving of humans has been proscribed from society by a unanimous agreement" (*RSW* 3). Rousseau would have happily remained with his fellows if they had allowed it. That he was *forced* to live at the margins of society indicates something about its choice-worthiness, as does his somewhat generous self-description (the "most sociable" and "most loving" of his species). For all civil society's corruption and hypocrisy, Rousseau never ceased to value the commitment to the activity of mutual perfection and the sentiments of love and sociability that it embodies. To give up on that commitment, as Rousseau did only after he was *forced* to do so by his fellows, is to give up on something important indeed.

Though the first walk concludes with Rousseau claiming to have found a tranquility in solitude that eluded him in society, the final walk gives us some reason to wonder about the truth of this claim. There, we find Rousseau confessing an ongoing need for social affection as well as revealing something about of the *kind* of affection he sought. His *promenade dernière* leads him back to Les Charmettes and his time with Mme de Warens, which he recalls with almost unqualified fondness. Only at this Edenic site, in the Oedipal embrace of his *chère maman*, could he "genuinely say that [he] had lived" and that he had done so "fully, without admixture and without obstacle" (*RSW* 89). Rousseau felt no opposition within or without: the lack of a need for pretenses with Mme de Warens or anyone else meant he could be his true self, and the lack of resistance from his environment meant he could show his natural benevolence "without obstacle." Life at Les Charmettes glided effortlessly along, as on a frictionless plane; the young Rousseau enjoyed fullness of social feeling without the trappings of social obligation. This was an existential limit point that may have never been surpassed, for Rousseau goes on to portray his philosophic life and the exile that followed it not as choiceworthy in its own right but rather as a kind of martyrdom he suffered for love of his mistress and maternal stand-in: he began his literary and philosophic career to find neither fame nor truth, but rather as a way of recompensing Mme de Warens for her generosity.[3] It was, then, his love of others that ultimately forced him from their midst. Philosophy itself was undertaken for non-philosophic reasons.

The disintegration of the boundaries between self and other that Rousseau ecstatically evokes at his *maison maternelle* is presented again in a revealing personal disclosure from the *Confessions*: "I am repeating myself. I know it; it is necessary. The first of my needs, the greatest, the strongest, the most inextinguishable, was entirely in my heart: it was the need for an intimate society and as intimate as it could be; it was above all for this that I needed a woman rather than a man, a lover rather than a friend. This peculiar need was such that the closest of union of two bodies could not even be enough for it: *I would have needed two souls in the same body*" (*C* 348; emphasis added). Rousseau again brings together the themes of unity and sociability, disclosing that his quest for comprehensive fulfillment—for a complete oneness with his surroundings—is felt most strongly as a social (and quasi-sexual) desire. The erotic longing for wholeness through connectedness that Rousseau evokes through the image of two souls inhabiting the same body is the first and most fundamental of his desires. It is not a compound passion that can be reduced into simpler or more fundamental elements, nor is it wanted because it might be useful in attaining some other and more basic good. Rousseau's characterization of his own desire is, rather, a clear and compelling statement about the character of the human good and how it is best realized. That which he sought was indivisible and intrinsic: self-transcendence is achieved via social interdependence, and social interdependence is achieved via self-transcendence. The themes of wholeness and connectedness are thus of a piece and must be understood together to be understood at all.

The desire to recapture natural unity through associational life is not restricted to Rousseau's autobiographical works and is poorly understood if it is thought to be the idiosyncratic private desire of a unique man. Indeed, Rousseau's diagnosis of alienation in *Emile* discloses that the entire species—humanity tout court—shares his need for deep emotional connection and suffers from its absence nearly as much as he does. We, Rousseau explains, are only halfway social: we are unable to rid ourselves of the lingering want of social connection but are equally unable to commit to its rigorous requirements. Our lives are therefore defined by a disproportion between what is good for us and what is expected of us: always "appearing to relate everything to others and never relating anything except to themselves alone," always "floating between his inclinations and his duties," always following a "composite impulse" that only reinforces our dissatisfaction, we die "without having been able to put ourselves in harmony with ourselves and without having been good either for ourselves or for others" (*E* 40–41). As in the *Reveries* and the *Confessions*, Rousseau links social interdependence to the restoration of psychological unity. However, this time he does so in a way that makes this reconciliation the aim of a broader social and political agenda rather than a personal desire. In order to restore ourselves to our original "harmony" we must find a way to remove the contradictions built into society's basic institutions, to neutralize the major sources of interpersonal division and social conflict. So long as we subsist in civil society, unity without is the essential condition of unity within.

| Rational Performances: Bourgeois Dividedness and the Crisis of Meaning

Rousseau's concern with halfway sociability and the dividedness that attends it is an extension of his critique of modern political thought and its restrictive conception of human relations. Rousseau's most important, though far from his only, interlocutors in this context were Thomas Hobbes and John Locke, both of whom sought to ameliorate the religious and political conflict that defined their century by restricting the aims of human community. The classical conception of political community handed down from Aristotle and his Christian heirs and assigns held that society was a partnership in virtue and a constitutive component of the human good. However, this conception had proven philosophically unsatisfactory as well as destructive in its practical effects. The religious persecution that had destabilized England and Europe as a whole revealed how unsuitable the traditional notion of political community was for modern times: far from inspiring feelings of fraternity or creating a brotherhood in Christ, it had instead loosed wild and sanguinary enthusiasms that undermined the sound functioning of society's basic institutions and turned God's children into enraged and bitter enemies.

Both Hobbes and Locke held that many of the disputes that had had such serious practical consequences were actually absurd on their face. The new science had exposed serious flaws in the teleological conceptions on which traditional notions of cosmos and society were based. The "good" at which political society was presumptively aimed was in fact an Aristotelian illusion with no ground in fact or nature. Human ends were expressive of subjective attractions and aversions but could not be justified by their correspondence to an objectively determined authoritative good—for there was no such good—and to argue over the nature of something that did not exist was the height of Peripatetic absurdity. Since the teleological conceptions of person and society could not make sense of political life, it was necessary to identify a more workable foundation for both concepts.

Both Hobbes and Locke found one in rational self-interest. A properly scientific account of human nature showed that it was necessary to begin from the premise of human selfishness, not the principle of sociability, to produce a more stable and more just political society. Human association was best understood not as an expression of our nature or as a constituent part of the good at which it naturally aims, but rather as an instrument to be utilized in the service of an essentially private felicity. Though this reconceptualization of human association and public life restricted the scope of political possibility and narrowed the motivational field of political subjects, it was claimed that this more scientific understanding of human nature and society could secure social stability and justice more effectively than could traditional notions. It so happened that the aim of political society was not the joint realization of the human good or the thick moral community that made that pursuit possible, but rather the protection of private holdings through the rule of law and the maintenance of social conditions that were favorable to mutually beneficial exchange. Such a system did not make inaccurate or heroic assumptions about human beings and their capacity for or disposition toward civic virtue, but instead claimed that, under the appropriate institutional conditions, directed rational selfishness could motivate the political agent to honor his covenants and obey the law. Modern political and social institutions thus sought to make men calculable by making them calculating, by tamping down the moral enthusiasm that had proven so unpredictable and destabilizing.

Hobbes was especially adamant in his attempt to reduce political life, and human association more generally, down to egoistic calculations. He rigorously rejected the classical principle of natural sociability, treating man's "aptness to society" as a function of his desire for self-preservation (*Lev.* XV, 95; XVII, 106).[4] He also flatly denied the classical belief in the existence of an authoritative human good: "There is no such *Finis Ultimus* nor *Summum Bonum* as is spoken of in the books of the old moral philosophers" (XI, 57). Eschewing the language of mutual perfection and adopting the patois of economics, Hobbes interprets love and friendship as essentially private phenomena, understood only by their effects on an agent's utility function. The desire for deep and serious communion is either reduced to instrumental considerations or viewed as a form of fanaticism—an illusory and dangerous longing to be purged rather than educated.

Following the "justly decried" Hobbes on this score, John Locke adopts a restrictive understanding of human community in the *Second Treatise of Civil Government*. While acknowledging that human beings have an "inclination" for society, he nonetheless explicates an asocial and utilitarian psychology and emphasizes the motives of "necessity and convenience" in his account of the formation of civil society (2*Tr.* 7, 42).[5] He also provides a depoetized and unsentimental account of conjugal society. Husbands and wives, Locke says, have no obligation to each other beyond what is necessary for rearing children, and once children reach the age of reason the conjugal bond "dissolves of itself" and both husband and wife are "at liberty" (7, 44). Underneath this restrictive and instrumental conception of human relations is a narrow conception of the human good. Indeed, Locke follows Hobbes in relegating the *Summum Bonum* to the philosophical junk pile: "The mind as well as the palate has a different relish; and you will as fruitlessly endeavour to delight all men with Riches or Glory . . . [as with] cheese or lobster. . . . Hence it was, I think, that the Philosophers of old did in vain enquire, whether *Summum bonum* consisted in Riches, or bodily Delights, or Virtue, or Contemplation" (*ECHU* 269).[6] Locke's denial of the existence of a consummate human good undermines the possibility of a political community—indeed *any* community—founded on its pursuit. Like Hobbes, then, he believed the path to justice and stability required a more modest conception of social relations.

Enter Rousseau, who found in the work of his predecessors a cure worse than the disease. Hobbes and Locke argued that rational self-interest fashioned an adequate ground for political community, but Rousseau countered that narrow selfishness—far from teaching us our duties—instead taught us the dishonesty necessary to evade them. The belief that egoism could serve as its own cure did not motivate citizens to become lawful, industrious, and tolerant; to the contrary, it had only succeeded in introducing another contradiction into the soul—that between speech and deed. *The Discourse on the Sciences and Arts* and *The Discourse on Inequality* are united by a concern to show that the model of human community advanced by Hobbes and Locke fails even on its own modest terms. In the former, Rousseau complains that the loss of "sincere friendships," "real esteem," and "well-founded trust" is due in part to the "suspicions, fears, coldness, reserve, hate, [and] betrayal" that hide underneath the "false veil of politeness" required by enlightened society (*DSA* 38).[7] No one acts as he speaks or speaks as he feels, and such widespread dishonesty contributes to a social atmosphere characterized by division, distrust, and bad faith.

The Discourse on Inequality develops and radicalizes this line of argument, arguing that rational self-interest is unable to solve the social conflicts it creates. "If," Rousseau thunders, "I am told that society is so constituted that each man gains by serving others, I shall reply that this would be very well, if he did not gain still more by harming them" (*DI* 194–95). Civil society introduces a zero-sum dynamic in which one person's gain always comes at another's expense and thus "necessarily brings men to hate each other in proportion to the conflict of their interests" (193). Those who follow the advice of Hobbes and Locke inevitably find that their interests are best served not by following the law but rather by "finding ways to be assured of impunity" (195). Because honest gains are always surpassed by dishonest ones, reason itself recommends criminality: there "is no profit, however legitimate, that is not surpassed by one that can be made illegitimately" (195). So long as private and particularistic considerations are harnessed to narrow instrumental rationality, they will mediate man's relation to the other and make his social life unstable and antagonistic. Association premised simply on the prospect of mutual advantage—friendship subject to Pareto optimality constraints—not only had failed to deliver the piddling felicity it had promised but had subjected us to debasing forms of personal dependence and made us miserable.

Rousseau was, of course, neither the first nor the last to argue against instrumental rationalism, and his novelty consists less in his insistence that egoism cannot solve its own problems than in his diagnosis of egoism's final effect on the psyche. He uses the language of *dividedness* to sum up these effects, arguing that the root cause of modern man's trouble is that he is at all times directed by two opposed masters—by interest and obligation, by desire and duty, by passion and reason, by self and society. These divisions force him to deploy his powers in opposite directions and to undo with one hand what was done with the other. All his exertions thus cancel each other out, and all his striving for power after power is simply so much sound and fury, signifying less than nothing.

I shall, however, be at pains to emphasize that to be divided in the Rousseauan sense is not simply to experience internal turmoil or to be of "two minds" at any given moment. Such experiences are inevitable and even characteristic of lives Rousseau himself considered exemplary. Dividedness is the condition of being *defined* by indecisiveness; it is to lack a principle of identity that provides a way of reconciling inner conflicts when they *do* occur. Thus, when Rousseau contrasts the divided bourgeois with those who are "something" and "one," he emphasizes that where the former spends his life "in conflict and floating" between unrealized possibilities, the latter follows a set of coherent impulses that give his life continuity and direction. Unified beings make decisions "in a lofty style" and stick to them, but the bourgeois—who delusively believes in the proposition that the human good is realized through the successful pursuit of narrow self-interest—operates under the false assumption that difficult choices do not need to be made (*E* 41). Acting on the basis of this false belief had left him in a kind of developmental purgatory where no particular vision of the good can be realized because all visions of the good are being simultaneously pursued. Like the democratic man of Plato's *Republic*, Rousseau's bourgeois is relegated to a haphazard and halfhearted pursuit of free-floating, disjointed, and unrewarding pleasures.

To be divided in the precise sense, then, is not simply to be uncertain about what to do in a moment. It is, rather, to be *truncated*, for to the degree that we lack the moral courage to confront and resolve the difficult dilemmas that life imposes, our lives will lack unifying purpose. Thus we find Rousseau complaining of the deeply impoverished character of modern man's moral experience in the context of his discussion of dividedness: he characterizes the life of the divided bourgeois as fundamentally meaningless and unpurposive, going so far as to call him a "nothing" (*rien*) (*E* 40). To be a bourgeois is to be a nonentity, a site of undeveloped possibility: this is why he "breathes" but does not "live," for he cannot give organized expression to his capacities for moral and social feeling. His obsession with self-preservation and his blithe disregard for love and virtue operate as a kind of affective anesthesia, diminishing the vitality of his passions and preventing genuine engagement with the human good. To follow the promptings of narrow self-interest, then, is not only to foment antisocial desires; it is to undermine the vitality of *desire itself*. Passional enthusiasm, and with it moral potential, are dried up at the source. All sentiment and social affection are reduced to a "secret egoism" that "prevents [men] from being born by . . . detaching them from their species" (*E* 312n). The condition of dividedness, then, does not simply reduce our stock of utiles so much as it lowers our threshold for experiencing pleasure.

Rousseau's critique of bourgeois society has met with considerable resistance in the twentieth century, with critics like Robert Nisbet (1943), J. L. Talmon (1952), and Isaiah Berlin (1990) viewing his alternative vision of human relations as illiberal Pollyannaism. Less distinguished commentators too numerous to count have scolded Rousseau for his utopian flights, arguing that his quest for wholeness through connectedness is at best futile and, at worst, more destructive of human happiness than the dividedness he blames. And it is indeed tempting to listen when we are told that there is no final harmony to be had, that the contradictions we face are built into the structure of the world and thus do not admit of final resolution, that conflict and division are coextensive with life itself, and that our experiences of reconciliation are momentary and misleading flashes rather than poetic intimations of the great unity of being. The prudent course, it is urged, is to accept our dividedness and attempt to manage its effects rather than eliminate its causes. Adopting this stratagem will ultimately maximize net satisfaction by inuring us to the false and dangerous charms of an unreasonable erotic enthusiasm.

But we can already see how misplaced this objection is, for though Rousseau's social theory is more ambitious in its aims than is the instrumentalism of Hobbes and Locke, it is motivated not by an optimistic belief in the infinite goodness and perfectibility of man but rather by a comprehensive critique of the crypto-utopian proposition that narrow self-interest can solve the problems that it creates (Melzer 1983). Rousseau denies that the fragmentation caused by the halfway sociability of modern life admits of the partial resolution sought by his critics, because he claims that fragmentation is itself *the product* of an attempted partial resolution. Unity is the essential precondition for healthy and productive human life, and a social theory that seeks anything less will be attended by all the frightful psychological and political consequences Rousseau diagnoses. What is more, Rousseau's conception of unity is not as utopian as it is made out to be: as will become clear, Rousseau was a long way indeed from believing that all the sources of suffering could be eliminated or that all conflicts could be neutralized. Even the best and happiest lives are full of travail; episodic frustration and discontent are part of the human estate and must be borne with that in mind. What he denies, rather, is that the causes of dissatisfaction in modern life can be accepted as the sunk cost of living in the best of all possible worlds.

Rousseau's very way of framing the problem of social and political order is thus a comprehensive response and challenge to the bourgeois alternative of Hobbes and Locke. The hope of creating a stable and just political society on the basis of narrow self-interest is a soul-shrinking and self-destructive dogma masquerading as a science of politics. It had succeeded only in multiplying the sources of human conflict, narrowing the scope of human desire, and undermining the psychological sources of virtue and social affection. Legitimate social institutions must offer deeper compensations than the empty felicity of Hobbes and Locke, and a satisfactory account of human relations must comprehend more than the impoverished and arid associations to which that anemic conception of happiness had given rise.

Rousseau's Third Way: Reimagining Self-Love and Human Relations

If Rousseau criticizes modern thinkers like Hobbes and Locke for failing to take the social passions seriously enough, he does so as a practitioner of and believer in modern science. Rousseau's own modernity is reflected in his strong rejection of the classical premise that man is naturally social and political (*DI* 95–96) and in his steadfast refusal to interpret man's sociability as evidence of its naturalness. To the contrary, Rousseau follows and even *radicalizes* the reductive, asocial, and materialistic tendencies of Hobbes and Locke. He argues that man in the state of nature is distinguished from other animals only in potentiality, claims that this man is a solitary and aconceptual brute whose natural needs are limited to "nourishment, a female, and repose" (116), rejects natural teleology, and founds his own social and political teaching on (properly understood) self-love. Thus, though Rousseau seeks to develop a more ambitious and more satisfying conception of human connectedness than do his modern predecessors, he does so by utilizing the conceptual tools and resources provided by modern science (Strauss 1953; Melzer 1983; Hulliung 1994).

Nowhere is Rousseau's effort to reinvigorate social life through a reinterpretation of broadly modern political principles more evident than in his revolutionary account of self-love. Though very pessimistic about the social utility of narrow self-interest, Rousseau insisted no less strongly than did Hobbes on the strength of human self-regard. Indeed, self-love defines and determines human life like no other passion and is thus the theoretical key to any effort to understand political and social life aright. It is therefore unsurprising to read in *Emile* that self-love (*amour de soi-même*) is a "primitive, innate passion, which is anterior to every other" and "the origin and principle" of all other desires. He goes on to say that "love of oneself is always good and always in conformity with order" and that we are perfectly justified in ignoring the well-being of others if our own is materially threatened (*E* 212–13). However, Rousseauan self-love has a dynamic and expansive character that allows for a far closer kind of social identification than Hobbes's static and restrictive conception would appear to allow. Whereas Hobbes, as we have seen, posits a very definite and ineliminable distinction between self and other, Rousseau holds that the boundaries of the self are elastic and hence can be stretched to incorporate another or many others. Self-love is itself malleable and susceptible to transformation and generalization. The capacity to extend and generalize self-love to include other beings—either individual persons or abstract entities like the state—is the psychological premise that enables the kind of intimate social connectedness Rousseau saw as a necessary condition of social as well as psychological unity. Through the lens of expansive self-love others may be viewed not as discrete from but rather as extensions of the self and its purposes; to deliberately harm the incorporated other would, in the limiting case, be as absurd and incomprehensible as deliberately harming oneself.

There is a second facet of Rousseauan self-love that both differentiates his conception from that of Hobbes and increases the emotional stakes of social relations: the emergence of *amour-propre*. Rousseau distinguishes this (much-debated) passion from what he calls *amour de soi-même* on the grounds that (1) it is *artificial*, or inactive in the native constitution of man, and that (2) it requires for its satisfaction some measure of *social recognition* and validation. The relativistic features of *amour-propre* make it both a uniquely powerful and uniquely dangerous spring of moral motivation in the context of Rousseau's psychological theory and open up social possibilities on which the more restrictive bourgeois conception of self-love would appear to foreclose. Indeed, Rousseau posits that *amour-propre* grows out of a non-Hobbesian developmental process through which we learn to recognize others as important sources of validation rather than as competitors or instruments of our will. Consciousness of the other begins not with an attempt to bend them to our preexisting purposes but, alternatively, with a desire to bend to theirs. What *amour-propre* wants above all is to obtain the recognition of others. Thus the source of good (and evil) is the desire for love and approval.

Properly trained, *amour-propre* has an expansive effect on the soul and suffuses the wellsprings of human vitality and power. It alters the human personality so fundamentally, and activates so many capacities relevant to the process of moral and social development, that Rousseau likens its awakening to a "second birth" (*E* 212). All meaningful social possibility—love, friendship, paternal and fraternal relations, and so on—requires the activation of *amour-propre*, for only after its birth can we begin to understand agency and intentionality, engage in the process of mutual esteem-seeking, and enter into emotionally rewarding social relations. The awareness of such possibilities gives us access to the consolations and hopes of the social world and serves as an invitation to "man's estate" (*E* 213). And yet this invitation is fraught with danger, for malignant *amour-propre* threatens to corrupt human character at its source and undermine the use of the very capacities to which it gives rise. Indeed, Rousseau claims that the desire for social approval and distinction is the cause of "all the evil that men do to each other"; further, he claims that its operations have transformed society from a cooperative venture into a site of vicious and underhanded contestation (*DI* 222).

It is, as an extensive and combative secondary literature will attest, very difficult to pin down precisely what *amour-propre* is and to isolate its effects on the human soul. Part of this is due to Rousseau's elusive and seemingly evolving presentation of the concept, but much of the difficulty we have in nailing down the impact of *amour-propre* is due to its intrinsic embeddedness in specific associational contexts. We rarely, if ever, observe *amour-propre* acting in isolation or hear it speaking its own language; it is always nested within particular forms of association and assuming their voices and tones. To put it a bit differently, the kind of recognition we expect or hope for from other people depends in large part on what kind of association we have or seek to have with them. In order to understand *amour-propre* correctly, then, it is necessary to understand how its demand for distinction changes as it interacts with other social passions and as it is embedded in different associational contexts.

Rousseau's expansive and relativized conception of self-love allows him to explore rather ambitious social and existential possibilities without having to deny the psychological salience of self-love. Thus he is attempting to utilize the conceptual resources of modernity in order to generate a conception of social life more rewarding than his predecessors had envisaged. The complex relationship Rousseau has with his modern forebears is captured perfectly in the first few pages of *Emile*, which both attacks and subtly confirms the largely materialistic bases of modern political thought: "One only thinks of preserving one's child. That is not enough. . . . It is less a question of keeping him from dying than of making him live. To live is not to breathe; it is to act; it is to make use of our organs, our senses, our faculties, of all the parts of ourselves which give us the sentiment of our existence. The man who has lived the most is not he who has counted the most years but he who has most felt life" (*E* 42). On the one hand, Rousseau is clearly critical of the crudely reductive and possibility-destroying tendency to boil everything down to the animal imperative of self-preservation. Because this narrow focus kills men before they are even born, he seeks to expand the scope of his own inquiry beyond these meager existential provisions. It is not enough for civilized man to use his "organs" and "senses" in the same mechanical way a beast does, for—as Rousseau makes clear in another context (*DI* 113–16)—human ends and human being are undetermined in a way that animal desire is not. Animals are moved by mechanical "instincts" which are peculiar to them and which admirably, if imperfectly, guide them toward their own good. Human beings, however, lack instincts in the strict sense. We are not, at least in the civilized state, passive conduits for alien forces; rather, we are self-conscious and self-determining agents who create the sources of our own desires and aid in the creation of our own moral identities. These identities serve us in much the same way that instinct serves the nonhuman animal: they provide coherence to thought and action and, if properly constructed, tend to guide us toward our own good. Because human being is by nature open-ended and malleable, the development of moral identity demands continued reflection on the character of our desires and their correspondence (or lack thereof) to our self-conception. The distinctively human power of identity creation is therefore taxing and dangerous (*DI* 115), but it is also exciting and generative of tremendous moral possibility. We develop and deploy our "faculties" and powers in the service of the "sentiment of existence," a diffuse and distinctively human pleasure that one takes in the conscious apprehension of his own life and being. It is the feeling of this "sentiment," the quotient of felt life, which a human being should aim to maximize; he should care less about living long than about living well, and the good life involves the activation and coherent direction of our capacities for rational thought and—most especially—for social feeling.

On the other hand, however, if Rousseau reopens a set of moral and social possibilities about which previous modern thinkers had expressed serious doubt, then he does so by redeploying the philosophical tools of modernity itself. If learning to feel the "sentiment of existence" is supposed to enrich human life in ways that Hobbes and previous modern thinkers had failed to take seriously, it is nonetheless the simple operations of our biological equipment—our "senses" and "organs"—that make that enrichment possible. No rational soul or divine essence is posited; no Natural Laws are invoked; no world of forms is apprehended; no noumenal realm is postulated; no immaterial substance is conjured (cf. Williams 2007). Feeling the "sentiment of existence" is surely a complex existential phenomenon that should not be squeezed into the cramped categories of crude materialism, but it still obtains in the sensible world and is susceptible to empirical analysis and rational explanation. For all its complexity and elevation, the sentiment of existence is still just a "sentiment" that does not transcend sensory experience so much as enrich it and channel it upward. Rousseau thus affirms Hobbes's tough-minded empiricism while claiming that Hobbes's failure to grasp the malleable nature of human being had led to an impoverished understanding of the sources of moral personhood. Hobbes was right to say that we learn using the senses, but he failed to teach us how to *feel*.

| The Natural Bases for Human Relations

The broad and exciting social possibilities that promise to gratify the sentiment of existence are not created by expansive self-love alone. Rousseau posits that two other forces in the soul connect us to others: sexual desire and pity. Like self-love, which undergoes an important transformation once it is placed in a social context, both sexual desire and pity differ greatly in their primitive and developed forms. In what follows, I briefly explain how these two natural passions develop, how they serve as the ground for love and friendship, and how they fail to realize the comprehensive satisfaction to which they point.

In the state of nature, the sexual passion is a direct expression of self-love and is shorn of intersubjective meaning. Sex carries no social or emotional significance because partners see each other—to the extent that they do so at all—as instruments of private pleasure rather than as sources of love and approval. Only when "physical" desire transforms into "moral" love does the sexual drive become an important spring of moral and social motivation (*DI* 134–45). Indeed, as we shall see in more detail in chapters 4 and 5, this transformation effects two important changes in the structure of sexual desire. First, in conjunction with the development of other cognitive capacities, it *refines taste*: whereas natural man does not distinguish between fit and unfit sexual partners, moral lovers do make distinctions like this on the basis of ethical and aesthetic criteria. It is by way of such distinctions that romantic love moves toward *exclusivity*, for once we have learned to esteem one person more than another our desire "gains a greater degree of energy" for our "preferred object" (*DI* 134). Second, the emergence of moral love greatly *intensifies* the desire for sexual communion. This intensification is due to the interaction of sexual desire and *amour-propre*: once we begin to view each other not as instruments of private satisfaction but rather as important sources of recognition and validation, the sexual act acquires profound and even revolutionary significance. In fact, Rousseau goes so far as to call the experience of exclusive romantic attachment *the* human good—it determines "the final form" of moral character and makes a person "as happy as he can be" (*E* 416, 419).

It is, of course, not simply the recognition of the beloved that one seeks when he selects a partner. Few human choices are subjected to as much scrutiny as the choice of a mate, and the assessments of others inevitably influence our decisions in this regard. When a couple marries, they make a *public* affirmation about who and what has final value in life; it is an announcement about what qualities of body and soul one most admires. Thus it is an announcement both about what kind of person one believes himself to be as well as about where he stands in the social order. Our mates are reflections of us in part because they are reflections *on* us, and part of why we seek out the specific persons we do is because they possess the physical and moral virtues deemed to be desirable by others. Thus do our liaisons take on even greater significance once they are embedded in and receive (or do not receive) validation from society's basic institutions. It is important, then, to recognize that love is both a private and public act; it involves the incorporation of two lovers as well as the incorporation of the newly formed marital unit into civil society's primary institutions.

Unhappily, both of these incorporative processes are beset by difficulties that ultimately overwhelm even the happiest and best-educated couples. The fusion of "two into one" that romantic love seeks (*E* 479) is ultimately undone by the disproportion between the idealized imaginary love object and the imperfect beloved. As husband and wife are forced by the very intimacy that they so desired to confront each other's flaws, they grow disillusioned with and alienated from each other. What is worse, the attempt to live together after love's passing proves as impossible as maintaining love forever: the feelings of resentment and distaste that set in make the transition from love to friendship very difficult. The fragile psychology of romantic love is not the only complication with which young lovers must deal. They must also cope with the process of integrating themselves into a larger society that is all-too-often corrupt and corrupting. The threats to happy marriage come from within and without: husband and wife must sustain the fragile illusions they have about each other in the face of social forces that threaten their collective happiness at every turn.

The sexual passion, though an especially powerful source of social connection, is not the only natural basis for human relations. Indeed, in *The Discourse on Inequality* Rousseau argues that we are also connected to other members of our species through pity (*pitié*). This sentiment, which like self-love exists "anterior to reason," inspires in human beings "a natural repugnance to see any sensitive being perish or suffer" (*DI* 95). Pity, however, is not simply an internal or emotional response to the sights and sounds of suffering. After sufficient development it can motivate a range of virtuous actions and generate sympathetic associations: pity, Rousseau claims, is the psychic basis for social virtues like "generosity, clemency, and humanity," adding that "benevolence *and even friendship* are, rightly understood, the products of a constant pity fixed on a particular object" (131–32; emphasis added).

If pity is the ground of friendship, then what type of friendship does it ground? In chapter 6 I shall emphasize two primary points. The first is to show that friendship lacks the psychological power to restore human beings to wholeness. On this point I shall be at pains to show that friendship operates somewhat at the margins of our psychic and social lives, and that it does more to relieve our sadness than to restore our happiness. The sentiments to which friendship gives rise—and the range of action it inspires—are circumscribed by the very circumstances that make it necessary. Friendship, thus conceived, provides a very real kind of comfort for divided beings, but the comfort it provides does not make us happy but rather makes our sadness a bit more bearable. It is, in fact, our ineliminable dividedness that makes friendship relevant and even important: fallen man needs friends, but much of the reason he needs them is *because* he is fallen. The second, related to the first, is to show that Rousseauan friendship is not a catalyst of virtue or moral perfection in the way that Joseph Reisert (2003) has persuasively argued. It is, rather, a palliative, a way of coping with life's inevitable disappointments and hardships. We need our friends not because they show us our good—for this we are needful of intellectual and moral *superiors*—but because they can sympathize with and console us in our failings, moral and otherwise.

| To Nature or to Denature? The Moral Ecology of the Just Regime

For the most part Rousseau chooses to paint his portraits of love and friendship in a domestic or private context, remote from the disruptions and disturbances of large-scale social institutions. Indeed, it often seems that considerable distance from large-scale social institutions and their corrupting tendencies is necessary in order to preserve sympathetic association, for when we incorporate fully into civil and political life we subject ourselves to the arbitrary private wills of others and to an overwhelmingly complex and chaotic system of social forces. Yet because these social forces are of our own making—because, however alien and hostile they may seem, they are themselves products of human agency—they may be restructured in a way that is conducive rather than injurious to human happiness. Indeed, it may seem that this restructuring is not only possible but *necessary*, for the household—

the site of domestic happiness—is not an independent entity free of social control; rather, it is itself a social institution that must be incorporated into civil society and exist in accordance with its laws and customs. Unless the society of which the household is a part is tolerably just, then it is only a matter of time before our domestic relations are corrupted by the sinister social forces around it.

Recently, a number of scholars have sought in various ways to show the compatibility of Rousseau's domestic and political visions. Most do so by reading the pedagogy of *Emile* into the political program of the *Social Contract*. Tracy Strong (1994, 138), for instance, claims that Emile's education *"requires and will generate, come what may, a political society"* because "that which makes him human requires that he be a citizen." Frederick Neuhouser (2008, 23) has also emphasized the politicizing functions of the work, saying that Emile's education "produces individuals who in the end can assume the role of citizen . . . in a manner consistent with . . . being a man." John Rawls (2007) and Joshua Cohen (2010) are at one with Neuhouser in pointing to the complementarity of *Emile* and the *Social Contract*. Still other scholars view Rousseau's novel *Julie* as providing an alternative, and perhaps more promising, bridge between the domestic and the political spheres. Nicole Fermon (1997, 119), for instance, claims that *Julie* presents a "vision of the 'private worlds' of citizens" that "fleshes out human aspects of the common life left out of *The Social Contract*"; she argues further that the household as depicted in *Julie* cultivates "sound moral habits" necessary to good citizenship.

Though I shall ultimately be critical of these interpretations for seeking a continuity between Rousseau's domestic and political visions that I do not think he provides, I also think that, in pointing to the irreducible multiplicity of man's social obligations and, hence, to the need to order them in some coherent way, they do help to recast Rousseau's understanding of the political problem in a more helpful light. That is to say, these various interpretations are right to point out that our different relationships—far from existing in vacuums—must instead be lived out at the same time and that we must find ways to reconcile the different, and often competing, obligations they impose on us. Political societies are complex and confusing places that necessarily place us under cross-pressures: the things we owe to ourselves, our parents, our children, our friends, our beloveds, and our fellow citizens are not always compatible, and the tensions that arise within our associational lives can have destructively decentering effects on our identities. This presence of such cross-pressures is especially problematic in the context of a political project like Rousseau's, which emphasizes both the need for and fragility of psychological and social *harmony*.

With this background problem in mind, I characterize Rousseau's political thought as an effort to balance the different and seemingly incompatible forces and obligations that constitute social life. I thus conceive of Rousseauan political society as a kind of "moral ecology" in which citizens, due to their embeddedness in a balanced and harmonious social environment, may approximate the psychological wholeness they would have enjoyed in the pure state of nature. On this conception, each citizen is an ordered whole existing within the larger ordered whole of the just society, attending to a coherent and jointly realizable set of socially defined obligations and, in so doing, discovering the internal unity that has eluded social man for so long.

Ultimately, however, the cross-cutting pressures that constitute social life overwhelm all efforts at comprehensive resolution, and the hybrid character of political life ends up producing the very dividedness it was set up to prevent. Citizens have a dual existence as both private selves and as public beings, and therefore they have attachments and obligations in both the political and the private spheres. The tensions that exist between these private and public obligations are never reconciled and are ultimately reproduced in the psyche, thus leading to the alienated self-centeredness Rousseau identifies in the *Social Contract* as both the cause and consequence of political corruption. The individuated self brought into being by social institutions is also torn asunder by the incommensurable obligations they impose on him. Rousseau temporizes brilliantly with this problem but cannot resolve it. It is important to add, though, that Rousseau's inability to resolve the problems his own thought creates is not, as has so often been claimed, evidence of his intellectual incoherence. It is, rather, the source of a rich and deeply coherent account of the sources of human fragmentation, dislocation, and disappointment. Rousseau gives us a way to reinterpret the very social experiences he so deeply problematizes.

| Men, Citizens, and Scholars: A Politic Digression

In arguing that Rousseau's solution to the political problem is "ecological" in nature I stake out a controversial position in the scholarly debate over the character of civic education, which is perhaps the central controversy in contemporary Rousseau scholarship. In *Emile*, Rousseau plots a course of education intended to reconcile self and society and claims that the "double object" of making a human being good, both for himself and others, might be achieved through one of two different educations. The first is civic or political education: it is "public and common" in character and creates "citizens" who are defined by their relation to and affection for their homeland. Citizens are "denature[d]" by their education, which "transports the *I* into the common unity" and makes "each individual . . . no longer one but a part of the unity." Such an education, though lauded by Rousseau, is nonetheless rejected on the grounds of impracticability. "Public instruction," he avers, "no longer exists and can no longer exist, because where there is no fatherland there can no longer be citizens. These two words, *fatherland* and *citizen*, should be effaced from modern languages" (*E* 40; see also Shklar 1969).

Because genuine civic education is unavailable in modern times, we are left with "the domestic education or the education of nature," which seeks to reconcile the tensions between self and society through the development of individuality and the establishment of intimate sexual connectedness. The result of this form of education is not a "citizen" who finds wholeness only by discovering his place in the polis, but a "man" who is "an absolute whole" unto himself (*E* 39). The attempt to make a man *and* a citizen out of the same person is doomed to fail: "One must choose between making a man and a citizen, for one cannot make both at the same time" (39). Rousseau, then, does not present the educations of "citizens" and "men" as interdependent parts of one pedagogic program but rather as discrete and incommensurable alternatives. They are different and uncombinable answers to the same question, not separate steps in a unified solution (41).

Despite Rousseau's insistence to the contrary, we have already seen that many contemporary scholars argue that the education given to the eponymous hero of *Emile* is best understood as an effort to reconcile the individualistic and broadly modern characteristics of "man" with the civic-minded virtues of the classical "citizen." In the introduction to his excellent translation of the *Social Contract*, Victor Gourevitch summarizes this increasingly popular position concerning the character of both Emile's education and Rousseau's intention as an author. "One important reason for regarding Rousseau as preeminently a political thinker," he holds, is "that we are moral agents by virtue of being citizens, or at least members of political societies; we are not moral agents first who then may or may not become political agents" (Rousseau 1997c, xiv–xv). This is a plausible statement of the view taken by Rousseau scholars of many different interpretive persuasions, and it suggests that Emile's full completion as a human being is contingent on his full incorporation into a political society and his becoming a "citizen." At one level this claim is quite correct: Emile's social consciousness could not properly develop were it not for some semblance of broader social order and decency; upon marrying his beloved Sophie, he must choose a country in which to settle and a set of laws to which he and his family are to be subject. The political is ubiquitous, and the impossibility of escaping it requires that Emile himself become political.

But does it require him to become a *citizen*? The necessity of social incorporation does not necessarily enjoin the necessity of incorporating after the specific manner of a "citizen" as Rousseau understands the term.[8] The Rousseauan citizen is defined by his devotion to the common good and is exemplified by the Spartan Pedaretus, who consoled himself after losing an election on the grounds that there were three hundred other citizens even more worthy than he. "This," Rousseau exclaims with relish, "is the citizen" (*E* 40). The difference between Pedaretus—whose identity is defined by the political institutions of his fatherland—and Emile—who has no fatherland and is told by his tutor not to run for political office unless he is *forced* to do so—could not be clearer (40, 473–75). I shall develop this line of argument further in chapter 4, where I show that the way Emile and his family integrate into and understand their role within political society is indeed at odds with Rousseau's thick notion of citizenship.

The attempt to turn Emile into a "citizen" leads not only to an inaccurate interpretation of *Emile* but also to an unduly restrictive account of Rousseau's intention as an author. The direct textual evidence most commonly cited in support of this view comes from the *Geneva Manuscript* and the *Confessions*.[9] In the former Rousseau remarks that "we do not really begin to become men until after we have been citizens," and in the latter he reports that he had come to understand that "everything depends radically on politics" and that "no people would ever be anything other than what it was made into by the nature of its Government" (*GM* I.2, 161–62; *C* 340). These passages make the point that political institutions are among the important determinants of moral character. But they do not say that they are the *only* or even the most important determinants of moral character, or that political institutions are exogenous and freestanding causes of subpolitical life. To arrive at this conclusion we are obliged to forget Rousseau's claims that the modern men were intellectually and morally incapable of authentic republican politics (*E* 39–41), that true civic education is no longer possible

(*E* 39–41), and that political institutions—far from determining the shape of the identity of a people in some simple, unidirectional way—should themselves be adapted to the preexisting cultural and climatological circumstances (*SC* III.8). It is one thing to say, with Rousseau, that everything depends on politics and quite another to say, as many interpreters of Rousseau seem to, that everything depends *only* or even *principally* on politics and that such dependence is nonreciprocal.

An important feature of the present interpretation is that the political association is treated as an important organizing force in social life without being made its *primum movens* and final justification. Rousseau himself turned his attention to politics because it grows out of social life and represents a systematic effort to resolve the complications to which social life gives rise. If politics is meant to solve or at least ameliorate the problems that inevitably arise in the course of shared life, then our first efforts must be directed to understanding the character of the "social problem" (Charvet 1973) which exists prior to politics and which brings it into being. It is, then, the antecedent problem of human association that leads Rousseau to theorize the political; far from looking to understand social relations in terms of politics, he sought instead to understand politics in terms of social relations. In so extensively treating the wide array of human relationships he does, and in treating the vast majority of them *outside* the agora and in relative isolation from the demands of political life, Rousseau asks his reader to consider not only what relation our private associations have to the polis but also what relation they have to one another and, indeed, to living a good life.

I believe that the attempt made here to comprehend political phenomena within the broader problem of human association allows not only for a more authentically Rousseauan understanding of politics, but also for increased explanatory leverage in understanding the character and consequences of *amour-propre*. N. J. H. Dent's (1988) pathbreaking work, developed in different directions by O'Hagan (1999), Rawls (2007), and Neuhouser (2008), distinguished *amour-propre*'s "healthy" and "malignant" forms in an effort to correct the older, and erroneous, idea that *amour-propre* is necessarily corrupt and corrupting. This characterization of *amour-propre*, though helpful in many regards, often makes us feel that the desire for social recognition is something monolithic and undifferentiated, that its effects are insensitive to context and felt uniformly across the entire social domain. The analysis here, however, points to the context-dependent character of *amour-propre*: the varied and complex responses that the desire for social distinction elicits show both that our associational life is itself varied and complex and that the kind of recognition we seek from others depends greatly on the associational context in which that relationship is embedded. We act and interact not just as equals and unequals but also as husbands and wives, citizens and subjects, parents and children, friends and enemies, and so on. The variety of our associational lives gives rise to variation in the ways in which *amour-propre* expresses itself, variation that is often concealed by conventional treatments but which nonetheless deserves our serious attention.

2 | Social Longing and Moral Perfection

When we turn to others, what is it that we want from them? It is not easy to see how to answer such a question, for the social motivations of human beings are mixed and manifold. There are all sorts of reasons why we invite other people into our lives, but the complexity of human desire—that fact that we want both different things at different times and different things at the same time—makes it difficult to know exactly what those reasons are or how much weight each one carries individually. The difficulty of determining what we want from others is in part attributable to the irreducible complexity of social life, for we associate with one another in many different ways—as friends, lovers, competitors, and the like—and find correspondingly different forms of satisfaction and frustration in these different forms of association. It is, however, also true because our social motives are themselves often obscure and indeterminate. We do not always know what we want from others when we enter into relationships with them. Sometimes this is because we do not know enough about our new associate to determine what needs an association with him will satisfy, but other times it is because we are ignorant of what our own needs actually are. It is, in fact, tempting to say that we *cannot* have such information. Indeed, since our needs themselves are at least partially a product of the associational environment in which we are embedded, such ignorance may well be a permanent condition. At the very least, it means that knowledge of self and of other are necessarily related phenomena: we must understand ourselves reasonably well in order to understand others and how they fit into our lives, and if we lack knowledge then we shall also lack a clear understanding of what it is we hope to accomplish in and through social relations. So long as we knowers remain unknown to ourselves, so, too, will the life of the other remain a mystery.

No less an authority than Thomas Hobbes invites his readers to reconsider the sources of their behavior and presents his own *Leviathan* as a sustained meditation on what he finds when he explores his own motivational field: "When I shall have set down my own reading [of human nature] orderly and perspicuously," he tells his reader, "the pains left another will be only to consider, if he also find not the same in himself. This doctrine," he rather importantly adds, "admitteth no other kind of demonstration" (*Lev.* Pr, 5). Hobbes's theories of human nature and political life are the results of rational introspection into his own motives, and the proper way for readers to test their soundness is to systematically interrogate their own social motivations and to compare the results to those of Hobbes. Learning how to look within and "read thyself" (*Nosce teipsum*) is thus the best—nay, the only—way to understand human nature, and anyone who wishes to challenge Hobbes's own reading of the passions must do more than engage in idle gainsaying or quibble with insignificant particulars (*Lev.* Pr, 4). He must present a more elegant theoretical alternative.

At least one reader took up Hobbes's challenge and believed that he had indeed developed a superior account of human nature and social motivation. That reader was Jean-Jacques Rousseau, who left aside "all scientific books" that "teach us to see men only as they have made themselves" and meditated "upon the first and simplest operations of the human soul" (*DI* 95). What he found there was a remarkably limited set of social motivations, one far more restrictive than the relatively exhaustive list provided by Hobbes, who in his haste to characterize human relations as naturally antagonistic had assumed the existence of human relations themselves (*Lev.* VI, 28–33). On Rousseau's accounting, however, the first human beings lacked both the inclination and the incentive to seek one another out. Drawing freely from nature's bounty and unable to conceive of anyone else taking an interest in his activities, natural man sought no emotional gratification from others and found the means of his physical subsistence without their help. Conflicts motivated by scarcity were brief and relatively infrequent, since nature provides plenty and men without pride ultimately have very little over which to fight. Lacking moral needs and possessing the power to satisfy his physical desires independently, natural man had no conceivable reason for social intercourse of any kind.

Because the utility-based motives of necessity and convenience cannot on Rousseau's view adequately explain the phenomenon of settled social relations, other factors must be at work. For Rousseau, the awakening of social sentiment effects a fundamental change in the structure of desire itself; the newly social subject is confused about what he wants because the desire for recognition—a new and powerful motivational force that will take much time and reflection to understand—has been loosed within him. Emerging with and from this desire to be viewed as valuable by others is a moral desire to *merit* such recognition. Whereas Hobbes and, following him, Locke account for social life and development in largely utilitarian terms, Rousseau argues that social desiring is in its first phases something indeterminate, vague, and highly confusing. When we turn to one another for the first time, it is not in order to satisfy some predetermined and exogenously given end. To the contrary, we have only the foggiest ideas about what purposes other human beings might serve or what needs they will help us satisfy. *Amour-propre* is both a cause and consequence of this confusion.

Rousseau's emphasis on the uncertainty out of which our desire for love and esteem arises has at least four important and somewhat neglected consequences for how human relations are theorized. First, his account affirms the *intrinsic* value of human relations, for if we enter associations without knowing what ends they can secure then we must have other and noninstrumental motives for seeking the company of others. Second, it highlights the fundamental albeit subterranean role that *sexuality* plays in motivating human connection more generally. As it turns out, the sexual passion informs moral and social development at virtually every stage—including and especially the earliest ones. Third, it provides a more *expansive and possibility-enhancing* conception of social relations than those provided by Hobbes and Locke, for attaching to the (well-governed) desire to be esteemed by others is the desire to be estimable. *Amour-propre*, that is, gives rise to a powerful perfectionistic imperative that leads healthy beings to develop and extend their being in ways that qualitatively enrich their lives. Rousseau's account of the psyche and his understanding of the emergence of social attachment are designed to reveal a richer and fuller set of human possibilities than are the more reductive models of Hobbes and Locke, whose theories had not explained human nature so much as explained it away. To the degree, then, that we wish not only to gain the good opinion of others but also to deserve it, the desire for recognition grounds a desire for moral perfection that proves crucially important to Rousseau's moral psychology. Finally, it allows us to see that the development of the social passions is at one with their *disaggregation*. To mature socially is to grow into the understanding that there are different forms of association—love, friendship, and so on—that satisfy different needs and create different expectations. This realization ultimately proves more important than it initially seems, for our ability to find comprehensive satisfaction hinges on the extent to which we are able to harmonize our various social roles and effectively negotiate with the irreducible complexity of living with others.

Though the novelty of Rousseau's noninstrumental account of social attachment is best glimpsed by contrasting it with the narrowly instrumentalist conceptions of Hobbes and Locke, we cannot forget that Rousseau is radicalizing the materialistic intuitions developed by his English forebears in the very act of questioning them. In his quest to provide a naturalistic explanation of human behavior that accounts for the full range of human drives and capacities Rousseau is careful not to assign a grounding function to obscure or rarefied psychic forces like eros or the desire for "extended being" (*E* 168; cf. Cooper 2004). Without denying the existence or indeed the importance of such forces, he nonetheless thinks them epiphenomenal products of still more fundamental psychological drives and seeks to account for their emergence in terms that are broadly congenial to modern materialism.

| Instruments and Obstacles: Hobbes, Locke, and Bourgeois Motivation

In his effort to reground moral and social behavior on less narrowly instrumental motives, Rousseau is forced to rethink the structure of human desire itself. His primary target is the rationalistic hedonism of Hobbes and Locke, which turns on the hinges of pleasure and pain and models human decision-making as egoistic computations of expected marginal utilities. Their respective moral-psychological theories each treat desire as the principal spring of action and conceive of it as something omnipresent, highly specific, and rigidly inflexible. This understanding of the human mind generates an instrumental understanding of human association, for it presumes—incorrectly on Rousseau's view—that human subjects enter into social relations with fully determined ends and purposes. The moral and social results of such a conception are as unacceptable as the conception itself, for it encourages us to view others as means to private ends, thus leading to the arid, unrewarding, and highly exploitative social practices Rousseau so memorably characterizes as destructive of city and soul alike.

Hobbes gives especially strong statement to the view that human beings are psychologically unequipped for sustained social intercourse. Without denying that men are susceptible to feelings of love and affection, he nonetheless affirms that such passions are unstable and hence insufficient to serve as a ground for civil society. "It is true," he avers in *The Citizen*, "that perpetual solitude is hard for a man to bear by nature as a man. . . . I am not therefore denying that we seek each other's company at the prompting of nature. But civil societies are not mere gatherings, they are Alliances, which essentially require good faith and agreement for their making" (I.2.n24). The "good faith" and "agreement" that make civil society possible are the results of a foresighted and careful coordination of selfish interests, not the spontaneous expressions of natural sociability or the passionate effusions of affectionate hearts. People do not honor their covenants made from a motive of love. Thus, while "mere gatherings" may well be animated by sympathetic fellow feeling, stable and effective associations are founded on the shared apprehension of common interests and are dedicated to the realization of some predetermined purpose discoverable by reason. Associational life thus conceived is an instrument of private felicity—a tool for achieving exogenously given ends—not a force capable of reconfiguring the structure of desire itself.

But it is not just the natural egoism of human beings that leads us to conceive of our associations in instrumental terms. The particular way in which human beings desire reinforces these selfish tendencies and further circumscribes our motivational field. Human desire is on Hobbes's accounting something infinite and definite, ubiquitous and precise. Desires, whether of attraction or aversion, are caused by encounters with specific and identifiable phenomena out in the world and always arise with respect to those same phenomena. To desire is necessarily to desire some *thing*, and to speak of a want without also mentioning its corresponding object is to speak of an effect without a cause. Hobbes's definition of felicity—"a continual progress of the desire, *from one object to the other*, the attaining of the former being still but the way to the latter"—underscores the insatiability of and lack of ambiguity in human desire (*Lev.* XI, 57; emphasis added). Desiring, then, is a process in which the want of one thing is replaced by the want of another; one's wish for some good X is satisfied (or frustrated) and instantaneously replaced by a desire for some other good Y. Our desires change if and when their "objects" change. Even the generalized anxiety lurking behind our specific attractions and aversions—that "restless desire for power after power" Hobbes puts in all men—is not itself felt *as* a generalized desire for something infinite and unrealizable in the world, but rather is experienced in a piecemeal, incremental fashion. To the degree that it is felt obscurely, it is to be disregarded as a dangerous and illusory longing for we know not what. We do not want something infinite—infinity, after all, is uncognizable—so much as we infinitely want finite things. Hobbes's phenomenology of desire thus presumes not only that men are always desiring but also that their discrete desires have a fairly clear and determinate character. The passions speak to human beings with extraordinary precision and irresistible persuasiveness.

Though Locke softens Hobbes's insistence on man's natural asociability and more openly acknowledges the necessity of traditional social virtues, his hedonistic moral-psychological outlook and instrumental conception of human association are Hobbesian in important and even essential respects. He, too, insists on man's natural selfishness, rejects the existence of a natural good (*ECHU* 269), holds that opinions concerning good and evil are statements of subjective preference rather than reports about the character of moral reality (259), acknowledges that hope of pleasure and fear of pain are the "hinges on which our *Passions* turn" (229), and claims that the fulfillment of desire—what he calls "Happiness"—is the fundamental aim of human action (258). Hobbes, it seems, may be more justly decried than dismissed.

Locke also follows Hobbes in giving to human desire a high degree of specificity and exactness. He understands desire as a felt absence, a "state of uneasiness" caused by the lack of some valued good (*ECHU* 251), and characterizes the anxiety of desiring beings not as an indeterminate longing for something comprehensive and all-encompassing but rather as a set of specific anxiet*ies*, a complex of discrete and distinguishable impulses: "We being in this World beset with sundry *uneasinesses*, distracted with different *desires*, the next enquiry will be, which of them has the precedency in determining the *will* to the next action?" (257). The practical problem posed by desire is one of prioritization rather than precise identification; we are not ignorant of what we want so much as of how to order our pursuits in a way that best suits our fundamental interest in happiness. Locke reiterates this point a few paragraphs later: "There being a great many *uneasinesses* always solliciting, and ready to determine the *Will*, it is natural, as I have said, that the greatest, and most pressing should determine the *Will* to the next action" (263). These passages reveal that Locke views human desire in much the same way as Hobbes, for we see in human being not a generalized anxiety or uneasiness but rather a series of specific and identifiable uneasiness*es*. Indeed, Locke's Hobbesian conception of desire as something infinite and definite is reflected in his very framing of the problem it poses: the difficulty with "Happiness," for Locke, is that we lack sound rules for determining which of our specific desires deserve priority over others, *not* that we want something indeterminate and enigmatic (e.g., wholeness or erotic transcendence). There is, then, nothing mysterious or vague about human ends themselves, for we are at all times beset by any number of discrete desires that make clear and distinct claims on our attention. We make mistakes not about the things we want but about the order in which we pursue them.

Hobbes's and Locke's disenchanting conceptions of desiring generate unsurprisingly and unapologetically instrumental conceptions of human association. For both thinkers, when we enter social life we do so with a full complement of predetermined interests, and when we seek others out it is in order to realize those interests. Thus conceived associations are products rather than sources—consequences rather than causes—of human desire. Because men are not doubtful about their ends, it is natural and even beneficial for them to employ one another as instruments in the service of their predetermined wants and needs. Of course these wants and needs are not necessarily sinister and need not entail the brutal exploitation of others (though for Rousseau that was their likely consequence), but the crucial point is that socialization thus conceived does not problematize the process of end-construction or ask us to rethink or revise our fundamental interests in any serious way. We shall see that Rousseau, without departing from the hedonistic essentials of Hobbes's and Locke's respective moral-psychological theories, seeks to rethink both what it means to desire and what it is that is desired, and in so doing to reconceive human relations as catalysts and creators of human desire rather than as simple instruments of its satisfaction.

| "Nature's Ignorance": Indeterminacy and Social Feeling

Hobbes and Locke turned to reason in order to solve the social problem both because they believed in the primacy of self-love and because they thought human passions too unstable and unpredictable a basis on which to build a political society. Rousseau, though as convinced as his predecessors of the centrality of self-love, nonetheless turns their pessimism about the human passions on its head. Indeed, Rousseau believes the passions must govern reason as often as reason governs the passions, for it is reason that teaches us to isolate ourselves from others and to think of them as instruments of our private purposes. Our natural passions, appropriately directed and developed, connect us to others in a very different and more sympathetic way: far from inspiring a taste for dominion, we instead learn to regard one another as beings entitled to moral respect, as sources of dignity who deserve fair treatment and whose well-being is a part of our own.

It is clear Rousseau regards Hobbes and Locke as sources of the erroneous doctrine that rational self-interest can solve the social problem, for he explicitly engages both thinkers on precisely this point at different places in his writing. A most interesting example occurs in *Emile* (103), where Rousseau criticizes Locke for misunderstanding the psychological mechanics of an important other-regarding virtue: liberality. Locke advises tutors to educate their pupils in the way of generosity by showing them that the liberal man always comes off better in the end. "As to the having and possessing of things," he tells us in *Some Thoughts concerning Education*, "teach [children] to part with what they have easily and freely . . . and let them find by experience that the most *liberal* has always most plenty" (81). Locke appears to be relying on something like the principle of operant conditioning: the child, rewarded repeatedly for generosity, will eventually develop a taste for giving to others. However, it would seem that there is in Locke's account a certain confusion of cause and effect, for it is not *due* to his liberality that the rich man "has always most plenty." It is wealth that makes a man liberal, not vice versa. Rousseau notes Locke's deliberate gloss and claims that it is only a matter of time before a child trained in a Lockean mode will discover it for himself and come to dismiss liberality as spurious. The lesson he will learn is not that it is good to be generous but rather that he should only give when he expects to be compensated with interest. Far, then, from inspiring genuine liberality, the self-regarding generosity Locke recommends instead creates a "miser" who practices a paltry and usurious liberality that "gives an egg to have a cow" (*E* 103). As a bon mot this can hardly be bettered, but Rousseau's clever parry is more than a witticism. Indeed, his retort is based on an instrumental understanding of reason that Locke himself accepted. Rousseau adds, however, that reason thus conceived does not and cannot solve the social problem because it inevitably subordinates the dignity of others to private purposes and destabilizes the social bond by making it contingent on considerations of narrow self-interest (*DI* 195–97). The calculations Locke commends to his tutor will produce only a mercenary virtue and will never serve as a stable foundation for human community.

Rousseau bypasses the coldness of instrumental reason and seeks instead to instill sociable virtue through a restructuring of the affective field. He turns to "the habit of the soul" rather than to rational calculation in order to teach the virtues essential to the maintenance of civil society and premises his account on the assumption that our initial social impulses are highly indeterminate (*E* 104). This indeterminacy puts our ends in doubt, thereby making it virtually impossible for us to use others as means to them. Rousseau takes up this argument at the start of Book IV of *Emile*, which marks the awakening of social sentiment and the revolution in self-understanding that it initiates. Before Emile's social desires are aroused, he embodies everything good and solid in the moral-psychological models of Hobbes and Locke. He cognizes the world in terms of pure usefulness—he knows the "what's it good for" in everything he does—and disregards everything whose utility cannot be shown. His ideas, however limited, are clear and distinct as far as they reach, and his mind is wholly devoid of prejudice (207). Emile has at age fifteen all "the virtue that relates to himself" and a moral disposition perfectly suited to his limited purposes: he "considers himself without regard to others and finds it good that others do not think of him. He demands nothing of anyone and believes he owes nothing to anyone" (208). Unaware of human will and the threat it poses to his self-sufficiency, Emile does what he wants but wants only what he himself can do. He is deliberate, industrious, prudent, resolute, courageous, patient, and moderate. He is, in short, a model bourgeois.

He is, of course, also profoundly unsocial. The instrumental psychology that allowed Emile to so effectively cognize the physical, depersonalized world of "dependence on things" will not suffice in the social realm, because consciousness of human agency introduces complications into the process of desiring that overwhelm the tidy cognitions of childhood. These complications are embodied in Rousseau's description of our first social desires, which he characterizes as highly indefinite: "A long restlessness precedes the first desires; a long ignorance puts them off the track. One desires without knowing what. The blood ferments and is agitated; a superabundance of life seeks to extend itself outward. The eye becomes animated and looks over other beings. One begins to take an interest in those surrounding us; one begins to feel that one is not made to live alone. It is thus that the human heart is opened to the human affections and becomes capable of attachment" (*E* 220). The first social impulse we sense within ourselves is subjectively experienced as all encompassing but utterly directionless. It is a compound passion, one that contains within itself a complex of distinct desires for different kinds of attachment. Of course, these desires can and ultimately must be distinguished in order to be developed in an "ordered" way (235), but a properly educated adolescent does not know the difference between love and friendship. He hence has little idea of how to give concrete expression to the "superabundance of life" within him that "seeks to extend itself outward." His first desire for communion with others is an undifferentiated and indeterminate want of connectedness; he has "an interest in those surrounding [him]" and he "looks over other beings" with a new intensity and feeling of recognition, but this recognition is limited by the ambiguity of the passion that actuates it. It is therefore the source of considerable confusion. He senses that others are good for something, but if pressed he could not explain the "what's it good for" in his new desire (207). He does not yet know exactly what he wants from others and is needful of much instruction if he is learn how to go about getting it. This newfound desire to be with and seen by others is thus not experienced as a precise and identifiable want or need—like a craving for a hot dog or a wish to take a nap—but as a generalized longing to project oneself into the world, to reach out beyond the narrow and narrowing restrictions of selfhood and connect with other beings.

Rousseau emphasizes the ambiguity in rather than the specificity of our initial social impulses and, in so doing, argues contra Hobbes and Locke that when we turn to others for the first time we lack a developed sense of what purposes they might serve in our lives. To treat others instrumentally presupposes that we already know what they are to us and what we want from them, but if we "desire without knowing what" it is we want from them, then we cannot say in advance what ends they might serve as a means to, what goods they can help us obtain, or how exactly we wish to be connected to them. We do not, in short, know what they are for, and yet they are still wanted, and deeply. The company of others has a value beyond its utility; we want nothing from them *but* them.¹ It will take time to learn to distinguish the different forms of recognition and the various needs to which they give rise, but this occurs at a later stage of moral development. For now it is enough to see that Rousseau's genesis of social attachment begins out of a salutary indeterminacy that shows how we can want others without wanting anything in particular from them. Human relations are desired by a healthy adolescent soul for their own sake rather than for their beneficial consequences.

The confusion into which we are thrown by our new and perplexing social longing raises the issue of self-knowledge and its relationship to sociability. Rousseau calls attention to the presence of identity confusion very early in Book IV, noting the physical and emotional changes that come with puberty: in addition to his "desiring without knowing what," we also find that Emile's "voice breaks, or, rather, he loses it; he is neither child nor man and can take the tone of neither" (*E* 212). Emile no longer knows what he is, what he wants, or how to explain his needs to others. He must adapt to the cruel irony of life as an adolescent—he has lost the ability to express himself at the very moment he most urgently needs it. The birth of the social passions has thus not only made Emile desire the company and recognition of others; it has also introduced the question of self-knowledge *as a question*, raising it in a way that makes necessary the assistance, care, and company of others. What he *is* from now on is social; he can no longer do anything—or at any rate anything interesting or important—without considering the interests and views of others. Human relations, then, are not instrumental but identity-constitutive; they give rise to the very desires they seek to satisfy, and do not help us get what we want so much as give shape and substance to desire itself. They influence our political views, our moral characters, our aesthetic orientations, even our physiognomies.² They count fundamentally for who we are and how we think of ourselves. The structure of human being is altered profoundly and irreversibly once the desire for the recognition and esteem of others is aroused.

| *Amour-Propre* and Moral Ambition

Rousseau connects the dawning of social sentiment and the development of moral personhood to reveal not only the indeterminacy but also the *intensity* of our first social desires. When we become social we not only want a new thing but also want it with a new depth and fervency, for as we are initiated into the mysteries of moral and social life we are gripped by a peculiar mixture of pride and shame—pride at our fuller participation in the human estate, and shame at our new needfulness and insufficiency. We begin to view ourselves as works in progress, as perfectible but imperfect beings in need of we know not what. Rousseau intimates something of this profound but enigmatic longing for perfection in his *Moral Letters*, which are addressed to his onetime and, it would seem, ongoing love interest, Sophie d'Houdetot.[3] "Have you," he asks his *belle amie*, "never felt that secret uneasiness that torments us at the sight of our misery and that becomes indignant about our weaknesses as about an insult to the faculties that exalt us?" He goes on to characterize the effects of this powerful psychic force, arguing that it "enflame[s] the heart with love of the celestial virtues" and "carries us into the empyrean next to God himself." This feeling, this "sublime going astray that raises us above our being," exalts the soul and "forbids us to have contempt for ourselves" or anyone else who is "a friend of justice and sensitive to the virtues" (*ML* 88–89). To be human is in some sense to wish to transcend humanity.

Though Rousseau sympathetically depicts this impulse in the *Moral Letters* and suggests that its development is necessarily tied to a full realization of the human good, he is more famous for calling attention to its dangers. Indeed, ever since Voltaire famously quipped that his perusal of the *Second Discourse* made him want to walk on all fours like an animal, Rousseau has been thought to counsel against the extension of this distinctively human desire. The more recent work of Laurence Cooper (1999) and N. J. H. Dent (1988) has, however, decisively undermined interpretations like this and suggests rather that Rousseau's depictions of *amour-propre*'s destructiveness are not to be viewed as claims about the essential malignancy of the passion itself but rather as evidence of its incredible force, one that can catalyze either the corruption *or* perfection of human nature. In order to see *amour-propre*'s moralizing force, then, it is necessary to examine its genesis, for in so doing we can glimpse both the destructive danger and the constructive potential to which it gives rise as well as begin to see how it might solve some of the problems its own emergence presents.

Rousseau begins his account on this score from the postulate of self-love, holding that "we have to love ourselves to preserve ourselves; and it follows immediately from this same sentiment that we love what preserves us." Our very first attachments to others are purely instinctual and instrumental: "Every child is attached to his nurse.... What fosters the well-being of an individual attracts him; what harms him repels him. This is merely blind instinct." Hobbes himself could not have said it better. However, during puberty the mechanical promptings of pure self-regard are complicated by the new and powerful realization that others exist and that they have *intentions* with respect to our well-being. The apprehension that other subjects exist and that they *mean* to do us good or ill looses the passions of hate and love, or rather creates passion proper: "What transforms ... instinct into sentiment, attachment into love, aversion into hate, is the intention manifested to harm us or to be useful to us.... We seek what serves us, but we love what wants to serve us. We flee what harms us, but we hate what wants to harm us. One is never passionate about insensible beings which merely follow the impulsion given to them. But those from whom one expects good or ill from their inner disposition, by their will ... inspire in us sentiments similar to those they manifest toward us" (*E* 213). One does not hate the tree branch that strikes his head, but he immediately despises the person who does the same with a baseball bat. The difference, of course, is that the latter's behavior is invested with malign intentions while the former is bereft of motive. The awareness of human intentionality thus transports us from a mechanical world moved by impersonal forces to a moral world governed by human will. The impact of this realization is difficult to overstate, but we can begin to understand something of its importance by noting that it is impossible for us to continue depending simply on things—on "insensible beings"—in order to subsist, for now we understand that our environment is structured not just by the uniform and harmonious laws of nature but also by the capricious and conflicting motives of other human beings. Our continued preservation and happiness now depend on our ability to discern the often-obscure intentions of others and gain favorable standing in their eyes.

Awareness of the existence of human will, of the fact that others have intentions toward other people and wish to do them good or harm, greatly raises the emotional stakes of social interaction and gives birth to perhaps the most dangerous passion in the human soul—*anger*. The importance of this emotion for Rousseau's psychological theory is suggested rather clearly by the fact that the epigraph to *Emile*—"We are sick with evils that can be cured; and nature, having brought us forth sound, itself helps us if we wish to be improved"—is culled from Seneca's treatise *Of Anger*. The frontispiece to the work also indicates anger's thematic importance: it depicts the solicitous

Thetis dipping her infant son Achilles—who would develop quite the temper—into the River Styx and thereby rendering him invulnerable. Though Rousseau appears to laud Thetis's care for her son and advises wise preceptors to emulate her salutary example by steeping their own pupils "in the River Styx," he subtly chastises her, along with the "cruel mothers" of modern times, for worrying too much about the mortality of their children (*E* 47; see also Scott 2012).

Obsessed with protecting her son from so many external dangers, Thetis failed to tend to his internal life and, in so doing, cultivated unawares the very passion which would prove his undoing. Her approach to education thus fails by its own standard. But such a failure was inevitable, since the standard it applies is the incorrect one: because mortality is a defining feature of the human condition, education is "less a question of keeping [a child] from dying than of making him live" (*E* 42). Thetis's well-intentioned efforts were therefore motivated by a misunderstanding of her child's true needs: in futilely trying to protect her Achilles from dying she prevented him from making productive use of the time he had, and in failing to understand how to educate his anger she made him its unwitting dupe. Jean-Jacques, far from seeking to render his Emile invulnerable and knowing how susceptible his nascent passions are to corruption, does not follow Thetis's flawed example but rather charts a new course directed by the theory of natural goodness. This theory puts the education of anger at the center of its pedagogy and, rather than seek to inure men to the troublesome effects of *amour-propre* by preventing its birth, elects instead to subject them to all its power and force (cf. *E* 235). This new path is the only one that can be trod, but it is rife with obstacles and dangers.

Anger and all its self-destructive consequences materialize when *amour-propre*'s wish to be recognized is thwarted by the will of another, and it expresses itself with particular intensity when recognition-seeking behaviors go ignored or affectionate feelings go unreciprocated. Rousseau claimed that the disposition to anger in children "requires extreme attentiveness," and the disciplining of this dangerous passion would appear to be one of Jean-Jacques's most important and most difficult tasks. This is because we are, on Rousseau's view, acutely sensitive to the refusals of others and disposed to interpret them as personal affronts, as hateful insults and denials of our worth. It is therefore not uncommon for us to attribute malevolent intentions to those who withhold their affection or otherwise frustrate our wishes. Our tendency to rashly attribute malicious intentionality to an intransigent other, even and perhaps especially when there is no clear reason to do so, is a form of demonization through which we administer punishment to him; it is how we rebuke him for refusing to love us as he is loved by us. It is also self-deception on the cheap: having been refused the recognition so earnestly sought, we discredit the motives of the other in order to convince ourselves that such love was not worth having in the first place.

Yet another danger that emerges with *amour-propre* is that our desire for social distinction leads us to seek recognition from the wrong sources. Just as governors make mistakes about how to effect their pupils' good, so, too, do human beings make mistakes about who and what is deserving of their affection. These mistakes have important consequences, for when the objects of our esteem are themselves inestimable we are inevitably led to think and act in unsociable ways. Indeed, domineering and antisocial behaviors (e.g., schoolyard bullying) are often motivated not by anger or malevolence per se but rather by a desire to be accepted by one's peers. In such cases it is not the wish to do harm but rather the desire to be loved that moves us to behave in aggressive and unsociable ways. Thus, unlike anger, which motivates us to harm others simply for the sake of harming them, misguided recognition-seeking might lead us to injure some for the purpose of impressing others. Like anger, the unguided or misguided desire for social distinction is a pervasive source of mischief in Rousseau's moral universe: we constantly seek false goods—wealth and titles of various kinds—in part because we believe that through their possession we will gain the affection of others (whose affection is in most cases not worth having), but in the pursuit of such things we are inevitably forced to undermine the interests of the very persons whose esteem we so desire. Thus does injudicious recognition-seeking help create the zero-sum power dynamics discussed in the previous chapter.

These two dangers hardly exhaust the problems that malignant *amour-propre* can cause, but they are highlighted here both because of their gravity and because they point up the depth and intensity of the desire for social recognition that is awakened with the birth of *amour-propre*. The antisocial tendencies that develop in their wake are, however, clearly perversions of *amour-propre* rather than fulfillments of its basic internal logic. Confronting the willfulness of others need not lead to anger overtaking the soul. Indeed, *amour-propre*—while the *source* of much evil—is not in itself evil. It is, to the contrary, a "useful but dangerous instrument" in the creation of moral identity, a passion that is susceptible to corruption without being corrupt in itself (*E* 244, cf. 252). Rousseau argues that the normal trajectory of healthy self-love is "toward benevolence" and that we are by nature disposed favorably toward the other members of our species (213). These natural sympathetic feelings are in principle reinforced rather than undermined by *amour-propre* because, once we understand that others recognize and have intentions toward us, it is immediately obvious that we should want that recognition to be positive and those intentions to be favorable. All things being equal, we would prefer to be remembered for the happiness we inspire rather than the threat we pose, and when we seek to dominate others we do so either because we are responding childishly to their intransigence or because our impoverished moral tastes have led us to look for love in all the wrong places. These problems emerge because we are exposed to human intentionality before we are in a condition to appropriately cognize it (214). Thus, when the healthy adolescent turns to others for the first time—when he *is able to* process the willfulness of others—he views them as important sources of recognition and validation. As an immediate consequence of the view he takes, he is disposed to desire their good opinion, even as he himself does not fully understand what it is he seeks. The desire for approval thus arises concomitantly with and necessarily attaches to the awakening of social sentiment.

The key to solving the twin dangers of anger and indiscriminate recognition-seeking is to forge a link between the desire for social approval and the desire to *merit* that approval. The crucial importance of this link emerges early in Book IV: "One wants to obtain the preference one grants. To be loved, one must make oneself lovable. To be preferred, one has to make oneself more lovable than another, more lovable than every other, at least in the eyes of the beloved object. This is the source of the first glances at one's fellows; this is the source of the first comparisons with them; this is the source of emulation, rivalries, jealousy. . . . With love and friendship are born dissensions, enmity, and hate" (*E* 214–15). With characteristic foreboding, Rousseau calls attention to the specifically comparative dimension of *amour-propre* and all the trouble it causes. Men want recognition for its own sake, and since the forms of recognition attaching to "love and friendship" are granted preferentially, not everyone attains the affection they so crave. Suffering feelings of exclusion, the malcontent may angrily lash out against or basely imitate those who won the love they were denied. The effects are uniformly destructive: competition becomes the basis for exclusion, which in its turn becomes the basis for great psychological and social conflict.

However, such dangers can be obviated to the degree that our comparative life is carefully developed, and our wish to be loved can be transformed into a wish to be *lovable*. This transformation, as it is explained in *Emile*, occurs in two stages: the first is to stabilize the sense of self-worth by subtly gratifying nascent *amour-propre*, and the second is to cultivate a passion for virtue by sublimating his sexual desire. With respect to the former, we may begin by noting that the sorts of interpersonal comparisons made by newly social subjects need not simply be the source of emotional turmoil but rather can actually strengthen their moral identities. Because it is not just "dissensions, enmity, and hate"—but also "love and friendship"—that grow out of *amour-propre*'s need to be recognized and respected, Emile's first comparisons are designed to stimulate his sympathetic impulses and thereby connect him to his species. He is exposed to the sights and sounds of poverty, and these early experiences inspire two kinds of comparisons that serve to stabilize his emerging moral identity as well. The first and most obvious comparison Emile makes is between himself and the person he is helping, and from this comparison he derives heartening reminders of his own puissance as well as the satisfaction that comes with providing a social service of indisputable worth (*E* 223, 229). This comparison solidifies a sense of self-respect that is still unsettled and hence susceptible to corruption because it helps Emile to see that, no matter how well-off some are, there are still others who require his assistance and care. With this in mind, it is worth emphasizing that the way in which comparative activity is introduced is of the first importance for the ultimate effect on the soul. It is essential to Rousseau that Emile be the victor in the first comparisons he makes with others, for if he were to think of himself as inferior it is very likely he would—just like the conventional pupil who is shown the magnificence of the rich rather than the destitution of the poor—become overwhelmed by envy and, ultimately, by anger (220). "Some are better-off," he would think, "and *someone* is responsible." Thus it is only after Emile's education in pity has established a reasonably stable sense of self-worth that it is safe for him to associate with the rich and magnificent.

Emile compares himself not only to the person who requires his assistance but also to those who could join him in helping the unfortunate but elect not to do so, whether out of laziness or contempt (*E* 224, 244–45). Here, too, Emile compares favorably to his fellows, but for a different reason: he prefers his position to that of others because he better exemplifies the standards of personal and moral excellence he shares with them. Reflecting on common standards of right and goodness and measuring his own efforts against those who occupy a social position similar to his own, Emile finds new reasons to love and cherish both himself as well as those who need his help. Comparative activity, properly structured, actually helps Emile clarify who he is to others and *to himself*: his moral identity, his sense of himself as a benevolent person, is stabilized by the contrast he observes between himself and those who share his social advantages. To be sure, this contrast will cultivate a sense of moral superiority, but it does so in a way that encourages him to think of himself as the kind of person whose own dignity is expressed by and conditioned on affirming the dignity of others.[4]

While the kinds of comparison embodied by pity help Emile cultivate habits of thought and action that are favorable to the species, this first step in the development of moral identity is only provisional and preparatory. The next and all-important stage is the sublimation of sexual desire. Indeed, the desire to gain the esteem of others and the desire to be estimable manifests itself with particular clarity and intensity in Rousseau's treatment of the sexual passion, which he conceives as an intrinsically moralistic and moralizing force in the human soul. Sexuality is a prodigious source of social energy and our sexual experiences have a decisive influence on the final shape of our entire personality; its education is therefore of the first moment. In the *Discourse on Inequality*, Rousseau genuflects fearfully before the "unrestrained and brutal" impulse that "makes one sex necessary to the other," noting that the sexual passion is so central to civilized man that it can override even his desire for self-preservation (*DI* 134).

Though the *Discourse*'s discussion emphasizes the dangers of the sexual passion, of special relevance here is the way Rousseau's distinction between "physical" and "moral" love helps us understand how sexuality builds the bridge between the desire for esteem and the desire to be estimable. "Physical" sexual desire is for Rousseau a direct expression of primitive *amour de soi-même* and, as such, a purely mechanical function of innate self-regard. Men and women in the state of nature engage without emotion or affection, seeing one another as instruments of private satisfaction. Considerations of compatibility, physical attractiveness, and moral character do not govern their relations. However, the desire for physical love is peaceable precisely because it is uninformed by complex, deeply felt desire. Natural man "waits for the impulsion of nature, yields to it without choice [and] with more pleasure than frenzy; and the need satisfied, all desire is extinguished" (*DI* 135). "Physical" sexuality is the psychic equivalent of scratching an itch.

All this changes, however, when "moral" love emerges and effects two related transformations in the structure of sexual desiring. The first involves the development of discriminatory capacities that sharpen aesthetic and moral taste. Whereas natural man does not distinguish between fit and unfit sexual partners, those under the spell of moral love consider questions of appearance as well as character when seeking an appropriate romantic object. The criteria we use to help us separate wheat from chaff—what Rousseau calls notions of "merit and beauty" (*DI* 135)—allow us to assess the physical and moral virtues of potential mates and to form preferences on their basis. It is by way of forming such preferences that romantic love moves toward *exclusivity*, for once we have learned to esteem one person more than another our desire "gains a greater degree of energy" for our "preferred object" (*DI* 134). It is important to note that both aesthetic and moral criteria—beauty *and* merit—are relevant to the selection of a partner.

The emergence of "moral love" not only refines but also intensifies sexual desire, and this intensification is due to its interaction with *amour-propre*. Once moved by the desire to be loved, men and women begin to view one another not as accessories to orgasm but rather as sources of personal validation. That is, as we become aware that others are observing us and as aesthetic and moral considerations begin to complicate the experience of sexual attraction, we start to view both our partners and the sexual act itself in a very different light. Coupling is no longer about the simple gratification of a purely physiological impulse, but rather about the acquisition of a unique and uniquely intoxicating form of recognition. To the moral lover, giving one's body to another is not simply or even a primarily physical act; it is, rather, the definitive way of sharing what is most deeply and fundamentally one's own. There is something paradoxical and, as Rousseau so often reminds us, potentially troubling about this kind of giving, for while it suggests something final and ultimate—that there is nothing beyond it that can be given—so, too, does it point beyond itself and toward something still more fundamental. The human good instantiated in the sexual passion is one at which sex only *hints* but at which *only* sex can hint, for the enchanting aspirations within and beyond moral love have—as we shall see below—a largely physical basis and must find final expression through the articulacy of action.

Because "moral love" utilizes aesthetic and ethical criteria in order to fix its affection on a particular object, so, too, does it indicate a strong connection—however attenuated in specific cases—between sexual and moral aspiration.

Indeed, Rousseau believes true love "will always be honored among men" because embedded in it are "estimable qualities without which one would not be in a condition to feel it" (*E* 215). Not even the most despicable Parisian dandy can entirely decouple the desire to be esteemed from the desire to be estimable. And though Rousseau does nothing to hide the dangers involved in the specifically sexual form of recognition-seeking—love "does not exclude odious qualities" and "even produces them"—he also argues such dangers are coextensive with the social enterprise and that they must be run in order for human beings to fulfill their moral potential (215). "How many great things," he exclaims in a discussion of moralized sexuality, "could be done by means of this motive if one knew how to set it in motion!" (390). So long as love facilitates consciousness of the "estimable qualities" qualities of body and soul—so long as there is a plausible connection between what is loved and what is lovable—sexual desire offers new and delicious inducements to virtue and thus can serve as a powerful catalyst of moral perfection.

| Grounding the Divine Heights: Sexuality and Sociability

In characterizing the first stirrings of sociability as both obscure and intense, Rousseau not only deviates from Hobbes's and Locke's moral psychology but also does much to recall Platonic eros (Cooper 2008). Indeed, the desire for moral perfection described above is a particular expression of a more general longing for perfection of a more fundamental, albeit more enigmatic, kind. For Rousseau as for Plato, the good that human beings seek through their relations is all-encompassing; furthermore, as Rousseau tells his Sophie, encounters with this good in its fullness carry us beyond our being and into the empyrean. Far, however, from following Plato in understanding human relations as the product of erotic desire, Rousseau instead views erotic desire as the product of human relations. And because he departs from Plato in denying the naturalness of eros he must therefore explain how it emerges from sources that are authentically natural. What, then, lurks underneath the indeterminate longings of the newly social adolescent?

A careful reading of the initial pages of Book IV of *Emile* shows how nascent *sexuality* plays an especially important role in grounding our first social impulses and lends them an intensity that is characteristic of eros. These pages describe the birth of the social passions, and Rousseau begins his analysis of this question with a dramatic pronouncement about the importance of love and sex. "How rapid is our journey on this earth! The first quarter of life has been lived before one knows the use of it. The last quarter is lived when one has ceased to enjoy it." He quickly clarifies what the interval between these two "useless extremities" is actually "good" for: "We are, so to speak, born twice: once to exist and once to live; once for our species and once for our sex" (211). The awakening of sexual desire is so crucial for Rousseau that it constitutes nothing less than a "second birth" in which man is "truly born to life . . . and nothing human is foreign to him" (212). Sexuality is essential to the ongoing process of self-understanding, for only through it can one access distinctively human pleasures, pains, and obligations. In short, sexuality makes us human.

Rousseau's decision to frame his treatment of the birth of social sentiment in terms of sexual development indicates that the two processes are closely related. Indeed, Rousseau comes to the point of arguing that the birth of *amour-propre* and all its peculiar longings is really the birth of inchoate sexual desire. "As soon," he explains, "as a man has need of a companion, he is no longer an isolated being. . . . All his relations with his species, all the affections of his soul are born with this one. His first passion soon makes the others ferment" (*E* 214). The following paragraph, which elaborates specifically and at length on the nature of romantic love, shows clearly that the "companion" now sought after is a lover rather than a friend: "The inclination of nature is indeterminate. One sex is attracted to the other; that is the movement of nature." Sexuality is crucial to social development not only because it is a powerful source of moral motivation but also because it sharpens the powers of moral and aesthetic discrimination we use in all the domains of social life. Love both presupposes and improves our ability to locate in others certain "estimable qualities"—considerations of merit and beauty—that would otherwise go unperceived or misperceived. Diffused, undirected sexual desire helps ground moral and social impulse; its operations and influence are not restricted to sexual life specifically but are rather felt in all the dimensions of moral life.

We, of course, know that the adolescent Emile does not know any of this and is in a state of constant perplexity both about what he is for others and what they are for him. On this point, we should recall how essential it is that he experience his first social longings in all their indeterminacy, for it is this indeterminacy that allows him to cognize his relations as intrinsic rather than instrumental goods. But there are still other reasons to delay the onset of specifically sexual desire, whose premature emergence is identified by Rousseau as *the* danger to be avoided in early adolescence. To this end, he undertakes an extended excursus on conventional sex education in order to show that it actually worsens the ill it was designed to resolve. It does so first by carelessly exciting the child's curiosity and second by refusing to satisfy it. Offended by the refusals of adults and enticed by their knowing grins, children search in secret for the knowledge their elders will not give them: "The lessons of decency given to [children], the veil of mystery that is supposed to be drawn over their eyes, are only so many spurs to their curiosity" (*E* 215). Efforts to conceal the great mystery of generation only sharpen the sight of prying eyes.

The effects of precocious sexuality are wide-ranging and destructive. For instance, premature gratification whitewashes other important social feelings, overwhelming with its wild force the still-developing system of social impulses and short-circuiting basic social sentiments like pity. This prevents us from understanding or entertaining—and thus from respecting—the interests of anyone but the love object. On this score Rousseau reports that young people who are "given over to women" too early are always "inhuman and cruel." The "heat of their temperaments made them impatient, vindictive, and wild. Their imaginations, filled with a single object, rejected all the rest. They knew neither pity nor mercy" (*E* 220). The sexual drive is so powerful that, if expressed too early, it crowds out other social sentiments that are also expressive of human nature and that are needed to enjoy a full and rich social life. Lovers who see and feel nothing but each other at too early an age never develop a full complement of social feelings and are unable to identify sympathetically with others. They are, in fact, often disposed to view the outside world and its impositions as so many threats to their bond and to either lash out against or attempt a complete retreat from "society." Even if well motivated, the strategy of escape would appear to be futile, for lovers do not and cannot exist in a social or political vacuum. They are, to the contrary, situated in a complex of social institutions with which they must come to terms in order to sustain their union. Thus it would seem that, to the degree that lovers wish to maintain their relation, they must develop the system of social impulses necessary for their healthy social incorporation.

Rousseau goes still further, arguing not only that precipitate sexuality short-circuits other important social feelings but also that it ultimately compromises the experience of love itself. Premature sexual activity is a prime cause of the moral and existential truncation of modern man. The sexual passion is simply too intense, too complex, and too overwhelming for young people, who remain "small, weak, and ill-formed" if they become sexually active at too young an age. It is particularly pernicious in cities, where young people "age instead of growing, as the vine that has been made to bear fruit in the spring languishes and dies before autumn" (*E* 216). Early initiation into the mysteries of sex exhausts man's vitality before it can truly express itself, stripping sex of its enchantment and robbing us of one of the greatest sources of happiness available to us. This loss is all the more serious when we consider that the passion of love—as we shall see in chapters 4 and 5—is highly unstable and must be supplemented by gentler social feelings (e.g., "pity and mercy") if the romantic association is to endure at all. If these feelings never fully develop, then resentment and even disgust are likely to follow upon the (inevitable) death of passion and undermine the union. It is in the face of such grave dangers that Jean-Jacques leaves Emile to dwell in aporetic confusion about the source of his desire. It is the first of many assists he will give to nature in the course of his pupil's moral and social development.

| Distinguishing Love and Friendship: The Many Faces of *Amour-Propre*

Because *amour-propre*'s need for social recognition expresses itself with particular intensity in the sexual situation, Rousseau seeks to delay for as long as possible the arousal of specifically sexual impulses. Indeed, one of the more puzzling aspects of Rousseau's treatment of the dawning of social sentiment is that he insists on the genetic priority of the sexual passion only to delay its expression until the last possible moment. Far from claiming that the first concrete manifestation of the social-sexual impulse should itself be sexual, he instead encourages the tutor to suppress his pupil's consciousness of sexual identity and to redirect his newfound need for companionship toward friendship rather than love: the "first sentiment of which a carefully raised young man is capable is not love; it is friendship. The first act of his nascent imagination is to teach him he has fellows; and the species affects him before the female sex" (*E* 220). A sentiment favorable to the species, and to all sentient creatures, must emerge before love even though such a sentiment is itself grounded at least in part in protean sexuality. Is this another of Rousseau's contradictions?

I submit that it is not, and for two reasons. First, Rousseau's claim that adolescents are capable of friendship before they are capable of love is not incompatible with his genetic claim that the desire for "friendship" emerges in part from inchoate sexuality. Because the set of responses and sentiments evoked by friendship are more tractable than the highly complex emotions associated with romantic love, Rousseau gives pedagogic priority to the former even though the latter has genetic priority. One must crawl before walking. Though it would appear that, in acting thus, Jean-Jacques works against rather than with the natural order, we shall see below that such appearances are somewhat deceiving. Second, it is clear that friendship and love are on Rousseau's accounting quite distinct associational phenomena that create different emotional needs and satisfy different kinds of human desire. Though want of both these forms of association share a common source, they become increasingly distinct as they develop and mature. The emergence of discrete social passions is more important than it may seem, for it helps explain a highly significant fact of social life, namely, that *amour-propre*'s demands are not uniform but rather vary according to associational context.

In privileging friendship over love it seems that Jean-Jacques is now working against rather than with natural developmental processes, for it appears that the indeterminate sexuality underwriting many of adolescent Emile's social impulses is now being actively suppressed by the tutor. However, by allowing his pupil to remain in aporetic confusion about the sources of his desires, Jean-Jacques claims that, far from violating nature, he is in fact its midwife and agent. On this score, Rousseau notes that nature itself only partially determines the specific moment for sexual awakening and thus allows for the influence of mores and education. A degree of indeterminacy is built into the *natural* structure of the sexual passion: the moment of its arousal and the character of its development are contingent on social and climatological factors which are being carefully controlled in Emile's education. Given that nature has left some room for environmental influence, Jean-Jacques claims that in exercising some discretion on his pupil's behalf he is actually nature's agent rather than its opponent: redirecting an inchoate sexual drive toward nonsexual objects "is not an artful untruth" but rather the best way to allow "nature's ignorance" to enlighten itself (E 219). We are reminded that "the time" of sexual maturity "is coming" but are told that to inform one's pupil too early is far worse than to inform him too late (if such is possible): "Nature's instruction is late and slow; men's is almost always premature. In the former case the senses awake the imagination; in the latter the imagination wakes the senses" (219, 215). Given space and time, our highly indeterminate want of social companionship unpacks itself and becomes discrete desires for specific kinds of companionship. The adolescent, then, is confused because nature wants it that way, not because his tutor is misleading him. In his redirection of diffused sexual energy Jean-Jacques is perhaps not in perfect accord with nature, but for Rousseau's argument to work it is enough that he not be in *dis*accord with it.

If the ordered development of the social passions leads us to friendship before romantic love, then it also requires us to distinguish *between* friendship and love. In so doing, it forces us to recognize that associational life is varied and complex. Though our initial social longing is itself highly indeterminate, there are immanent within it several discrete desires for different kinds of association that have their own particular requirements and are directed toward the fulfillment of distinct psychological needs. Human beings identify with one another in all manner of ways—as lovers and beloveds, parents and children, friends and siblings, superiors and subordinates, citizens and subjects, competitors and fellows—and the kinds of recognition and fulfillment we seek from these various forms of identification are different and distinguishable. What the confused adolescent lacks—and what he gains through the process of social development—is a sense of exactly how others figure into his life and of what kinds of expectations are appropriate to particular interpersonal contexts. Much of what social development *is*, then, is the gradual disaggregation of the undifferentiated desire for recognition into several discrete desires for distinct kinds of love and recognition. At the very heart of socialization is the realization that different kinds of relationships offer different kinds of satisfaction. The development of sociability, on Rousseau's account, is then quite literally the transformation of the original social *passion*—the as yet undifferentiated want of companionship—into discrete, identifiable, and educable social *passions*. Though this first and highly indeterminate social passion has a largely sexual basis it nonetheless contains within it a whole host of discrete social desires that can be meaningfully distinguished from the specifically sexual desire.

The capacity to distinguish between love and friendship has important implications for how we think about *amour-propre*. Because social attachment is not a monolithic or undifferentiated psychic phenomenon—because there are distinguishable and discrete forms of connectedness with different psychic bases—neither is the desire for social distinction something that assumes the same form or behaves in the same way. Different kinds of relationships serve different purposes and speak to different needs in the psychic economies of healthy human beings. Thus the degree and kind of recognition that we seek is in many ways contingent on the specific associational context in which it is embedded. This finding, it must be admitted, is hardly counterintuitive. In arguing as he does, Rousseau is in accord—for him, perhaps, a rare accord—with what might be called common sense, for no special genius is needed to see that human beings find themselves in different sorts of relationships, that such relationships have different psychological sources and effects, and that these relationships help to structure the behaviors and desires of those who are embedded in them.

Curiously, the very feature of *amour-propre* that is evident to virtually anyone who has reflected even momentarily on his own associational life remains undertheorized in Rousseau scholarship. Most scholarly treatments characterize the emergence and development of *amour-propre* as a unidimensional transformation from a self-love that has its origin in natural needs into one that has its origin in arbitrary opinion. In seeking to explain this transformation, the focus has been on the *fact* of social observation—the realization that others, whoever they may be, are *watching us*. Judith Shklar, N. J. H. Dent, and Frederick Neuhouser have all provided very sophisticated and helpful statements of this broad problematic and have gone on to adduce many of the psychological possibilities and pathologies that attend the ever-increasing awareness of others and an ever-increasing desire to gain their esteem. What is important in such cases is to know *that* we are being observed, not *who* is doing the observing. As a general characterization of *amour-propre* this is correct and even useful as a way of fixing ideas about the kinds of psychic dislocations that can result from the phenomenon of social observation. But to focus simply on the fact of observation in the abstract is to assume that the effects of *amour-propre* are felt uniformly across the entire field of social interaction. It is to assume that we would like to know whether we are being observed but are uninterested in knowing who, exactly, is doing the observing.

It will be a guiding concern in the following chapters to show that this assumption conceals meaningful variation in the way *amour-propre* expresses itself, that it in fact matters a great deal who exactly is watching us. The way in which we identify the observer—whether we are under the gaze of a lover (or prospective lover), a friend, a parent, a teacher (or student), a fellow citizen, a stranger, or a child—is of the first importance for what we do and how we go about doing it. Not all social anxieties are created equal. Because the differentiation of the social passions is at one with their development, it becomes necessary to look more closely at the various forms of social recognition that recur in Rousseau's oeuvre, and to look specifically at their respective psychological consequences. In so doing, we shall see that the various forms of connectedness have different psychological statuses, are felt more or less intensely, and in consequence are more or less useful in their contribution to the preservation of human wholeness.

3 | Pity and Human Weakness

"There is, besides, another principle which Hobbes did not notice, and which—having been given to man in order to soften his vanity or the desire for self-preservation before the birth of vanity [*amour-propre*]—tempers the ardor he has for his own well-being by an innate repugnance to see his fellow-man suffer" (*DI* 130).[1] In his first sustained criticism of Hobbes, Rousseau charges the great systematist with a serious error of omission. In his effort to reduce all human behavior to the mechanical promptings of rational self-interest, Hobbes had failed to notice a psychological principle that encourages human beings not to harm one another. The failure to account for this mysterious tendency had led Hobbes and his acolytes to an unduly restrictive understanding of human nature and of the social situation; by naming it Rousseau believes he can not only improve on Hobbes's theory but also reveal the true origin of "all the rules of natural right" (96). Rousseau speaks, of course, of pity, a sentiment that produces a natural aversion to the spectacle of suffering and that is "appropriate to beings as weak and subject to as many ills as we are" (130). On Rousseau's accounting it is neither Hobbes's hedonistic calculus nor Aristotle's principle of natural sociability, but rather a native sensitivity to the distress of other living beings, that lies at the basis of moral and social life. Indeed, he claims that from pity "*alone* flow *all* the social virtues" and that "benevolence and even friendship" are best understood as "the products of a constant pity fixed on a particular object" (131–32; emphasis added). Thus pity, understood aright, is not only a restraint on the uglier expressions of unadulterated self-love; it is also the foundation of sympathetic social identification, a more or less comprehensive list of social virtues ("generosity," "clemency, [and] humanity" are the ones given by Rousseau), and a particular—and particularly important—form of association in which such virtues find expression.

Though Rousseau was hardly the only moral philosopher of the eighteenth century to insist on the importance of sympathy, his account of this central passion is distinctive for both its ambitiousness as well as its ambiguity. In the *Second Discourse* he invokes pity as a kind of moral-psychological panacea, arguing that it is operative in the earliest stages of human development and that it serves a series of important socializing functions. However, his actual argument on these points is at best suggestive and often borders on complete collapse. The sentiment itself appears more or less out of nowhere—it emerges not as the product of reasoned argument or plausible empirical observation but rather from the black box of Rousseau's private meditations on "the first and simplest principles of the human soul"—and the account of its importance to human life falls far short of substantiating the remarkably strong claim that it *alone* is the source of *all* the social virtues (*DI* 95). What is more, the premise that pity is especially important to and appropriate for beings "subject to as many ills" as humans are appears to be in tension with what is perhaps the central argument of the entire work—that man is naturally strong and independent and that the majority of his "ills" are his own creations. If the theoretical usefulness of pity is grounded in the postulate of man's essential frailty, then Rousseau's famously idyllic characterization of life in the state of nature would appear to be misleadingly simple. One is hard-pressed to see how the operations of pity could be at all useful for a being as indolent and cognitively simple as Rousseau's natural man (e.g., *DI* 105). Even by the end of the *Discourse on Inequality* it is not entirely clear how the unique situation of the human being—the environment in which he is embedded and the specific complex of capacities that express and confine his nature—creates the especial need for a sentiment like pity. It is then Rousseau's own characterization of the natural human condition that seems to delimit the utility of pity.

Rousseau's paradoxical characterization of the human condition as being one of both weakness and strength has important consequences for how we understand human relations. We saw in the previous chapter that Rousseau was concerned about the self-serving sociability and lack of moral energy he believed to be characteristic of his age; we also saw that one of his principal aims as an author was to reinvigorate his readers' sense of moral and social possibility. This aim is especially evident in the *Discourse on Inequality*, which he imagined being performed in front of the entire "human race" rather than perused by pedants in the cold isolation of the ivory tower (*DI* 103).[2] Yet remaining mindful of both the moral transformation Rousseau sought to effect in his readers as well as the performative or public character of the *Discourse* makes the invocation of pity doubly paradoxical, for a continued emphasis on the weakness and vulnerability of human nature could have the perverse practical effect of creating in his audience a deadly moral fatalism rather than a more expansive sense of possibility. Rousseau himself indicates an awareness of this problem in the *Preface to Narcisse*, observing that "so many reflections on the weakness of our nature often serve only to turn us away from generous undertakings" and that incessant harping on "the miseries of humanity" ultimately results in moral passivity (25).[3] Rousseau's own utterances thus beg an important motivational question: how can we be expected to energetically pursue our own perfectionistic impulses when the very author encouraging us to do so is also constantly reminding us of our own basic and ineliminable weakness?

This question has recently been put rather forcefully to Rousseau by Clifford Orwin (1997a, 1997b) and Richard Boyd (2004), who both worry that Rousseau's insistence on the importance of pity diminishes human possibility in politically destructive ways. Boyd (2004, 525, 529) is especially concerned about pity's tendency to induce moral passivity, arguing that it turns us into "voyeurs" who not only find ourselves unable to actively assist the needy but also take positive *delight* in their suffering. Orwin (1997a, 10–11) blames pity for lowering moral horizons and inaugurating a politics of class warfare which valorizes the blameless poor at the expense of the hard-hearted rich. Both accounts charge that pity cannot generate the moral energy necessary to inspire citizens to take action against injustice.

Such objections are not without face plausibility, but a more comprehensive look at Rousseau's understanding of the human condition, and of pity's place within it, helps to show that Rousseau never intended for pity to perform the kinds of functions that Boyd and Orwin assign to it. Indeed, since—as we have already seen—Rousseau turns to moralized *amour-propre*, grounded in protean sexuality, in order to generate the moral energy and ambition that both critics find absent in pity, he has already addressed the motivational problems that they charge him with ignoring. In order to understand the role of pity in moral life, then, it is important to see how it works in conjunction with *other* social and ethical impulses. That is the task of this chapter. In particular, I am interested in how the "low" and more egalitarian features of pity supplement and, in certain instances, even serve to correct the "high" ambitions created by moralized *amour-propre*.

Because Rousseau is especially concerned to diagnose and depict the kinds of suffering that occur when our highest and best desires are frustrated, much of pity's usefulness as a moral sentiment is not in contradiction with, but rather depends decisively on, the existence and activity of our most ambitious moral and social aspirations. It is, after all, most especially in the wake of failure that we are in need of consolation and care. Commiseration takes some of the sting out of failing to live up to the expectations we have for ourselves and others, and it is in the act of lamenting our shared imperfections that the hope of our "frail happiness" arises (*E* 221). Far, then, from conceiving of pity and the perfectionistic drives of moralized *amour-propre* as polar opposites or uncombinable forces, Rousseau views them as dialectically interdependent and interlocking impulses which address themselves to different, though related, psychological and social needs. Pity is therefore especially appropriate for human beings not simply because we are by nature weak and frail, but also because the logic of human development requires that we learn to boldly—if sometimes unsuccessfully—aspire to large and great things. To be human is for Rousseau a difficult and frustrating thing; our grandest ambitions point to a horizon in constant retreat. The disappointments that attach to this dynamic cannot be overcome by means of historical progress or erotic transcendence; they are, rather, constituent features of our social and moral lives that we must learn to manage. It is against this backdrop that Rousseau's insistence on pity's especial importance must be understood.

Provided that Rousseau can appeal to the moral force of pity without undermining his commitment to elevating man's moral and social aspirations, to what functions can he assign it in the context of his broader theory of human relations? I shall develop two major arguments on this score. First, I shall be at pains throughout to emphasize the *negative* character of pity. In both the state of nature and the state of society, one of pity's primary functions is to soften the harsher expressions of self-love. Thus, in rounding out Rousseau's account of moral and social motivation, pity helps to ameliorate some of the dangers—most notably false pride and fanaticism—to which moralized *amour-propre* exposes us. We already know Rousseau believes it necessary to develop rather than stifle our perfectionistic moral drives because they are the source of "the most sublime virtues," but below we shall see he is also aware that such drives require softening because they, left to their own devices, cause socially destabilizing forms of intolerance and even sanguinary violence. Pity and the set of virtues that grow out of it remind us that we share the imperfection of the afflicted (or, in many cases, the guilty) party; in so doing, it serves to moderate the harshness that often attaches to our moral assessments.

Second, pity is a positive catalyst of social togetherness, but it catalyzes associations of a necessarily attenuated kind. The form of identification embodied by pity has peculiar dynamics that simultaneously enable and limit human community: one who pities another apprehends that he is both like *and* unlike the suffering other—alike insofar as he realizes that he, too, is in principle subject to whatever misfortune the aggrieved party suffers, but different insofar as he also realizes that he does not suffer *in fact*. The dual presence of likeness and difference, of equality and superiority, characterize the psychic experience of pity and put limits on the forms of association that are actuated by it. We are forced by the apprehension of difference that is implicit in pity to recognize the discrete, individuated existence of the other being—we must recognize the other's otherness. This kind of recognition, though it can provide a genuine source of comfort and community, nonetheless cannot satisfy our need for *unity* with and through one another.

In arguing thus I understand pity as playing a coequal role with the sexual passion in structuring man's moral and associational life, and I seek to show how it both supplements the moral and social motivations that grow out of sublimated sexual desire as well as how it ameliorates some of the dangers to which those motivations give rise. If the sexualized morality of perfection speaks to the aspiring, bold, and "high" expressions of our nature, then pity keeps us connected to the vulnerable, imperfect, and "low" sides of ourselves. The extent to which we can integrate the dynamic tensions created by these two distinct but interdependent impulses is an important determinant of our ultimate happiness. In the chapters following this one, we shall see how and why we fail at this task as well as the dislocations that result from those failures.

| The State of Nature: A State of Weakness?

Though Rousseau insists on pity's especial utility for the human species, a first glance at his picture of man in the state of nature hardly bears that insistence out. If anyone is to be pitied it is the troubled and restless "civil" man, whose self-defeating way of life is contrasted with natural man's independent and peaceable existence. Indeed, the autarchic contentment of natural man's life is consistently contrasted with the hyperactive mischievousness of the *Second Discourse*'s reprehensible villain. Rousseau thematizes the stylized contrast between "natural man" and "civil man" to the advantage of the former and, in so doing, forces the reader to view himself in a new and less flattering light. Natural man is strong and free while civil man is weak and dependent; natural man is content with little while civil man is unhappy with much; natural man assists those he pities while civil man retreats to safety; natural man does not care what others think while civil man lives only in the eyes of others; natural man "hardly has need of remedies" while civil man needs the constant attention of doctors; natural man is at harmony with himself and his environment while civil man is at war with both; natural man naps peacefully under the same tree that provided his meal and sips water from a babbling brook while civil man rushes futilely toward a retreating horizon (*DI* 110, 105).

Such comparisons are a rhetorically effective way to expose the absurdity of the social situation and to inspire in readers a moralized indignation at their own condition, but they problematize Rousseau's insistence on the especial importance of pity. To the degree that human beings are naturally strong and independent in the way Rousseau's portraits of life in the state of nature suggest, it becomes very easy to wonder about the utility that a sentiment like pity could have for him: pity, as Rousseau himself notes, is appropriate for "weak" beings that are subject to "many ills," not for free and capable individuals who successfully satisfy their own needs (*DI* 130). In order to reconcile this tension it is necessary to consult both the *Second Discourse*'s depiction of the state of nature and its account of pity, for they reveal that Rousseau understates the difficulties of life in the former and overstates the activity of the latter. These exaggerations are part of an anti-Hobbesian rhetorical strategy intended to inspire in less attentive readers a moralized indignation at their own condition. More "attentive readers"—those with "the courage to begin again"—will not fail to discover that the forms of weakness and vulnerability that beset natural man, though different than those that are experienced in civil society, are nonetheless no less definitive of his basic condition (98). So, too, will they discover a conception of pity that, far from inspiring active benevolence, instead serves to restrain the uglier manifestations of pure self-love.

Close attention to the argument of the *Discourse on Inequality* shows that vulnerability and weakness are conditions of life in the state of nature as well as in civil society. Men are constantly subjected to the harsh and unrelenting necessities imposed by "infancy, old age, and illnesses of all kinds" (*DI* 108). These conditions are "sad signs" of his basic weakness: putting aside the problems posed by the "inclemencies of the weather and the rigor of the seasons" with which all animals must deal, Rousseau notes that humans have unusually long periods of gestation and infancy, thus leaving mothers and children more vulnerable to prey than other animal species (106, 108, 112). Though he attempts to lighten the weight of this specifically human burden by adding that "if infancy is longer among us, then so is life [and] everything remains approximately equal in this respect," this qualification is transparently and even suspiciously unconvincing: because the likelihood of dying during infancy is a function of the absolute rather than the relative length of the period of dependence on the mother, and because the period of such dependence is longer for humans than for other animals, it follows that human infants are more likely to perish than are their animal counterparts (109). We are beset by still more limitations. For instance, our bipedalism, touted by Rousseau to be one of our chief advantages over other species, proves far less beneficial than initial appearances suggest. Indeed, the primary benefit of having two legs is that we can carry our children as we flee from quadrupedal predators who—precisely because they are quadrupeds—run more swiftly than we do. In addition, we do not have fur and thus are more susceptible to the ill effects of cold weather (112).

The question of disease deserves special attention in this context, for Rousseau's claim that illness "belongs principally to man living in civil society" must be understood as part of his broader rhetorical strategy to highlight the way in which civil man creates many of his own problems. He begins his discussion of sickness by posing a seemingly rhetorical question whose answer is in fact anything but obvious: "I shall ask whether there is any solid observation from which one might conclude that in Countries where this art [of medicine] is most neglected, the average life of man is shorter than in those where it is cultivated with the greatest care" (*DI* 109). Note that Rousseau proposes a testable hypothesis to settle the matter; what is needed is a scientific investigation into the utility of a particular branch of applied science. He thus appeals to the authority of science in the very act of interrogating its usefulness. Note also that the hypothesis he advances is a null: he expects medicine to have *no* effect on life expectancy, not a negative effect as his rhetoric implies. Rousseau's critique of medicine is thus more qualified than it first appears.

But what evidence does Rousseau provide in support of this (qualified) claim? The "observations" made on this score are offered as provisional rather than definitive explanations, and they are known by Rousseau himself to be far from solid. For instance, while suggesting that natural man is generally healthy, Rousseau is in fact very careful not to deny that sickness exists in the state of nature or that the illnesses suffered there are often fatal. He claims instead that natural man has fewer *sources* of illness than does civilized man—far different from claiming that he is sick less frequently—and that he "*hardly* has need of remedies" (*DI* 110; emphasis added). These hedges suggest Rousseau's own awareness that life in his state of nature, far from being easy, is in fact full of hardship.

Indeed, the more Rousseau appears to deny such hardships the more evident he makes them. Seeking some empirical basis for his claims regarding natural man's health, Rousseau appeals to the experience of wild animals: he says the testimonies of hunters show that it is common to find animals that "have received extensive but very well-healed wounds," but that it is extremely rare to discover sick ones. The implied conclusion is that humans, like animals, may be injured in nature but rarely, if ever, fall ill. Yet the empirical evidence on which this *reductio ad animalia* is based is once again curiously—indeed, almost perfectly—shoddy. The reports Rousseau cites, even if they are true, certainly do not show that illnesses are not prevalent in the state of nature, for hunters might fail to find sick animals not because there are none to find but rather because sick animals go into hiding in order to (among other reasons) protect themselves from predators. The testimonies of "hunters" would thus appear to be especially untrustworthy on this question. One might also explain the apparent absence of sick animals by hypothesizing that ill animals are less likely to be seen because they, without the aid of modern medicine, are simply quicker to die. Both explanations are compatible with the facts Rousseau reports and, far from suggesting the general health and robustness of natural fauna, instead point up their essential vulnerability and susceptibility to nature's many dangers. Thus the conclusion that a "sick savage" has "nothing to fear except for his illness" is manifestly unwarranted, for he is at the mercy of indifferent natural forces and has "hunters" of his own from which he must protect himself (*DI* 111).

Just as Rousseau understates the difficulties of the state of nature in order to illustrate its advantages, so he overstates the activity of pity in order to show its naturalness. We can begin to see his exaggerations on this head by noting that the argument for natural goodness does not require expressions of active benevolence. In contrast to the Golden Rule, which imposes positive duties by obligating us to "*do unto others as you would have them do unto you*," Rousseau's careful formulation of the principle of natural goodness—"*do what is good for you with the least possible harm to others*"—makes clear that pity modifies behavior only by *restraining* the way in which we pursue our good. The only "duties" goodness imposes are those of forbearance, and even these do not bind absolutely: pity bids us not to harm others unless we deem it necessary to do so. Thus a healthy savage refrains from "robbing a weak child or an infirm old man" only where he believes he can find his subsistence elsewhere (*DI* 133). Rousseau also emphasizes pity's negative character when he introduces the concept in the context of a critique of Hobbes, whom he chastises for "failing to notice" sentiments that—"under certain circumstances"—"*restrain* the ferocity" and "*temper* the ardor" of natural self-love (130). Having failed to notice that "salutary *restraint*" which prevents the expression of self-love's uglier and more callous manifestations, Hobbes had falsely concluded that men, left to their own devices, would savage one another over the most insignificant affairs (133; emphasis added). The role of pity in the state of nature, then, is to minimize the damage men would otherwise do to one another.

Though the argument for natural goodness requires only an economy of violence, Rousseau's rhetoric of pity provides for a seemingly limitless benevolence. He takes it to be "very certain that pity is a natural sentiment" that carries us "without reflection to the aid of those whom we see suffer," and he claims it is evident that savage man "is always seen heedlessly yielding to the first sentiment of humanity." Though pity would now seem to be inspiring men in the state of nature to actively assist one another, the evidence adduced on this score is, as with the discussion of medicine, far short of convincing. Though claiming that savage man is "always seen" following the impulses of pity with no thought of his own good, the only example of anything like positive benevolence that Rousseau provides occurs outside the state of nature. He tells us that in "riots or street fights . . . the prudent man moves away; it is the rabble, the marketwoman, who separate the combatants and prevent honest people from murdering each other" (*DI* 132). At best, this illustration is evidence of the mediating effect of calculative reason—for the crude marketgoer who risks life and limb is contrasted with "the philosopher" who is able to ignore the sounds of murder by "argu[ing] with himself a bit"—but it pretty clearly cannot prove that *natural* pity moves men to actively assist one another.

I emphasize the defectiveness of Rousseau's characterizations of the state of nature and the sentiment of pity not because he was unaware of them but precisely because he *was*. Both arguments are predicated on a "natural man"/"civil man" polarity, a hyper-stylized rhetorical construct intended to make readers see with new eyes the moral and social world that they themselves have built. The function of these rather bad arguments in the text, which we must remember is being *performed* in front of the entire human race, is almost entirely rhetorical: they exaggerate certain contrasts between natural and civil life in order to make those contrasts evident to the less discriminating members of Rousseau's audience, who may lack the philosophic acumen of Plato or Xenocrates but who nonetheless require salutary moral instruction and an account of their nature that is compatible with the truth. With this in mind it should be clear that Rousseau's illustrations are detachable from the actual theory of natural goodness—which stands or falls independently of provisional empirical hypotheses. Indeed, insofar as the theory of natural goodness requires the activity of pity so, too, does it demand an awareness of human vulnerability that, while not inconsistent with the arguments of the *Discourse on Inequality*, is nonetheless not fully accounted for within it. For this account we must turn to *Emile*.

Pitying the Fool: Sympathy, Society, and the Human Condition

Unlike the *Discourse on Inequality*, which invokes the importance of pity while concealing the conditions of life that would make it useful, *Emile* puts the human struggle front and center. Again, rhetorical considerations help explain this shift in emphasis: given that the eponymous hero of the work—unlike the asocial protagonist of the *Second Discourse*—is to become fully social and hence must assume all the difficulties socialization entails, Rousseau's choice to emphasize the challenges of being fully human is hardly surprising. For we see that even when all the problems human beings have created for themselves are assumed away, as they are in the pure state of nature or in Emile's education, Rousseau both characterizes the human condition as one of weakness and travail and holds that pity is an especially appropriate socializing sentiment for beings constituted as we are: "Men are not naturally kings, or lords, or courtiers, or rich men. All are born naked and poor; all are subject to the miseries of life, to sorrows, ills, needs, and pains of every kind. Finally, all are condemned to death. This is what truly belongs to man. This is what no mortal is exempt from. Begin, therefore, by studying in human nature what is most inseparable from it, what best characterizes humanity" (*E* 222). Here, as in the *Discourse on Inequality*, the contrast between natural man and civil man grabs the reader. The inequalities we experience and accept as natural—that some are kings and others are subjects—are in fact not natural at all. Yet the substance of the contrast might surprise the reader of the *Discourse*, for what is genuinely natural—what truly defines us as a species—is no longer our independence but rather our shared fragility and vulnerability to injury. It is in our common need of assistance that we are best able to see "the identity of our natures with theirs" (*E* 221). Human life and contentment are fragile things, and it is in the not uncommon circumstance that our best-laid plans go awry that we most acutely feel our weakness as well as a sense of connection with those beings who are compromised in the way we are.

If weakness is in some way definitive of the human condition tout court, then it is especially so for men in civil society, whose hearts have been sensitized by settled social relations. Thus, while the specific challenges faced by Emile and savage man are very different—the former does not have to forage for food or fight off bears, but the latter does not have to win the heart of a woman or cultivate the good opinion of others—both lives are defined by their respective challenges in ways that point up the usefulness of pity. The primary difficulties that Emile will face have more to do with his emotional and interpersonal life than with his physical subsistence or basic safety, for as we have seen his turning-toward-others is motivated primarily by a desire to love and be loved rather than an inability to meet his basic needs. Emile's "weakness," then, consists largely in his newfound need for interpersonal validation. This need, as Rousseau makes clear earlier in his analysis of the birth of social sentiment, is not perverse or destructive but rather natural to and coextensive with social life proper: "It is man's weakness which makes him sociable; it is our common miseries which turn our hearts to humanity; we would owe humanity nothing if we were not men. Every attachment is a sign of insufficiency. If each of us had no need of others, he would hardly think of uniting himself with them. *Thus from our very infirmity is born our frail happiness*" (*E* 221; emphasis added). To enter society is to understand and accept one's own physical and emotional weakness. It is also to recognize and love that same weakness in others, and to draw from the disconcerting realization of shared vulnerability the chance of a "frail happiness." Our weakness is thus a consequence and a cause of the social situation.

Such claims go a long way toward suggesting the importance of a sentiment like pity, which allows us to enter into sympathetic community with our more unfortunate fellows (and we are *all* unfortunate) and to view the weakness of others not with hostility or contempt but rather as a reflection of our own fragility. In fact, the apprehension of one's own personal susceptibility to misfortune is essential to the proper development of pity, as Rousseau makes clear in his first "maxim" of sympathetic association: "*One pities in others only those ills from which one does not feel oneself exempt.*" The hardness of the privileged toward the poor is often a product of their failure to recognize the fragility and arbitrariness of their own good fortune. They feel secure in their social positions and regard "abasement and poverty as a condition alien" to them. Lacking an experiential or imaginative foothold in a lived reality characterized by privation, the rich are unable to enter into sympathetic association with the unfortunate. "Why," Rousseau asks, "are kings without pity for their subjects? Because they count on never being mere men. Why are the rich so hard toward the poor? It is because they have no fear of becoming poor." Emile, however, will be "exposed to the vicissitudes of fortune" and will "understand well that the fate of . . . unhappy men can be his, that all their ills are there in the ground beneath their feet" (*E* 224). Able to imaginatively transport himself outside himself and know that there are "beings like him who suffer what he has suffered," Emile will expand the circumference of his own understanding and find meaning in the sympathetic identification he is able to achieve with them. It is, then, through the mechanism of pity and the related awareness of our own personal vulnerability that we are softened to the plight of the unfortunate.

The strength of our identification with the least fortunate of our species also reinforces our awareness of the limits of human nature. Rousseau frequently reminds his reader that human being, for all its expansiveness, nonetheless has boundaries that must be respected. Jean-Jacques, for example, tells his pupil to "restrain your heart within the limits of your condition," to "study and know these limits," and that man is "unhappy only when he forgets his human estate" (*E* 445). These limits are most commonly neglected when considerations of pride or malignant *amour-propre* compromise the honesty of our self-assessments and lead to an inflated estimate of our own importance, or when they interfere with our moral judgment and cause us to treat others disrespectfully. However, an active sense of pity counteracts these antisocial tendencies by revealing the fragility of our own happiness, by keeping us in touch with our essential vulnerability, and by reminding us that we have done less to deserve our good fortune than we are prone to believe (244–45).

Pity for the unfortunate can, however, activate false pride and thereby degenerate into contempt and hatred. The tendency to glorify oneself at the expense of others is so pervasive that even the impeccably educated Emile is not immune to it: having been shown by his tutor the madness of civil society, Jean-Jacques worries that his pupil may draw the self-congratulatory conclusion that he is "'wise, and men are mad.'" The distortion that pride introduces into social cognition is "the error most to be feared" because it short-circuits healthy associative impulses and replaces them with false, self-serving, and hateful delusions. In order to prevent this self-destructive error from setting in, Jean-Jacques arranges for his pupil to be publicly humiliated (*E* 244–45, cf. 172–75). From such experiences Emile learns not only worldliness but also that not even he is exempt from the vicissitudes of fortune. Because the madness of the world can touch him, too, he learns to judge the unfortunate less harshly—fate may have been still crueler to others than it has to him.

| Growing the Self: Pity and the Ordered Development of *Amour-Propre*

Though cultivating the sense of pity creates certain dangers with respect to *amour-propre* and how one views himself vis-à-vis the other, Rousseau is clear that these risks can and *must* be run. In order to persuade the reader of his account of the soul's development Rousseau employs a stylized rhetorical device quite similar to the "natural man"/"civil man" distinction of the *Discourse on Inequality*, namely, an ongoing comparison between Emile and a conventionally raised boy—between "my pupil" and "your pupil" (Scott 2012, 448–49). This comparison is especially important at the beginning of Book IV, which marks the birth of *amour-propre* and all its attendant complications. In fact, it is at this point in the text when Rousseau invokes the specter of "your pupil" by inviting the reader to imagine "two young men, emerging from their first education and entering into society by directly opposite paths" (*E* 228). Rousseau claims that the apparent advantages enjoyed by the conventionally raised pupil are in fact the catalysts of his own corruption: "Does he wander through a palace? All his questions tell you that he is ceaselessly comparing himself with the master of the house; and that all that he finds mortifying for himself in this parallel makes his vanity rebel and thus sharpens it" (228). Exposure to pomp and magnificence reinforces rather than resolves the problem of *amour-propre*, for, far from putting us in a position to extend our self-love in healthy and productive ways, it instead inspires resentment toward the more fortunate as well as a distaste for one's own social position. In fact, malignant *amour-propre* requires absolute validation and cannot tolerate disapproval of any kind. "Your pupil," once exposed to "the disturbing glances of a serious man" or "the scoffing words of a caustic man," is unable to abide their slights: "Were he despised by only a single man, that man's contempt instantly poisons the others' applause" (228). The way in which we compare ourselves to others leads us to resent them and to despise ourselves. This is a recipe for failure.

Though it is necessary to restrain *amour-propre*'s tendency to seek an unreasonable degree of validation, the provision of appropriate restraints is by itself insufficient to educate this naturally expansive passion. By now it should be clear that Rousseau does not wish to prevent *amour-propre* from being born but rather to allow for its healthy development and extension (*E* 214). He must therefore find a way to accommodate its demand for recognition. When he reminds us that "as soon as *amour-propre* has developed and the relative *I* is constantly in play, and the young man never observes others without returning to himself and comparing himself with them," he does not mean to criticize but rather to simply acknowledge its relativizing tendency (243). This "useful but dangerous" instrument thus needs to be gratified as well as restrained, for it is not at all difficult to imagine those who are systematically denied the social affirmation they so crave—those, for example, who are economically and socially disadvantaged—would be at least as susceptible to feelings of envy as the petulant young fop described above. Negotiating *amour-propre*'s demand for distinction thus requires maintaining a fragile balance between too much and too little recognition. Having been placed at the tiller, Jean-Jacques now must steer between the Charybdis of false pride and the Scylla of diffidence. Ever aware of the fragility of human things, Rousseau gravely intones that if the tutor loses sight of his course for even a moment "all is lost" (212).

How, then, to chart the rocky course between two intolerable extremes? The pedagogic trick is to stabilize the emergent moral personality *by way of* comparative activity, and pity aids in this task by accommodating the need for high relative standing while discouraging us from tyrannizing others or demanding what they are unable to give. It is for precisely this reason that Rousseau gives pride of place to pity in the context of Emile's education: he claims it is "the first relative sentiment which touches the human heart according to the order of nature," and on that basis he makes it the first passion in which Emile will receive an education (*E* 222). Pity gratifies our nascent *amour-propre* by teaching us to prefer our own station to those occupied by others. The experience of inequality is not so bitter when it works out in our favor, and the experience of pity gives us fresh reasons to focus not on the advantages we have been denied but rather on the good fortune we enjoy:

> Imagination puts us in the places of the miserable man rather than in that of the happy man. We feel that one of these conditions touches us more closely than the other. Pity is sweet because, in putting ourselves in the place of the one who suffers, we nevertheless feel the pleasure of not suffering as he does. Envy is bitter because the sight of a happy man, far from putting the envious man in his place, makes the envious man regret not being there. It seems that the one exempts us from the ills he suffers, and the other takes from us the goods he enjoys. (221)

The sweetness of commiseration comes in part from the understanding that we do not suffer as severely as does the person we pity; in pitying another, we remind ourselves of our superiority over them. These pleasing confirmations of our own puissance reinforce our sense of self-worth and moral competence. This feeling of power and strength thus has a stabilizing effect on our *amour-propre*. We now enjoy both an absolute and a relative sense of our own self-worth—absolute because it is intrinsically pleasant to care for others, and relative because we see clearly that the object of our pity is less well-off than we are. Confident in our own moral standing vis-à-vis others, we can tend to their good without worrying that our own is compromised.

Rousseau is very candid, perhaps surprisingly so, about what would seem to be a kind of perversity in the experience of pity. His candor on this score opens him to a serious objection: if pity presupposes and even finds pleasure in the suffering of others, is it not itself a subtle kind of antisociability whose internal logic, like that of malignant *amour-propre*, requires for its satisfaction the subjection of others? On this account pity is cunningly predatory, a veiled form of ressentiment that reinforces one's sense of superiority at the expense of others' well-being. So thought Nietzsche, who saw pity as the impulse of a soul at war with its own tyrannical drives: " 'Pity for all'—would be harshness and tyranny for *you*, my dear neighbor!" (*BGE* 60).[4] I take Nietzsche to mean not only that pity is a form of self-tyranny because it unreasonably represses the self's instinctual drives, but also that it is a form of tyranny over others because it consigns them to a position of inferiority and dependence. Pity is thus nothing but war by other means, the will to power's expressing itself despite itself.

Such an objection, however, fails at the very least to meet Rousseau on his own ground, for it does not take into account that pity requires not just feelings of difference but also feelings of sameness or unity with the suffering being. We are far less likely to be cavalier in disregarding the feelings of others when those feelings are recognizable to us or when we have an experiential foothold in the lived reality of the suffering other. It also fails to see, as Jonathan Marks (2007, 730–31) has noted, that the perversity built into pity—and there is *some* perversity—is self-limiting and thus will not give rise to socially destructive attitudes and behaviors in the way that malignant *amour-propre* does. As a way of seeing this, let us recall from note I to the *Discourse on Inequality* that *amour-propre* in its corrupt form conceptualizes happiness in terms of social status and a zero-sum game: because all status gains are relative, an increase for one is necessarily a detriment to those around him (*DI* 195–96). We thus find ourselves locked in a never-ending struggle for distinction that finally issues in a tyrannical demand to be "sole master of the universe" (195). What is critical about unmoored *amour-propre* is its unsatisfied and unsatisfiable character: it *stops at nothing* to attain the recognition it so demands and, as a condition of its fulfillment, is even willing to destroy the very persons whose recognition it desires.

Rousseauan pity, however, is repelled by the sight of suffering and even more so by the idea of *causing* it. Emile's example helps to show how *amour-propre* informed by pity becomes beneficent and magnanimous rather than destructive and tyrannical, and how the psychological perversity is—unlike the tyrannical drive for total mastery—self-limiting. In the early part of his social education Emile is exposed not to the rich and powerful but rather to the poor and unfortunate (*E* 229). These spectacles pluck his heartstrings and inspire him to engage in charitable activity. The comparisons he is led to make are certainly flattering to pride, but they also teach him to feel the satisfaction that comes with providing a social service of indisputable worth (223, 229). Unlike Locke's self-serving little gentleman and Nietzsche's weepy Christian hypocrite, Emile neither insists on profiting from acts of charity nor defines his own happiness with reference to the suffering of others. He shows respect both for himself and for others by giving active expression to his sympathetic impulses. In Rousseau's moral universe, only compassion—whatever its other limitations—is capable of producing this psychological result.

| Pity and Perfectionism: Compassion, Fanaticism, and Moral Disgust

By charting a course between the twin dangers of diffidence and false pride, Rousseau seeks to show how pity serves to correct the erroneous internal logic of corrupt *amour-propre*. But it must be remembered that even healthy expressions of this problematic passion are prone to excess and thus are in need of regulation. We saw in the previous chapter that the moralized passions loosed by the drive for recognition generate a perfectionistic impulse that is essential to human life. And yet we must follow Rousseau in recognizing that this sentiment, too, can inspire unsociable feelings and behaviors: morally serious persons—seeing the grotesque imperfections of their fellows and interpreting social life as a vulgar charade—are prone to become disdainful, haughty, and unsociable. There is, of course, more than a note of disdain in Rousseau's own work, and his own example surely suffices to show how love of one's species can lead to moral disgust with one's contemporaries. The *Letter to D'Alembert*'s sympathetic treatment of Moliere's famous misanthrope Alceste points to precisely the same problem. Even the exemplary Emile may look with antipathy at the failings of his brethren after "considering his rank in the human species and seeing himself so happily placed there"

(*E* 245). Of course, the dissociative and antisocial tendencies to which all morally serious persons are susceptible need not be any more severe than the rebarbative crankiness of a Mr. Darcy, but in Rousseau they take on Swiftian tenacity and depth. In his investigation of the phenomenon of moral disgust, he commonly reasons from a most extreme and most difficult case: that of the religious fanatic (see Trachtenberg 2009).

It is on some level not surprising that Rousseau would find it necessary to address himself to the question of fanaticism, for the questions of religious toleration and persecution were never far from the eighteenth-century mind. Virtually all of Rousseau's philosophical contemporaries had weighed—or in Voltaire's case, cashed—in on the matter, with all emerging as champions of religious toleration and freedom of thought. The distinctiveness of Rousseau's account on this head is thus best glimpsed by comparing it to the entry in Diderot and D'Alembert's *Encyclopedia* on "Fanaticism," which was composed by Rousseau's friend Alexandre Deleyre and which appears to articulate the collective opinion of the philosophes as a group.[5] Like Rousseau, Deleyre sees fanaticism as a dangerous social force with roots in superstition: it is a "blind and passionate zeal" that undermines compassion and causes people "to commit absurd, unjust, and cruel acts" without "shame or remorse" (Diderot 1967, 393). He notes that "truth makes no fanatics," punctuating his entry with a mocking prayer in which he beseeches an unnamed deity to "enlighten your zealots, so they might at least take care not to confuse holocaust with homicide" (401). If superstition is the disease, then enlightenment is the cure: fanatics attack their enemies "with a kind of joy and comfort" not because they are naturally cruel but rather because they have been blinded by absurd dogmas (393). More rational and tolerant attitudes would reduce sanguinary violence and give to men the kindly dispositions and the "tender and compassionate hearts" that enlightened social commerce requires (401).

Rousseau's complex response to Deleyre and "the philosophist party" that he viewed as an agent of intolerance itself reveals a hope of disciplining—and hence of capitalizing—on the wild *enthousiasmes* of the fanatics as well as an acknowledgment of their real social danger. He recognizes with Deleyre and the *philosophes* that the roots of moral anger are in social institutions rather than nature, agrees with Bayle that "fanaticism is more pernicious than atheism," and holds it is unsociable so far as it is "sanguinary and cruel" (*E* 312n). So, too, does he insist on the necessity of religious toleration in his treatment of civil religion in the *Social Contract*, arguing that citizens who follow the "sentiments of sociability" prescribed by state religion cannot be punished for the private beliefs they hold about questions of doctrine (*SC* IV.8, 130). Through the intolerance of bizarre cults, religion, which ought to be a catalyst of sociability, had become quite the opposite. Rousseau, then, is in at least qualified sympathy with his colleagues about the dangers of fanatical moral energy and the intolerant attitudes it engenders.

Yet Rousseau is distinguished among his contemporaries for his willingness to subject the partisans of toleration and enlightenment—"the philosophist party"—to the same level of critical scrutiny that he applies to the Christian sect. Thus he can say that Bayle was correct as far as he went, but that he did not go far enough:

> What he did not take care to say, and which is no less true, is that fanaticism, although sanguinary and cruel, is nevertheless a grand and strong passion which elevates the heart of man, makes him despise death, and gives him a prodigious energy that need only be better directed in order to produce the most sublime virtues. On the other hand, irreligion—and the reasoning and philosophic spirit in general—causes attachment to life, makes souls effeminate and degraded, concentrates all the passions in the baseness of private interest, in the abjectness of the human *I*, and thus quietly saps the true foundations of every society. (*E* 312n)

"Truth does not make any fanatics," says Deleyre. Rousseau heartily agrees. But this, he adds, is precisely the problem with the "philosophic spirit" in its soul-shrinking modern form. The rationalizing—which is not to say rational—temper of the philosophes actually magnifies rather than ameliorates the problem posed by intolerance, for it replaces a misplaced but correctable hatred of evil with a stubborn indifference to the good. This moral indifference, motivated by the restrictive conception of self-love developed by Hobbes and Locke and endorsed by the philosophes, destroys human relations by counseling the pursuit of narrow private interest and weakening the affective bonds that would otherwise unite us. Thus, though Rousseau understood that the social and political costs of loosing strong moral passions could be high, he nonetheless held that the costs of neutralizing those same passions are higher still: moralized *amour-propre* is a "useful but dangerous instrument" that *can be* "sanguinary and cruel" but is also the source of "prodigious energy" that produces "the most sublime virtues" (*E* 244, 312n). To diffuse that energy is to destroy all higher human possibility and to create an intolerably unstable social situation: reasoning from a narrow idea of their own interests, human beings inevitably see they have more to gain by taking advantage of others than they do by sacrificing for them and they act accordingly. To the degree this is true, instrumental rationality cannot solve its own problem and society cannot subsist without a concern for virtue: a nation of devils, however ingeniously designed, is fated to be unjust because of reason's tendency to find loopholes in its own solutions. Thus it is one thing to say, with Rousseau, that fanatical moral desiring can be injurious to society and quite another to say with Deleyre and the philosophes that society would be better off without fanaticism. Faced with two options he knows to be imperfect, Rousseau prudently chooses the one he thinks better.

If the costs of short-circuiting man's ethical impulses are prohibitively high, how does Rousseau propose to discipline moral disgust and prevent it from turning violent? In addition to more specific institutional solutions (e.g., proposing a civil religion with fewer and more sensible articles of faith), Rousseau turns to pity in order to strengthen our identification with the misguided and unfortunate and so to soften the harshness of moralized *amour-propre*. The intolerance motivated by fanaticism relies in many respects on the demonization of the other, on a visceral hatred of his grotesque and incomprehensible way of life. We should not, however, say "incomprehensible," for something unrecognizable does not register a strong emotional reaction precisely because it is not recognized. The demonized other, on the other hand, is seen as something malignant and disgusting, as not only undeserving of respect but as deserving of *dis*respect. And our hatred is only magnified when that other intransigently refuses to adopt the way of life or the manner of thinking that would enable us to view them as being like us, for now they are not simply different but *disobedient*.

Pity combats the demonization of the other that fanaticism inspires, for embedded in it is a mechanism of sympathetic identification that allows us to view the imperfections of others with greater gentleness. In searching for commonality with those who think differently we are reminded of how difficult it is to discover the truth concerning religious matters—indeed, any matter—and of the shortcomings of our *own* understanding. We, of course, know that we ourselves have erred in the past but are disposed to believe the best about our own intentions and view our past mistakes as motivated by good faith efforts to discover the truth. More than any other sentiment, pity allows us to extend to others the generosity that we naturally give to ourselves; through its operations we are able to "extend *amour-propre* to other beings" and "transform it into a virtue" instead of allowing its unsociable forms to take root (*E* 252).[6] Far from blaming or hating those who see things differently, we see our own errors—our own fallibility and intellectual weakness—reflected in theirs, and we experience feelings not of frustration but rather of solidarity and togetherness. These feelings of sameness may not and often should not overcome the urge to persuade the other of the mistakenness of his view—friends can and do disagree—but it will make it almost impossible to hate or to seek to punish him for that mistakenness.

The way in which pity blunts the prickly exterior of virtue is best seen in Rousseau's wildly popular novel *Julie*, and most especially in the personality of the work's heroine. Julie takes virtue seriously and seeks to share her enthusiasm with her entire circle of associates, who affectionately tease her for her bombast and eventually take to calling her a "charming preacher" (*J* 332). Her case is instructive in this context because, were it not for her all-too-active sense of compassion, she would for at least three reasons seem to be especially susceptible to fanatical and evangelical excess. First, she is a woman and therefore (says Rousseau) generally prone to emotional excess (*E* 377–82). Second, she is distinguished even among her gender for her passionate enthusiasm and is thus extremely susceptible to very strong emotions, both positive and negative. Finally, she is highly moralistic and, as such, is disposed to feelings of ethical disgust. Taking all this into view, we might plausibly wonder why Julie is not *more* prone to evangelical excesses than she already is. However, we see she is able to restrict her tiresome homiletics to a small circle of intimates and to express her moral zeal through charitable and humane action rather than through useless and self-righteous speechifying or, worse still, through violent and hateful denunciations.

Appropriately enough, Julie's moralistic temperament and ability to govern her own fanatical desires show up most clearly in the context of her description of her own religious awakening, which occurs during her nuptials. Recounting her illumination to her former lover St. Preux in order to discourage his hope of carrying on an adulterous affair with her, Julie claims that when she entered the church she was "seized" by a "never before experienced" emotion that was akin to "terror." Moved by the gravity and seriousness of the marital bond, she experienced a "sudden revolution" that reminded her of her moral obligations and gave her fresh energy to discharge them. Her divination and the new self-understanding inspired by it leads

Julie to feel "scorn and indignation" for the "vain sophisms" of the "philosophers" who, through their moral laxness and encouragement of adultery, seek to "obliterate human society." Drawing the letter to a close, Julie assumes moral authority over her former tutor and, in a fit of evangelical zeal, exhorts St. Preux to rededicate himself to Christian morality: the "best way to discover what is good is to seek it sincerely, and one cannot thus seek it for long without going back to the author of all good. It seems to me I have been doing this . . . and you will do it better than I once you decide to follow the same road." It is difficult not to hear the tones of moral disgust in Julie's letter. She is full of self-loathing for having failed in her duties but has plenty of spare sanctimony for the philosophers, who destabilize society in order to glorify themselves and whose specious arguments only serve to undermine sound morality. She even momentarily exalts in the penalty awaiting these vain scribblers, saying—in the heat of an angry moment—that they and their disciples will be punished "before the author of all justice" (*J* 295, 296, 298).

And yet these notes of antipathy, jarring in isolation, only serve to add necessary tension to the touching and consonant (if perhaps belabored) melody that the whole letter sounds. Julie's address to her former lover, though steadfast in asserting the sad conclusion that "Julie de Wolmar is no longer your former Julie," is nonetheless full of sympathy and efforts to ease the suffering the letter is sure to cause the weepy St. Preux. While she sternly lectures her former lover for his moral failures, she also shares directly in that sense of failure. She participates in his sense of loss so as to diffuse it and, while confidently reporting the results of her illumination, nonetheless intimates a subtle awareness that the improvements owing to it may prove unstable: "Yesterday one was abject and weak; today one is strong and magnanimous. By observing oneself in two such different conditions, one better appreciates the value of the condition that has been recovered, and in consequence one becomes more attentive to maintaining it" (*J* 300). In admitting that she shares—or at least shared—St. Preux's weakness, she remains mindful of her essential likeness with him and thus of her own ongoing vulnerability. Her temporal presentation—her noting the difference between "yesterday" and "today"—further underscores this point by raising an unanswered question about *tomorrow*. If drastic transformations like Julie's illumination can be effected so quickly, how certain can she be that she will not sink back into her former condition and again become the object of pity herself? Far, then, from viewing her old flame as worthy of contempt for his having morally strayed, Julie creates a community of consolation with him because her active sense of compassion shows her that she is not immune from the ills St. Preux suffers.

| Attenuated Sympathies: Pity and the Mediation of Difference

The sympathetic communion Julie attempts to establish with St. Preux betokens a signal shift in the character of their relationship. Informing her old tutor that "all is changed between us" and that "Julie de Wolmar is no longer your former Julie," Julie tries to soften the blow by telling him that all is not lost: "If you are losing a tender lover then you are gaining a faithful friend, and, whatever we may have said during our illusions, I doubt that this change is to your disadvantage" (*J* 300). The transition from love to friendship—if it is ever completed entirely—promises to be difficult, for it involves a fundamental change in the dynamics of social recognition. Shared understandings about the boundaries of relationships must be renegotiated, but such negotiations take place against a backdrop of previously established expectations and hopes that prove very difficult, perhaps impossible, to efface. It is a social manifestation of a problem Wittgenstein would later call "the dawning of an aspect," and which he would represent with the famous "duck-rabbit" image.

The "duck-rabbit" is puzzling because, depending simply on how it is viewed by the subject, it can be plausibly described as either a duck or a rabbit. Wittgenstein, interested to understand the different ways we utilize the concept "see," sums up the problem thus: "The expression of a change of aspect is the expression of a new perception and at the same time of the perception's being unchanged." The change in the report of what the subject sees is due to a change in the understanding; it involves a combination of perception and cognition, a mixture of "seeing and thinking" (Wittgenstein 1958, 196–97). The image, though utterly unchanged, has for the perceiver a set of associations and meanings that it did not before.

I raise the "duck-rabbit" problem not to resolve it so much as to show its relevance for Julie and St. Preux, who are seeking to transition from love to friendship and as such must learn to "see" each other very differently despite the fact that they are *not* especially different. While age and smallpox do effect changes in the lovers' physical appearance, their basic moral dispositions—Julie's mysterious "conversion" notwithstanding—remain largely the same throughout the novel. They must confront that continuity, which served as the source of their romantic union, and learn to re-cognize each other despite it; the same people must come to view each other differently. This can be, as the novel's narrative makes clear, a very difficult transition to undertake. Part of the reason for this extreme difficulty is that love and friendship are for Rousseau two very different things and, as such, awaken very different kinds of moral and social impulses.[7] Julie signals her awareness of the great distance between these two forms of association in a letter to her "inseparable" cousin Claire, where she avers that the distinct office of friendship—as opposed to that of love—is to console others in their suffering. "Are you not aware," she asks her cousin, "that the communion of hearts imbues sadness with a sweet and touching something that contentment does not know? And *was friendship not specially given to the unhappy to relieve their woes* and comfort their sorrows?" (*J* 332). What lovers do *as* lovers creates a high, aspirational moral energy that arouses the hope of mutual perfection. If, or perhaps when, this hope is frustrated, lovers are often far less able to console each other in their disappointment than are their friends, for because lovers are commonly *the source of* each other's deepest frustrations they often prove to be poor shoulders on which to cry. There are, of course, a great many exceptions to this rule, but the general inability of lovers to console each other in many cases shows up most readily in the tense and resentful exchange between Julie and St. Preux immediately following their forced separation. Suicidally depressed and bitter, St. Preux lashes out angrily at his beloved: "Answer me, now, deceived or deceitful lover: what has become of those plans contrived in such secrecy? Where are those vain expectations with which you so often baited my naïve credulity? Where is that holy and desired union, the sweet object so ardently wished for, with which your pen and your mouth flattered my wishes? . . . Give me an account, ingrate, of the charge I have entrusted to you: give me an account of myself after leading my heart astray into that supreme felicity you have shown me and are now taking away" (157). Julie responds to these vehemently expressed (and not entirely unfair) charges not with sympathy but rather by accusing her lover of cruelty and lamenting her own misery. St. Preux and Julie view each other as responsible for the unhappiness they share and thus are unable to effectively sympathize with the plight of the other. Again, this is a not uncommon phenomenon among lovers, who have more occasions for conflict precisely because they seek to share everything.

The activity characteristic of friendship, on the other hand, is gentler, sweeter, and less generative of conflict because its aims are more modest. Friends qua friends do not seek wholeness through each other so much as comfort in their condition of dividedness; their special office is to "relieve [the] woes and comfort [the] sorrows" of their unfortunate fellows, to create community through the mutual apprehension of their respective imperfections. The experience of friendship and the capacity for pity are thus clearly and even intimately bound up with each other, for friendship is predicated specifically on the desire to ameliorate another's suffering. Julie's letter to her inseparable cousin gives us an intimation—one which will be explored in depth in chapter 6—of the meaning of Rousseau's rather odd-sounding claim that friendship, rightly understood, is the product of pity fixed on a particular object (*DI* 130).

However, because the feelings of commonality that enable pity are also necessarily limited by it, the relation of friend to friend would also seem to be attenuated in ways that romantic associations may not be. Indeed, Rousseau's analysis of pity in *Emile* discloses that when one pities another he does so with the recognition that the other suffers in a way that he does not. More revealing still, the disproportion between the condition of he who pities and he who is pitied is in fact a source of *pleasure* for the former: "If the first sight that strikes [Emile] is an object of sadness, the first return to himself is a sentiment of pleasure. In seeing how many ills he is exempt from, he feels himself to be happier than he thought he was" (*E* 229). And again: "Pity is sweet because, in putting ourselves in the place of the one who suffers, we nevertheless feel the pleasure of not suffering as he does" (221). To pity another is thus to simultaneously claim an equality with *and* a superiority over him: while one recognizes that he could *in principle* be subjected to the same afflictions as the aggrieved party, he nonetheless feels considerable satisfaction in the realization that he does not suffer *in fact* or *reality* (223–24).

Pity, then, is as much a consolation for he who offers as for he who receives it. It is a "resource for a rainy day" because it recognizes a de facto inequality between he who pities and he who suffers (*E* 223). One feels a sense of superiority over suffering beings, and if he has the strength to deliver them from their disappointments, he delights doubly in the heartening reminder of his power and potency. If pity is the "first relative sentiment that enters the human heart," as Rousseau claims, then it follows from this that the idea of mutual attachment is formed in the context of relationships in which we are the stronger rather than the weaker party. Our affection for others is a function of their misfortune as well as an edifying aide-mémoire of our own strength and moral competence. The pleasures that attach to sympathetic communion are motivated not only by the delight one takes in the feeling of oneness with others but also by the heartening reminders of one's own puissance. We pity because we know we are not exempt from the sufferer's ills and because we delight in the fact that we do not suffer as he does. Again, these are only intimations and are intended to anticipate arguments to come. The peculiar dynamics of pity and their associational consequences will be explored more thoroughly in chapter 6.

| Becoming Social: Conclusions

Having now surveyed the psychological ground on which Rousseau seeks to build social sentiment, we are now in a position to draw some preliminary conclusions about Rousseau's moral-psychological theory and the kind of relationships that grow out of it. I have been at special pains to show how *amour-propre*, the sexual passion, and pity develop and interact with one another and, in so doing, give rise to a complex of desires for various kinds of recognition. In arguing thus, I have perhaps more than most emphasized the role of sexual desire specifically, which, properly developed, is the chief source of man's social and moral energy. Indeed, it was shown that social desiring as such emerges from a largely sexual basis and that moralized sexuality catalyzes a perfectionistic impulse that draws out man's highest and best aspirations. Yet this same impulse, even developed aright, can easily degenerate into moral disgust and antisocial forms of intolerance; its sharp edges must thus be rounded off by pity, which counteracts the excesses of moralized anger by establishing a sense of connection between the judger and the judged. As pity supplements and in some ways counteracts the harmful excesses of man's perfectionistic impulse, so, too, does that perfectionistic impulse combat the moral complacency and resignation that can result from a too-active sense of pity. Though Rousseau himself took a rather circumspect view of the human condition and did not shy away from characterizing it as one of weakness and vulnerability, he was nonetheless acutely sensitive to the fact that an overemphasis on such characteristics can lead to ethical fatalism and a posture of indifference toward one's own moral growth. Thus there exists in the properly educated mind a kind of dynamic tension between sexual passion and pity, between a belief in our capacity for growth and an awareness of our limitations.

Though *Emile* shows that the desire for recognition from and association with other human beings issues from a largely sexual source, it also shows how the development of the social passions is at one with their disaggregation. Thus, to develop socially is to understand what one wants from particular individuals in particular associational contexts. In the next chapter, I begin my survey of the various forms of association that Rousseau treats in his oeuvre and show how, whether considered individually or together, they fail to satisfy the desires to which they give rise. In making this argument I will build on what has been established and will seek to show (1) the moralized and moralizing character of sexuality as it manifests itself in *Emile* and *Julie*, and (2) that the attenuations built into pity have important and underappreciated consequences for how Rousseau theorizes friendship.

4 | Romantic Love in *Emile*

I adore myself in what I have made.

—ROUSSEAU, *Pygmalion*

Nowhere is Rousseau's effort to expand human possibility through social relations more evident than in his account of romantic love, and nowhere in his oeuvre is this account better worked out than in *Emile*. In this wildly successful treatise-cum-novel Rousseau not only articulates the most comprehensive statement of his intellectual system but also provides a vision of domestic life so attractive that even one of his most codgerly critics has conceded that it "represents a profound understanding of the conditions of a happy marriage" (Orwin 1997a, 6). That "marriage," of course, is the one between the eponymous hero and his beloved Sophie, who after an extended and very carefully managed courtship are united at the conclusion of the work. In leaving his audience to ponder the ultimate fate of his *beaux amants*, however, there is a significant sense in which Rousseau ends the work precisely where things get interesting, for it is well-known that falling in love is far easier than staying that way. This would seem to be especially true in the context of Rousseau's own moral universe, where the traps and snares are many and the consequences of falling into them are ruinous.

In order, however, to understand the extent to which we may consider Emile and Sophie's marriage successful, we must be able to answer a still-more-fundamental question: what would count as a success? We need to know what ends the marital relation is supposed to realize before we can know how effectively it realizes them. With this in mind, I propose that Rousseauan marriage is designed to directly instantiate the human good through the limit experience of romantic love and the creation of a comprehensive form of social incorporation. The nature of moral love is such that the union created in and through marriage is *and must be* an erotic fusion of souls, a joining of "two into one" (*E* 479). Any romantic relation that demands less disrespects the expansive character of human being by truncating the healthy growth of the passions and, thereby, compromising the experience of the human good. This argument will build in particular on the conception of moralized sexuality articulated in chapter 2 and show its pedagogic relevance in the context of Emile's education, but it will also reintroduce and further develop the account of wholeness that was introduced in chapter 1.

In developing this account, a more detailed engagement with secondary scholarship concerning both the function of the marital relation and its role in Emile's education is unavoidable, for though *Emile* has (after long neglect) become central to Rousseau interpretation there remain serious questions regarding both its basic meaning and broader significance. Judith Shklar (1969) structured what is now the most important controversy among readers of *Emile* by calling attention to Rousseau's distinction between "men" and "citizens" and by arguing that the eponymous hero's education was intended primarily to preserve his natural independence and, thereby, to create a "man." Scholars as diverse as Okin (1979), Cassirer (1989), Melzer (1990), Todorov (2001), and Gauthier (2006) have articulated some variant of this hypothesis and consequently tend to view Emile as a detached cosmopolitan rather than a fully incorporated social subject. A second wave of research, however, has noted the deeply *social* character of Emile's education, and has attended to the ways in which it prepares him for incorporation into a political community (Bloom 1979; Strong 1994; Wingrove 2000; Neuhouser 2008). Whatever their disagreements, these scholars are unanimous in their rejection of Shklar's claim that the educations of "men" and "citizens" are incommensurable alternatives and in their insistence that Emile's education is successful only to the degree that his experiences as human being and political subject are compatible. In arguing thus many scholars have emphasized the political functions of marriage, holding that its significance is in its creation of an autarchic household that catalyzes allegiance to the regime. The important fact about the family is its role as an agent—*the* agent—of political socialization. This understanding of *Emile* has provided cause both for celebrating Rousseau's teaching (e.g., Schwartz 1984) and for censuring it (e.g., Fermon 1997), but what unites these approaches is their viewing sexual union as preparation for what it is *really* important: citizenship.

Though such claims improve on independence-focused interpretations by calling attention to the social-sexual character of Emile's education, they also obscure much of what is interesting in Rousseau's treatment of marriage by viewing it as a tool of political socialization rather than a direct instantiation of the human good. My more "domestic" reading is amply substantiated by Rousseau's strong and continued emphasis on the sexual passion, and what we will see below is that it is also confirmed by the specific way in which Jean-Jacques directs Emile and his beloved Sophie to incorporate into political society. The regime Emile chooses for his family is not and would not be the one outlined in the *Social Contract*, but rather one that makes far less stringent demands on his time and attention. Emile does not have the specifically *civic* virtue of the citizen, but the acquisition of virtue in a different and more universal form is of the first moment for his education. The development of the sexual passion, it is important to add, is central to this education in virtue: the moralization of this passion facilitates Emile's universal benevolence and moral taste by facilitating consciousness of the beloved's moral character. In arguing thus, I depart from Bloom (1993, 108), who neglects the moralizing dimension of love, and Reisert (2003, 80), who views sexuality as a "threat" to virtue.

It is in light of the foregoing that we may return to the question of whether the pedagogic plan laid out for Emile actually works. Does love-through-marriage obtain for Emile the comprehensive satisfaction—the natural wholeness *and* the social connectedness—that he so desires? Unfortunately, I believe we must answer this question in the negative. Perhaps more troublingly, we must do so because of Rousseau's own understanding of love: he makes love a creature of the imagination, but the necessary disproportion between Emile's imagination of Sophie and the girl herself ultimately serves to undermine their love. So, too, does the sexual act pale in comparison with the imagination of it, with the result that the very consummation of a romantic relationship initiates its decay. Thus *Emile*, which works through a marriage's "best case," nonetheless enacts a tragic conception of romantic love whose ultimate consequences are spelled out in *Emile and Sophie*, an unfinished and posthumously published sequel to *Emile*.

Though this tragic interpretation of *Emile* is significant in its own right, it can be wondered what implications it has for Rousseau's more general political theory. Though I will delay full consideration of this question until chapter 8, I shall conclude this chapter by making some suggestions about how the failure of Emile's education might be reproduced in the political realm, and why the limits exposed within *Emile* may have consequences for the political world outside of it.

| Men, Citizens, and Rousseau's "Double Object"

At the beginning of *Emile* (41), Rousseau posits a "double object" which is to serve as the end or purpose of his pupil's education: "What will a man raised uniquely for himself be for others? If per chance the double object we set for ourselves could be joined in a single one by removing the contradictions of man, a great obstacle to his happiness would be removed." In order for Emile's education to be a success, he must learn to be both good for himself and for others. This means he must be (1) civilized, which is to say that he has social relations and all the moral and intellectual capacities these relations imply, and (2) natural, which is to say that his social relations have not corrupted his native goodness. Rousseau, however, stacks the deck against the realization of this dual objective by assuming a contradiction between civilization and nature. On his account, we are "swept along in contrary routes by nature and by men" and our educations reinforce rather than resolve our divided state. The consequence is that we live "in conflict and floating during the whole course of our lives" and die "without having been good for ourselves or for others" (41). Resolving the contradictions between self and other, between nature and society, is no easy task. To this end we must make an important choice: we must create a "man" or a "citizen," because it is impossible to simultaneously create both (39, 41).

Though it is clear up front that Emile must be a man or a citizen, there is some ambiguity about which he ultimately becomes. Secondary scholarship is divided on this score, with scholars interpreting Rousseau's equivocation in two primary, but only partially adequate, ways. One interpretation pioneered by Shklar (1969) tends to make Emile a "man" whose education is designed to protect him from the scourge of personal dependence. Gauthier (2006, 33) succinctly summarizes this view: "Emile is to be raised for independence." Okin (1979, 407) articulates a similar interpretation in the context of a feminist critique of *Emile*: "Rousseau's prescribed education for Sophie is in total contrast with that prescribed for Emile, who is to be as independent . . . as possible." Arthur Melzer joins the chorus, claiming personal dependence is the "true villain of Rousseau's analysis" and arguing on Rousseau's behalf that "all personal dependence, all social power . . . is self-contradictory and enslaving" (1990, 70n, 74). He goes on to explain that, once ensconced in rustic repose, the happy lovers are "protected . . . from the need to depend on others" (93). Melzer fails, however, to note not only that Emile and Sophie must incorporate into political society and are therefore *not* free of "the need to depend on others," but also that they must still depend on *each other* in a profoundly personal way. Thus, to emphasize the dangers of personal dependence is also to obscure a very important aspect of *Emile*, namely, that Jean-Jacques turns to a specifically personal form of dependence—sexual or romantic love—in order to realize his double object. If this task is to be completed, Emile's intellectual and affective capacities must find expression in a meaningful and lasting form of association.

If escaping the perils of deep interdependence were truly the aim of *Emile*, Rousseau would not have needed to write Books IV and V of the work. At age fifteen Emile knows how to "live free and depend little on human things," and he possesses all the "virtue . . . that relates to himself" (*E* 208). Yet such independence is merely a prelude to a larger and more complex pedagogic task: "This [the onset of *amour-propre*] is the second birth of which I have spoken. It is now that man is truly born to life and now that nothing human in foreign to him. Up to now our care has only been a child's game. It takes on true importance at present. This period, where ordinary education ends, is properly the one where ours ought to begin" (212). Emile's tutelage thus does not take on "true importance" until it is time to make him part of a larger social whole. In order to call his education a success, he must be connected to others in some meaningful way.

But what form should that connectedness ultimately take? A diverse group of scholars more sensitive to both prongs of the "double object" claim that Emile's *political* relationships are the ones of ultimate importance. On this view, Emile's highest and best capacities find expression in the experience of citizenship. Strong (1994, 138) explains that Emile's final perfection *"requires and will generate, come what may, a political society* . . . that which makes him human requires that he be a citizen." Frederick Neuhouser (2008, 23) echoes this sentiment, arguing that Emile's education "produces individuals who in the end can assume the role of citizen . . . in a manner consistent with . . . being a man." Bloom, too, emphasizes the political character of *Emile* by noting that its pedagogy serves as "the outline for a possible bridge between the particular and the general will" and thereby prepares human beings for "the most comprehensive human order, political society" (Bloom 1979, 27). Jean-Jacques's task is thus not an effort to make a man *or* a citizen but a man *and* a citizen. The most influential—and the most compelling—attempts to build this "bridge" use sexuality as the primary means of doing so. On this view, the sexual relationship is significant because it prepares individuals for full incorporation into political society. Thus we are led to view Emile's romantic relation to Sophie as preparatory for the higher calling of politics. On this score, Schwartz (1984, 97, 70) observes that because "men are sexual, they must as a consequence be political" and concludes that "romantic love is less exalted than . . . patriotism." Wingrove (2000, 61) makes a similar claim, arguing that Emile's and Sophie's relationship discloses the endogeneity of politics and sexuality: "Emile and Sophie enact a political relationship that is not just like (or even not much like) Rousseau's democratic republicanism, but that is continuous with it." In these accounts and others, the political is the axis on which Emile's world turns.

These "political" interpretations of *Emile* improve on their predecessors by acknowledging the importance of the social and political dimensions of Emile's education and pointing to the importance of the sexual passion as a catalyst of sociability. Yet in order to read the sexual teaching of *Emile* into the republican political program of the *Social Contract*, it is necessary to attribute to Rousseau understandings of politics and citizenship that he actively resists. He holds that true civic education is neither available to nor appropriate for his young charge, arguing that "public instruction" requires the exchange of one's "absolute existence" for "a relative one . . . with the result that each individual believes himself no longer one but a part of the unity and no longer feels except within the whole" (*E* 40; cf. *SC* II.7). Rousseau's desubjectivized citizen is defined by his social position and his relationship to political society. If he abandons his role as a citizen then "he is no longer fit for anything" (*E* 41).

Emile, in contrast to the citizen, has neither a particular social station nor a fatherland (*E* 40, 466, 473). Even at the end of his formal political education he makes cosmopolitan pronouncements that would confuse and infuriate any decent Spartan or Roman: "Rich or poor, I shall be free. I shall not be free in this or that land, in this or that region. I shall be free everywhere on earth . . . wherever there are men, I am at the home of my brothers; wherever there are no men, I am in my own home" (472). Unlike the citizen, who is rudderless without his *patrie*, Emile has the intellectual and moral dexterity to occupy any number of social positions. "Let," writes Rousseau, "my student be destined for the sword, the church, the bar. I do not care. Prior to the calling of his parents is nature's call to human life. Living is the job I want to teach him" (41). This is not to deny that Emile could find within himself a general will, for as Rousseau (*SC* II.3, 61) reminds us, a will can be general with respect to one's family while being particular with respect to his state; it is, rather, to deny that such a will must be general *at the level of political society* in order to call his education a success.

Indeed, by the time Emile and his tutor come to the study of politics, the proverbial heavy lifting has already been done. The crash course in politics does not add to Emile's happiness so much as it *secures* the happiness he has already won. Thus, unlike "the Lacedaemonian Pedaretus"—that paragon of citizenship whose "sincere" love of *patrie* consoled him after losing an election—Emile knows enough not to run for office in the first place: "If we were kings and were wise, the first thing that we would want to do for ourselves and others would be to abdicate our royal position and become again what we are" (*E* 40, 467). Attaining a position in the government would be harmful both for the young man and for others, and thus cannot satisfy the double object in the context of Emile's education. It is therefore unsurprising to see Jean-Jacques give his political instruction a decidedly apolitical end: "Let us consecrate the two years until your return to choosing an abode in Europe where you can live happily with your family, *sheltered* from all the dangers of which I have just spoken to you" (457; emphasis added). Emile's travels, and the political education that is their fruit, are devoted to the domestic purpose of finding a regime that will leave Emile and his beloved to their conjugal bliss. He wants a regime from which he can effectively "shelter" himself, not one that demands his presence in the assembly. The best regime absolutely is thus not the best regime for Emile. He is not committed to the regime he chooses; rather, he chooses the regime he does because it requires no commitment.

To the degree that Emile *is* committed to his regime, one sees through the attenuated relation he has to his political society that the basis of that commitment bears little resemblance to that of "the citizen" as Rousseau conceives him. Though Jean-Jacques tells Emile to "leave everything" if the state calls him to service, it is still true that Emile, like Plato's philosopher-king, must be *compelled* by others to join in the tumults of the assembly (*E* 475). Because Emile knows he will not find happiness in the shadows of the just, his tutor gives him a very circumscribed conception of the common good, one that is consistent with his duties to man qua man but inconsistent with the requirements of "citizenship" as Rousseau understands the term. Emile's political duty is to "vivify the country and reanimate the zeal of the unfortunate village folk" (474). However, his benevolent treatment of an injured peasant he encounters on the road while traveling to see Sophie shows he is satisfying these requirements well before he knows anything about politics proper. The kindness Emile shows in this instance is certainly a kind of service to the common good, but it is motivated less by the partial sentiments of citizenship than by a respect for the "rights of humanity" (441). Such cosmopolitan considerations are alien to the citizen, who is immediately motivated by his specifically civic duty. Unlike the citizen, who does good to friends and harm to enemies, Emile's first and most important duty is to hurt no one (39, 445). Of Emile, then, it seems correct to say that he will live in a political society but will not be constituted by it, and that he will be happy despite politics rather than because of them.

Our examination of the relevant scholarly literature has left us with a puzzle of sorts. It shows that the individualistic line of interpretation pioneered by Judith Shklar is deficient in signal respects, but it also reveals that the more "social" readings of Tracy Strong and others suffer from no less serious defects. Thus the literature points to the need for connectedness, but it points in the wrong direction. In the next section I argue that Rousseau turns to romantic love in order to satisfy the double object. In doing so, he prepares his pupil not for a life of independence or republican politics but rather for a life of domestic repose, one that entails complete—and completely personal—dependence on his beloved Sophie.

Beyond Men and Citizens: Rousseau's Sex Education

We have so far seen that Emile's education is designed to incorporate the other in a way that is consistent with the requirements of natural self-love, and that neither independence nor citizenship gives answer to these dual requirements in a satisfactory way. So, too, have we seen in earlier chapters that Rousseau also rejects the instrumental approach of Hobbes and Locke, whose appeals to narrow self-interest generate only a mercenary virtue that "gives an egg to have a cow" (*E* 103). The self-serving sociability of the bourgeois clearly will not do. But what will?

Many have found in the sexual passion a way of grounding the robust and enduring associations that Rousseau sought to depict in and effect through his writing. Bloom (1993, 108), for instance, has claimed that the sexual component of Emile's education is reminiscent of Aristophanes's characterization of eros in Plato's *Symposium*: "Rousseau presents in all seriousness what Aristophanes presents half-jokingly . . . that is, that love is the quest for one's other half which, once found, restores the lovers to perfect wholeness." This parallel is somewhat useful, as it both calls attention to the sexual-social character of Emile's rearing and reveals the comprehensiveness of the communion he hoped to construct on that basis. Emile and Sophie are not seeking mere mates but—like the Rousseau of the *Confessions*—are looking for their "other half" (*E* 479, see also 377). However, Rousseau departs from Aristophanes's amoral and nonhierarchical conception of eros-as-wholeness, arguing instead that sexuality is inherently moralizing and moralistic. Considerations of virtue, far from being irrelevant as they are for Aristophanes, are instead essential to the process of erotic recognition and attraction. Thus when Jean-Jacques puts an imaginary object of desire—"Sophie"—in Emile's mind, his purpose is to unify the processes of sexual and moral maturation and to show how ethical criteria are necessary to identify one's "other half." Emile's Sophie, whoever she is, must be physically *and* morally beautiful.

Emile's turn to sexual desire should not be at all surprising, for we have already seen in Rousseau's distinction between "physical" and "moral" forms of love the profound psychological and moral power he gives to the phenomenon of exclusive romantic recognition. And it is precisely because *amour-propre* expresses itself so strongly in the romantic situation that Rousseau identifies sexual desire as both the most promising and the most dangerous socializing force in the human soul. Though the dangers of moral love are laid bare in the *Discourse on Inequality*, these are not viewed as a reason to consign sex education to the margins of Emile's pedagogy. To the contrary, the perils of sexuality are the best reasons imaginable for putting it front and center. Thus Emile's healing education is distinguished by the degree and the kind of attention it gives to this most fundamental want: "We are given treatises on education consisting of useless, pedantic, bloated verbiage . . . and we are not told a word about the most important and most difficult part of the whole education—the crisis that serves as a passage from childhood to man's estate. If I have been able to make these essays useful in some respect, it is especially by having expanded at great length on this essential part, omitted by all others" (*E* 416). Sexual education is the "most important" and "most difficult" part of human education, and Rousseau believes his *Emile* to be "especially" useful because of the priority it assigns to this neglected topic. We should thus not be surprised when the narrative expands "at great length" about the sex education that Emile receives, or when Jean-Jacques makes the search for a suitable mate the end of his pupil's education. This quest commences in Book IV, which begins with a dramatic flourish: "How rapid is our journey on this earth! The first quarter of life has been lived before one knows the use of it" (211). The next paragraph makes it quite clear what the "use" of life really is: "We are, so to speak, born twice: once to exist and once to live; once for our species and once for our sex." The onset of sexual passion is a "second birth" that enables the development of Emile's social consciousness and makes him available (susceptible?) to the charms of intimacy.

Though the explosive compound of *amour-propre* and nascent sexuality threatens to unhinge him as an adult (*E* 212), these are risks that can and indeed *must* be run. If the onset of sexual passion costs Emile his childish felicity, it promises to compensate him with something far greater. Sexual desire does not just signal a transition to a new phase of life but instead constitutes the call to *life itself*: "This is the second birth of which I have spoken. It is now that man is truly born to life and now that *nothing human is truly foreign to him*" (212; emphasis added). Before he felt the pull of sexual attraction, Emile "breathed" but did not "live"; he had not yet "felt life" (42). But through exclusive romantic union with Sophie, Emile will gain access not only to the most intense happiness available to him (447) but also to knowledge of his true nature: because it is only through love that "nothing human [can be] foreign to him," love is Emile's guide in the Delphic quest for self-knowledge. For Rousseau as for Plato, the erotic leads unawares to the point of philosophy. Rather than teach Emile to pursue philosophy as a way of life, however, Rousseau sexualizes the human good itself. The experience of romantic love therefore serves as something of a *Finis Ultimus* for Emile: through it, he might learn not only how to be good for Sophie but also how to be good for himself in a self-conscious and existentially enriched way (447). Yet Rousseau's own conception of love problematizes the realization of these pedagogic objectives. The very intensity of the sexual passions makes them difficult to educate, and Rousseau, foreshadowing a tragic end, comments at several places that any small misstep could derail the entire education (e.g., 212, 416).

| The Dynamics of Romantic Love: An Erotic Tragedy?

Rousseau's teaching on romantic love reflects his ambiguous position within the history of political thought. Though the seriousness with which Rousseau treats the phenomenon of human connectedness in its various forms is more redolent of classical than modern thought, the psychological assumptions he adopts are far closer to those of his modern forebears (Strauss 1953, 252–55). Thus, while Rousseau took the human desire for "intimate society" more seriously than did, say, Hobbes or Locke, his insistence on man's natural asociability is correspondingly more trenchant. How, then, to account for our deepest social longings? The treatment of sexuality in the previous section provides part of the answer, but it remains to elaborate more fully the psychology of romantic love and to assess its robustness. On this score, the mechanism of interest is the *imagination*: love, Rousseau tells us, is a "sweet illusion" that has its basis in the imagination rather than in nature. The issue is whether love thus understood can forge a durable bond between Emile and his beloved. Though the work's end suggests an affirmative answer, Rousseau's own treatment of romantic love indicates otherwise (see also Bloom 1993, 137; Gauthier 2006, 44–47).

Rousseau tells us repeatedly and explicitly in *Emile* that love is imaginary rather than real. It exists only to the degree that our imaginations are active: "What is true love itself if it is not chimera, lie, and illusion?" (*E* 329). Even more pointedly, Rousseau observes that with love, "everything is only illusion. I admit it. But what is real are the sentiments for the truly beautiful with which love animates us and which it makes us love. This beauty is not in the object one loves; it is the work of our errors" (391). The connectedness that love makes possible is thus founded on a kind of stupidity, but it is a tremendously ennobling kind of stupidity: it "suffuses our hearts with all the virtues" that we blindly attribute to our beloved, and refines that "sensual and coarse passion" which bewilders and tortures civilized man. The prospect of loving and of being loved ennobles us by providing new and delicious inducements to self-perfection: "How many great things could be done by means of this [sexual] motive if one knew how to set it in motion!" (390). The connection between love and virtue is strong.

Yet treating love as a product of the imagination ultimately circumscribes its possibilities quite narrowly, and Rousseau discloses these limits in the most telling way. Emile's natural sexual drive is indiscriminate, so his sex education seeks less to suppress his nascent passion than to channel it upward. It is about the cultivation of taste, not the repression of desire. To this end, Jean-Jacques inflames Emile's imagination by putting in his mind a "model of perfection" endowed with all the distinctively female virtues, and he attaches the name "Sophie" to it. This imaginary model is designed to fix Emile's desires on a single object and to make him "disgusted" with those who do not measure up to it: "It suffices that he everywhere find comparisons which make him prefer his chimera to the real objects which strike his eye" (*E* 329). The immediate purpose of providing Emile with this model is to protect him from the lubricious coos of salacious Parisian ladies. Rousseau knows how dangerous a young man's introduction into civil society is, and Emile must be made to see the lascivious but empty charms of the parlor for what they are. The solution to this problem, however, seems rather *too* effective: won't the *real* Sophie, no matter how considerable her virtue, also suffer by comparison with Emile's imaginary version of her?

Anticipating the objection, Rousseau claims that "it is unimportant whether the object I depict for him is imaginary" because "we love the image we make for ourselves far more than we love the object to which we apply it" (*E* 329). Yet he reveals the importance of the fact that Emile's "model" is imaginary in the very act of downplaying its significance: "If we saw what we love exactly as it is, there would be no more love on earth. When we stop loving, the person we loved remains the same as before, but we no longer see her in the same way. The magic veil drops, and love disappears." Intimacy is highly injurious to illusion, and a stubbornly imperfect reality erodes even the most powerful psychological projections. When we stop loving, it is partially due to the disproportion between our perfect standard and our imperfect beloved.

Rousseau exposes this disproportion and its troubling implications at the moment Emile is introduced to Sophie: "At the name Sophie, you would have seen Emile shiver. Struck by so dear a name, he is wakened with a start and casts an avid glance at the girl who dares to bear it. 'Sophie, O Sophie! Is it you whom my heart seeks? Is it you whom my heart loves?'" (*E* 414). In a state of deep anxiety, Emile goes on to compare Sophie's every feature to those possessed by his imaginary beloved, concerned that "if my heart yields and I am mistaken, then I shall never recover in all my days" (415). Of course, Emile is and *must* be mistaken: Sophie is not and cannot be the Sophie who exists in his imagination. But he nonetheless "surrenders" as soon as he hears her speak: "It is Sophie. He no longer doubts it. If it were not she, it would be too late for him to turn back." Emile proceeds to "swallow with deep draughts the poison with which she intoxicates him," and in that instant he bids farewell to his naïve independence. Emile now suffers from a new kind of naïveté: he is desperately in love with a girl to whom he has not even spoken. The reader, however, has been warned. We know that the Sophie Emile sees is patently *not* the one he dreamed up and that it is most assuredly "too late for him to turn back." In emphasizing the importance of Emile's initial encounter with Sophie I follow Rousseau himself, who cautions us not to regard his detailed depiction of this event as a "frivolous game." Those who ignore his warning fail to see "that a first impression as lively as that of love . . . has distant effects whose links are not perceived in the progress of the years but do not cease to act until death." Read in light of Rousseau's intimation that Emile's first encounter with Sophie is more troublesome than initial appearances suggest, such observations give us reason to regard the apparently happy ending of the *Emile* with some suspicion: if the "effects" of first impressions can remain latent for years, then there is no good reason to believe that they have been fully disclosed at the end of the *Emile*, or that the marriage according to nature will proceed and grow as happily as it began.

In addition to the disproportion that exists between the perfect model and the imperfect beloved, we find a similar gap between anticipating consummation and the act itself. Sex pales in comparison with the imagination of it: the "supreme happiness" of consummation is "a hundred times sweeter to hope for than to obtain. One enjoys it better when one looks forward to it than when one tastes it." Indeed, during the courting phase Emile is "as happy as a man can be." Unfortunately, the pleasure of imagining consummation and the pleasure of engaging in it cannot be combined: "The *whole value of life* is in the felicity that he tastes. What [before consummation] can be added to his happiness? Look, consider, imagine what he still needs that can accord with what he has. He enjoys all the goods that can be obtained at once. None can be added except at the expense of another." The sexual act itself, then, can only come at the "expense" of the extraordinary felicity provided by imagining it. The consumption of a romantic relationship initiates its decay. Jean-Jacques, cognizant of all this, vows not to "shorten this happy time in your life. I shall spin out its enchantment for you. I shall prolong it as much as possible. Alas, it has to end, and end soon. But I shall make it last forever in your memory and make you never repent having tasted it" (*E* 419; emphasis added).

Emile and Sophie, unaware of the possibility that they would ever "repent" anything, blissfully abandon themselves to their shared illusions. Jean-Jacques does not (yet) explain the nature of love to his pupil and his beloved, allowing them to enjoy "the most charming delirium that human souls have ever experienced" (*E* 426). He has good reasons for withholding this lesson: though love is an illusion, to experience it *as* an illusion is to cheapen the experience itself. To make love an abstract phenomenon to be dissected and apprehended through reason, rather than a sentiment to be felt and enjoyed, is to prematurely decrease its appeal. We must be deceived fully in order to love fully (see Bloom 1993, 91, 113). Jean-Jacques knows that to understand love is to sacrifice it, but yet again Rousseau the author has informed the reader in ways that Jean-Jacques the tutor has not informed his pupil (*E* 426). He even invites us, informed in ways that Emile and Sophie are not, to let our imaginations "wander without constraint" in contemplating the fate of "two young lovers who . . . are untroubled as they yield themselves to the sweet illusion delighting them" (424). The reader who does so carefully must surely be struck that the source of their profound delight cannot endure.

Jean-Jacques does eventually inform Emile that his delirium cannot last. Before they leave Sophie and begin their extended travels, Jean-Jacques speaks forcefully to him about the nature and scope of love: "Before tasting the pleasure of life, you have exhausted its happiness. There is nothing beyond what you have felt. . . . You have enjoyed more from hope than you will ever enjoy in reality. Imagination adorns what one desires but abandons it when it is in one's possession . . . if nothing changes from without, the heart changes.

Happiness leaves us, or we leave it" (*E* 447). Rousseau finally tells Emile what the reader has long known. Romantic love begins to decay the moment it is consummated, and nothing can reverse this process once it has begun. Jean-Jacques's impassioned discourse does not take hold, however, and he finds it necessary to again inform Emile—this time very unceremoniously—of the unsustainability of his love for Sophie. He reminds the lovers on their wedding day that their bond "can only become weaker," and he adds that the only way to extend their mutual attraction over the whole course of life is to disjoin obligation and love (475–76). Unfairly but unavoidably, the responsibility of managing love's first fires falls to Sophie, who is informed (in confidence) that shared pleasure is necessary but not sufficient to make the marriage endure: since "enjoyment wears out pleasure," the only way to extend the marriage is to "make her favors rare and precious." However, not even the most artful coquetry can prevent the inevitable decay of love, and the resulting void must be filled with the consolations—however partial—provided by friendship and the "sweet habit" of conjugal solicitude (479).

Because Rousseau never enters into the psychological particulars of how the transition from love to friendship occurs, it is difficult to know whether these compensations will be sufficient to console the young lovers in their loss. Yet Rousseau's own moral psychology suggests that such a transition will be more difficult than Jean-Jacques lets on. Rousseau grounds his conception of friendship in pity (*DI* 131; cf. Reisert 2003, 78–85), but Rousseauan pity possesses conceptual features that ultimately tend to work against the kind of connectedness that Jean-Jacques seeks to effect. Though his ultimate aim is to fuse Emile and Sophie into a single organic unity (*E* 479), Rousseauan pity requires the existence of two discrete persons. We pity others both because we know we are not exempt from the sufferer's ills but also because we delight in the fact that we do not suffer (223–24). Pity thus unites us with others while recognizing the imperfect and attenuated nature of that union. Pity, and by extension friendship, would thus seem ill suited to sustain Jean-Jacques's hope of uniting Emile and Sophie into a single "moral person" (377), for the individuation required by pity violates Rousseau's own conception of a healthy gendered relationship. The transition from love to friendship—a journey Emile and Sophie must make in order to stay together—thus appears to be more difficult than initial appearances suggest.

The work concludes with Emile informing Jean-Jacques that Sophie is pregnant and requesting that he be involved in the rearing of their child: "My master, congratulate your child. He hopes soon to have the honor of being a father. . . . But remain the master of young masters. As long as I live I shall need you. I need you more than ever now that my functions as a man begin. You have fulfilled yours. Guide me so that I can imitate you. And take your rest. It is time" (*E* 480). Emile's curious request recalls the creation language in Genesis 2:2: both God and Jean-Jacques "take their rest" while remaining intimately involved with their respective creations. When read in light of Rousseau's previous remarks about the sustainability of romantic love, the biblical analogy seems to hold: Rousseau's creation story, like the Bible's, suggests that a *fall* is imminent.

| Fallen Man (and Citizen): The Perils of Social Incorporation

Provided that the end of *Emile* does not augur well, we should not be surprised that Rousseau provides an account of "the fall" consistent with his belief in man's natural goodness in *Emile and Sophie*, the unfinished and posthumously published sequel to *Emile*. In this work Emile and his beloved move to Paris following the deaths of their child and her parents, and Sophie, coaxed by Emile's flagging romantic attentions, has an affair with another man and becomes pregnant with his child. Driven to hysteria by the news, Emile abandons his family and, following a series of bizarre, almost picaresque adventures, finds himself alone in the world. This tragic end was foreshadowed in *Emile*, for it was brought on by precisely what Jean-Jacques warned of: the waning of Emile's sexual passions. Indeed, we find in the sequel that not even Sophie's virtuous coquetry could stoke the flames of imagination: "This was no longer the time when my heated imagination was looking for Sophie, and rejected everything else. I was no longer looking for her, I possessed her, and her charm now served to embellish these objects of affect, as much as it had disfigured them in early youth. But soon these same objects dulled my desires by diffusing them. Worn out little by little by all these frivolous pursuits, my heart was imperceptibly losing its early resilience and was becoming incapable of warmth and vigor" (*ES* 202). The cooling of Emile's passions leads, inevitably and necessarily, to a process of decline that reaches its nadir in Sophie's dramatic confession of her unfaithfulness.

This tragic decline was undoubtedly accelerated by the questionable choice to move to Paris, a decision that not only sped up the process of decay but also magnified the severity of its effects. In explaining his strange choice to move his family to the seventh circle of Rousseau's moral universe, Emile refers vaguely to "business" he had in the capital but adds that his primary motive was to provide a change of scenery that might help Sophie recover. This explanation is manifestly unpersuasive, for one does not rehabilitate an ailing spouse by moving to Gomorrah. A more compelling alternative—one that explains both Emile's decision to move to Paris as well as his diminished desire for Sophie—is boredom. Though he was under no obligation to go to Paris and knew from experience to stay away, he moved there anyway and, once there, wasted no time in making the acquaintances of "too attractive liaisons" that isolated him from his wife and encouraged her infidelity (*ES* 202–3). Emile, it would seem, was unhappy in the country and needed sexual and social stimulation that his wife could no longer provide. We may blame Paris, but only for accelerating a process that was already well under way.

This interpretation of the decision to move to Paris helps point up the broader problems with both of the strategies of social incorporation that are available to Emile and Sophie. The strategy of isolation proves ineffective: left to each other in rustic repose, life becomes intolerably boring after romantic illusions are undermined by the harsh realities of running a domicile. However, integration into a larger political community also poses decisive problems. In Paris, indeed in *any* large political society, the problems come both from within and from without: couples must worry not only about sustaining the fragile illusions that enable their collective happiness but also about protecting themselves from the chaotic swirl of social forces that threaten their bond. We know, of course, that the City of Light is especially deadly to good morals, but it is distinguished from other communities not by the fact that it corrupts but rather by the speed with which it does so. The move to Paris thus leads us to the melancholy insight that neither the isolated nor the integrated household can endure. One cannot be a part or apart.

Bad luck also clearly affected Emile and Sophie's prospects for a happy life, but the decisive role accorded to accident speaks directly to the fragility of *Emile*'s pedagogic project. In order to endure, love must descend from the "celestial regions" to terra firma, it must survive the journey from the perfect imagination to the imperfect real world. Surviving such a descent requires a robustness and solidity that Emile and Sophie possess individually without sharing in tandem. Their misfortunes—even those not directly related to Emile's dwindling desires—serve to underscore the fragility of their union. Human love is simply too frail to survive sustained exposure to the vicissitudes of fortune. Its maintenance requires either extreme good luck or the perpetual interventions of an omniscient tutor. The happiness enjoyed by men of goodwill but of average abilities is never secure; the world is too great, too strong, and too complex for middling natures. They, or rather we, require a kind of assistance that cannot be reasonably expected and that, even when obtained, proves insufficient. This is the teaching of *Emile*.

| Why Cast the Tragic Veil?

The disquieting conclusion I have just found in *Emile* is, while discernible from the surface teaching, nonetheless not the work's surface teaching and even appears to contradict its surface teaching. Thus it is necessary to ask what reasons Rousseau would have for veiling the tragic character of his great bildungsroman. At least part of the answer is contained in his very choice of literary form: in choosing to write an educational novel Rousseau not only describes but enacts the educational process depicted in the work (Scott 2012). Insofar as readers are provided with an account of the development of their own passions that reveals their own natural goodness and are given "models of perfection" to which they may compare themselves and one another, they are themselves treated to a Rousseauan education no less than Emile and Sophie are. The imaginary pupils Rousseau presents to our understanding do much to expose the emptiness of bourgeois social life and to enlarge our sense of social possibility, and in so doing they seize control of the reader's moral imagination in the same way that the idea "Sophie" did for Emile and the fictional Telemachus did for Sophie.

The fact that such images ultimately prove problematic for both of the happy lovers is doubtless worrisome for the careful reader, but not decisively so, for he knows that the noble failure embodied by Emile and Sophie's imaginary romance is more meaningful than the hollow success achieved by more conventional understandings of love and marriage. It is nobler because it points corrupt readers—and all of us are corrupt—in the direction of virtue and away from the morally destructive individualism of Hobbes. To this end Rousseau simultaneously flatters and elevates our romantic hopes. His romance shows us how the desire for love arouses the desire to be lovable and hence the desire to be virtuous. Emile and Sophie find what is best in themselves through each other, and their touching example—even if it fails to endure—is for that reason worthy of genuine admiration. They are not a perfect template for the reformation of domestic life, but they remind us all of what is highest and best in us and in so doing provide a much-needed form of moral guidance.

Yet after all this has been said, we must acknowledge that this is something of a consolation prize. More attentive readers—ones with "the courage to begin again"—also see Rousseau's quiet confirmation of the very individualism he is criticizing (*DI* 98). While the experience of love is salutary because it is conducive to the development of individual virtue, it nonetheless fails to establish the affective basis for lasting human community; to make virtue the final reward of love is to replace a public or shared good with a private one. *Emile* sought to establish a kind of reciprocal governance between persons but in the end established it within them. Neither Emile nor Sophie ever became fully sociable in the way that the double object required; they loved their perfect images, not the imperfect other. In loving thus they became unwitting instruments of each other's private moral improvement, but they failed to ever love each other *as others*. Love thus emerges from *Emile* both as a futile aspiration and as our "last best hope" in the quest to preserve our natural wholeness. It shows that there is no going back to the state of nature, but also that there can be no final reconciliation of the natural and the social. The decisive and even tragic difficulties to which romantic love is subject would thus appear to have serious consequences for how we understand Rousseau's broader social and political theory. Though it will not be until chapter 8 that I articulate a model of domestic life that *would* be appropriate for Rousseau's political vision, I shall anticipate the analysis to come—and sum up the analysis already finished—by considering the question of political obligation in the context of Emile's education.

| The Household and the Polity: Conclusions

Emile teaches not only that Emile's love for Sophie is unsustainably fragile but also that the romantic-marital relation is the ground of Emile's attachment to his country. Taken together, these findings suggest something very unsettling about the extent and the robustness of Emile's sense of civic duty: if affection for one's regime is derived from the affection he has for his family and if affection for one's family is bound to decline, then it would seem that connection to the state would inevitably disintegrate as well. This, however, is too quick, for since Emile's affection for his family is itself the product of his appreciation for the good and the decent in their universal forms, then perhaps these same cosmopolitan moral sensibilities should, even in the absence of strong family ties, connect him to his fellow countrymen and dispose him to take sympathetic and beneficent action toward them. Thus, before concluding our discussion of Emile and his relation to political society, it is necessary to see whether the universalistic moral commitments to which he subscribes are sufficiently strong to connect him to his political regime and his fellow countrymen even in the absence of domestic ties (Neuhouser 2008).

We can begin to see our answer by noting that the very cosmopolitanism that connects Emile to his countrymen also prevents his having any especially strong regard for them. His concern for them is a particular expression of a universal concern for the species and is emblematic of the equal moral respect to which men qua men are entitled, but neither one's fellow citizens nor his particular state deserves special preference. The regime as the regime means nothing to Emile. His universal morality makes him as bad a patriot as he is a good neighbor.

To flesh out these conclusions, we need to recur to the above analysis of Jean-Jacques's explanation of Emile's political duties as well as to look briefly at *Emile and Sophie*. On this score, recall that Emile chooses at his tutor's behest to remain in his homeland not because his presence will be demanded in the assembly but rather because it almost certainly will *not* be. He subjects himself to the laws of his country because the "simulacra of laws" found there best approximates his initial wish to "live in independence" with his beloved Sophie. Thus the political education Emile receives does not transform his affective field or reorient his relation to the political community in the same way that the education of the classical citizen does. Rather, his cosmopolitan moral outlook leads him to view his obligations to his state as deriving from his obligations to humanity as a whole. And even though Jean-Jacques finds it necessary to correct the "extravagant disinterestedness" with which Emile initially views those obligations, he approves the cosmopolitan attitude underneath it and encourages his pupil never to forget that all men—fellow countrymen or not—deserve equal moral respect.

But the universal duty of moral respect is not enough to keep Emile connected to his homeland, or indeed to anyone in particular, and the second letter of *Emile and Sophie* shows why. Writing his tutor from a remote, isolated location, Emile explains why he chose to leave his homeland and family following his wife's infidelity. Characterizing his feelings of isolation and betrayal, Emile writes, "I have drunk the waters of oblivion. The past is fading from my memory, and the universe opens before me. That is what I said to myself when leaving my fatherland. I was ashamed of it, and I owed it only contempt and hatred. Happy and worthy of honor in my own right, my country and its vile inhabitants victimized me and plunged me into disgrace. By breaking the bonds that attached me to my country, my patriotism extended over the whole earth, and I became more of a man by ceasing to be a citizen" (*ES* 221–22). Emile reveals here how fragile his connection to the state is, acknowledging the derivative character of his political identity by blaming his "fatherland" for rupturing the relation he had to it. He had no other motive to remain where he was once the possibility of happy marriage had passed, and even goes so far as to *blame* his homeland and its "vile inhabitants" for Sophie's infidelity. He left his country not indifferently, but with strong feelings of victimization and indignance, in order to spread his patriotism "over the whole earth." Tracy Strong (1994), eager to find Emile's inner citizen, claims the young man is simply deceived about his own feelings, but this is precisely the conclusion his education would have led him to draw. Incorporation into a particular political community—even the one his tutor had recommended for its relative justice—had contributed to the undoing of the romantic relation on which happiness depended, confirming Emile's initial suspicions about subjecting himself to the chaotic swirl of social forces that constitute political life. Far from being compensated for the sacrifice of independence that comes with settling down in a particular place, Emile is punished for it; his experience shows him that the costs of incorporation outweigh the benefits. He thus decides to extend his patriotism "over the whole earth" and becomes a roving, itinerant traveler—one without roots or settled social relations, one who treats his fellow men with disengaged beneficence without being emotionally or psychologically invested in any of them. Emile is benevolent in order to remain independent, and if he extends his hand to his fellows it is only in order to keep them at arm's length.

By the end of *Emile and Sophie* it is clear that Emile's own self-understanding far more closely resembles the disengaged and asocial pose that Rousseau himself strikes in the *Reveries* than it does the robust social sensibility of the classical citizen. The quasi-Stoic posture he assumes is a function not just of the breakdown of his romantic relation—though this breakdown defines Emile's life in much the same way that, as we shall soon see, St. Preux's frustrated love for Julie defines his—but of the recognition of the irreconcilable tension between his own cosmopolitanism and the comprehensive embeddedness of the true citizen. Emile's universal morality reveals the arbitrariness of the partiality that citizens show for one another, and in so doing it undermines the strong identification that a good political society requires. Citizens love those within the city's walls and regard outsiders with suspicion and contempt (*E* 39). Cosmopolitan universalism does not lead to citizenship but to disengagement, social isolation, and relative independence. It is not the answer to the question posed by *Emile*.

What, then, does the failure of the social and political component of Emile's education tell us about the more general question of the relationship between the household and the polity? We must begin to answer this question by acknowledging that *Emile* appears to assert their complementarity. Criticizing Socrates's attempt to eliminate the nuclear family, Rousseau holds that the philosopher's error was to reason "as though it were not by means of the small fatherland which is the family that the heart attaches itself to the large one; as though it were not the good son, the good husband, and the good father who make the good citizen!" (*E* 363). Though this passage is often taken to reveal the ultimate compatibility of Rousseau's domestic and political visions (Fermon 1997; Schwartz 1984, 51), it is clear that Rousseau is defending the general idea of the household per se and not any specific set of domestic arrangements. He says that a private household of some kind is necessary to the possibility of good citizenship; he does *not* say that a household like Emile's is the one necessary to the realization of that possibility.

In fact, Rousseau's other writings strongly suggest that a home like Emile and Sophie's is patently not what he has in mind for the society of the *Social Contract*. In the *Discourse on Political Economy*, for instance, Rousseau praises the households of the classical world, and of ancient Rome in particular, for their politicizing capacity: in serving as "so many schools of citizens" they managed to underwrite rather than undermine civic virtue. But he quickly adds that the complementarity Rome established between the household and the polity was a "continual miracle" that "the world should not hope to see again" (*DPE* 21–22). One reason Rousseau is pessimistic about rediscovering the civic potential of the household is that the ascendance of Christianity (among other developments) has decisively undermined the ideal of citizenship (e.g., *E* 38–40; *SC* IV.8). Perhaps more important, however, is that the idea of the household itself has changed in ways that affect its ability to serve as a site of civic education: the classical household did not contain within itself a conception of the best human life but was rather the "realm of necessity" (e.g., Arendt 1998, 28–31). As such, its function was not to instantiate the good but rather to provide the material preconditions requisite to its realization in the *public* realm. The household thus existed for the sake of the city—not vice versa. We, however, have seen that Emile and Sophie's domestic retreat embodies a compelling—albeit not unproblematic—vision of the good that does not require for its fulfillment an experience of citizenship in a just polity. His household is a substitute for meaningful political life, not a basis for it.

5 Romantic Love in *Julie*

In *Emile* and its unfinished sequel, Rousseau articulates a psychological theory about the dynamics of romantic love that highlights love's imaginary character and the tragic limitations that such imaginariness imposes. He also shows that the psychological difficulties attending the marital relationship are aggravated by the necessity of social incorporation: whether in the bustling salons of Paris or the suffocating hush of the farmhouse, even our impeccably educated lovers cannot, for all their individual merits, seem to make things work. Theirs is a best case, and its failure is suggestive of broader problems with romantic association in particular and, perhaps, of human association more generally. Yet *Emile* is not Rousseau's only, or perhaps even his final, word on romantic love. To readers of Rousseau's own time, in fact, it was not *Emile* but *Julie* that cemented the great Genevan's reputation as a knower of things romantic. In the wildly popular epistolary novel, of which Rousseau claimed only to be the "editor," the same tragic dynamics seen in *Emile* are reproduced in an illicit romance that occurs between an aristocratic pupil (Julie) and her bourgeois tutor (St. Preux). Unlike Emile and Sophie, St. Preux and Julie are not perfectly educated. Also unlike Emile and Sophie, they are not allowed to choose their own spouses and thus are never formally united: learning of his daughter's intention to wed her bourgeois tutor, Julie's staunchly aristocratic father emphatically opposes her plans and intervenes violently in order to prevent them from coming to fruition (*J* 142–43). This turn in the narrative, though compelling from a dramatic point of view, denies the reader the opportunity to directly observe how St. Preux and Julie would have fared in the event of their union and makes it more difficult to generalize from Emile and Sophie's very different case.

In seeking to generalize, then, one must reason from a counterfactual and, in such cases, there are inevitably plausible arguments on either side of the question. On one hand, there is no denying the unique and even miraculous character of St. Preux and Julie's love for each other. They seem never to tire of expatiating on the exceptional character of their connection, and in one of the more affecting—and prescient—passages in the novel, Julie tells St. Preux what all lovers long to hear and say: "Our destinies are forever united, and we can no longer be either happy or unhappy if not together. Our souls have, so to speak, touched at every point, and we have everywhere felt the same cohesion" (*J* 44). Such grand pronunciamentoes would be easier to dismiss if they issued only from the lovers themselves, but one finds nearly all the principal personages in the novel deeply impressed by the intensity of Julie and St. Preux's relationship. It frequently occasions jealousy in Claire and astonishment in Milord Edward; the latter, himself an erstwhile admirer of Julie, says he has "seen nothing so extraordinary" as the connection shared by the two lovers, and he is so moved by the depth and charm of their love that he offers them romantic asylum in England (161–64). What is more, we find at the work's end that Julie and St. Preux never stopped loving each other—that in fact their love *had* endured despite all the obstacles that impeded its full growth and development. On the basis of all this, there is a strong temptation to conclude that St. Preux and Julie's love is exceptional—that it is "outside the rules" that confined and ultimately undid Emile and Sophie—and that its indestructibility consists in its very distinctiveness.

After all this has been said, however, there is still plenty of room to question such a conclusion. The lovers' self-assessments, while often insightful and always earnest, are also untrustworthy. Their correspondence, as Rousseau himself acknowledges in the work's second preface, is full of exaggeration, self-deception, and childish rhodomontadizing (*J* 11). In lucid moments, Julie herself wonders about the robustness of the love she and St. Preux share, recalling the circumspection that Rousseau expresses as his own in *Emile*. "To me," she tells an increasingly randy St. Preux early in their courtship, "the slightest alteration of our present situation can only be for the worse. No, even were a happy bond to unite us forever, I know not whether the surfeit of happiness would not soon be its demise" (42). Julie's pessimism about her prospects for felicity—even *in* a marriage—is striking, especially in light of St. Preux's naïve unwillingness or inability to conceive of the passing of his love for Julie (e.g., 94–95). The assessments of others prove somewhat unreliable as well: Julie's cousin Claire believes the generous view that Milord Edward takes of Julie and St. Preux's relationship is less the product of disinterested observation than of the passionate attachment he feels for his friends (167). This attachment—precisely because it is so passionate—recommends Milord Edward's zeal in friendship more than his acuteness of judgment. Rousseau himself cannot resist poking fun at the affable bombast of the soi-disant sage, appending an affectionately derisive remark to some of Milord's more affectedly abstract ruminations: "I like the muddle of this letter, in that it is totally in good Edward's character, who is never so philosophical as when he behaves foolishly, and never reasons so much as when he does not know what he is talking about" (431n). Milord always means well but rarely knows how to help.

Finally and perhaps most decisively, it would seem that Julie and St. Preux's love endures throughout the novel not in spite of but *because of* the obstacles that impede its development. If Rousseau is clear about anything in *Emile*, it is that love has a life cycle—it grows, matures, and dies. Applied to the novel, this theory suggests that the very circumstances that conspire to arrest the development of Julie and St. Preux's love also keep it from dying. The image of Julie calcifies in St. Preux's memory because intervening circumstances prevent him from perceiving or coming to terms with the disproportion between the perfect image and the imperfect person. Had their relationship been given space to grow, it is difficult to believe that the outcome would be different from or preferable to what happened to Emile and Sophie. These, to be sure, are only prima facie considerations, but they are compelling enough to cast sufficient doubt on the view that the uniqueness of St. Preux and Julie's attachment is sufficient to guarantee its long-term success.

I incline toward this more circumspect view and below I will give it more systematic and persuasive exposition. More specifically, I intend to establish two general propositions. The first is that there is little reason to believe that Julie and St. Preux's love is immune to the processes of decline that undo Emile and Sophie and appear to beset all romantic relationships. The second, following from the first, is that if St. Preux and Julie's love is liable to break under the weight of habit—if their imaginary conceptions of each other are effaced by the harsh and unflattering lights of reality—then the transition from love to friendship would seem to be difficult and ultimately impossible for such intense lovers. Thus *Julie* confirms and builds on the tragic teaching of *Emile*.

In arguing thus it will be necessary to closely examine Part I of *Julie* in light of the possibility raised by Milord Edward (called Bomston hereafter) early in Part II: he offers St. Preux and Julie romantic asylum in England, where they can enjoy their love sheltered from the "gothic maxims" of Julie's implacable and barbarous father. St. Preux is predictably enthusiastic about the whole affair, but Julie—after seeking the counsel of her "inseparable" cousin Claire—refuses Bomston's offer. Her rejection is grounded in her (and Rousseau's) pessimism not only about the durability of love but also about the possibility of friendship after love has faded. Julie herself betrays a certain circumspection concerning the ultimate fate of their union consistent with the theory announced in *Emile* but inconsistent with relevant alternative hypotheses. What is more, St. Preux's reaction to his tryst with Julie more than justifies her pessimism: as the psychological theory of *Emile* predicts, St. Preux's affections for Julie begin to diminish immediately after consummation. The necessity of love's passing requires us to consider the possibility of transitioning from love to friendship as well as the possibility of transitioning from friendship to love. *Julie*, however, casts doubt on both of these propositions: the memory of lost love creates resentment rather than affection and renders bitter the "sweet habit" of conjugal solicitude, and friendship cannot become love because it is characterized by a form of transparency precluded by the illusions of love.

| Should I Stay or Should I Go? Julie's Divided Loyalties

The first movement of *Julie* is also its most romantic. The opening theme—"I must flee you Mademoiselle, that I can see"—introduces a visual metaphor and suggests that we are blind while under love's spell (*J* 25). The coda—an angry St. Preux protesting the forced separation from his lover—reintroduces visual language but for a different and even contradictory purpose: as he repeats "What! Not *see* her again!" in increasingly mournful tones, there is a suggestion that he is blind *without* love and that death in the service of intense passional commitment is preferable to life spent under the anesthesia of petty pleasures (151; emphasis added). To this tension *Julie* joins many others, and a central debate among critics of the work is less about whether it possesses a bipolar or dialectical structure than about what specific opposition best explains the tensions in the text. For Schiller (1979) they were "intellect" and "sensitivity"; for Starobinski (1988), "transparency" and "obstruction"; and for Shklar (1969), "inclination" and "duty." Starobinski, though he offers a dialectical interpretation of *Julie*, has some reservations about doing so. He confesses that "some ambiguities remain" after his dialecticized interpretation is complete: "Are the antithetical terms, passion and virtue, ever really reconciled? Is passion really transcended? Does the synthesis really take place? . . . All these questions must be asked, and the difficulty of answering them points up the danger of accepting unreservedly a 'dialectical' interpretation such as the one sketched here" (114, cf. DeMan 1979).

I join Starobinski in such concerns, and to them I add that *Julie* seems to be less about the resolution of problems than about their fundamental intransigence. And to be sure, one such problem *is* the tension between virtue and happiness. But it is neither the only nor the most important problem the text confronts. Indeed, the difficulties faced by the novel's principal characters—the internal contradictions, the feelings of alienation and isolation, the self-deception, the crippling emotional dependence—are not presented as accidental or transient conditions that admit of synthesis or final resolution, but rather as perennial and ineliminable features of their (and our) individual and collective lives. *Julie* teaches that these enemies must be fought but can never be defeated. They crowd the text and animate all the action; they are always lurking underneath all the delusions, mistakes, errors in judgment, and deficiencies in self-knowledge that propel the plot forward. It is to their rhythm that the tragedy marches inexorably forward, and it is on their terms that Julie's symbolic sacrifice/suicide occurs. Her death, of course, is meant to remind us of Jesus's, but in the end we find that Julie's desires were decidedly un-Christlike, for she loved and physically desired St. Preux all along. If God exists then He was either unwilling or unable to cure Julie's illness. His earthly stand-in, Wolmar, tried his best but, in the end, could only throw up his hands. For all his machinations and foresight, not even he could resolve the difficulties that threaten and finally undermine the fragile happiness of which human beings are capable.

But we must ask: are our difficulties as stubborn and severe as that? It is one thing to say Rousseau's characters make things difficult for themselves and quite another to say there is no good solution to the problems they face. Things may have turned out differently and, yes, perhaps even more happily. What, for instance, if Julie had accepted Bomston's offer to give her and St. Preux an estate in England? We, of course, want to believe things might have been different had the lovers been united; we are on their side and, as Rousseau's heirs, are enlightened enough to prefer his voluntaristic theory of marriage to the "gothic maxims" that prevent their union. However, Julie does *not* accept Bomston's offer, choosing instead to stay in the Vaud with her parents. The entire novel turns on this decision and becomes incomprehensible if we cannot understand why Julie did what she did. Of course, she offers an account on this score and it is plausible enough: she expresses concern about her mother's health, her father's violent temper, and their advancing age. She is, in addition, almost certainly worried about the prospect of her increasingly enfeebled *maman* receiving another beating at the hands of the "best of fathers" (*J* 143). "The question," she tells Bomston, "is not whether I have the right to order my life against the will of those who gave it to me, but whether I can do so without mortally aggrieving them, whether I can flee them without casting them deep into despair" (170). "Can I," she goes on, "pitilessly desert those thanks to whom I breathe, who sustain the life they have given me, and make it dear to me . . . ? A father approaching sixty! A mother forever sickly!" To such considerations she appends the now foregone conclusion: "My parents will make me unhappy . . . but for me it will be less cruel to lament in my misfortune than to have caused theirs" (171). Julie would leave, but her heart bids her stay.

Such considerations are not inapposite, and they are offered sincerely. The "shame and regret" of desertion and neglect very possibly would have presented an insuperable obstacle to Julie's happiness, especially given her extreme susceptibility to feelings of moral guilt (*J* 170). Yet her rationale ultimately creates as many questions as it answers, and even the most charitable interpretation of her account shows that it fails to resolve the concerns it addresses. Indeed, the arguments she offers on behalf of staying with her parents cut both ways, and they might actually be advanced even more forcefully on the other side of the controversy. If, for instance, she is concerned about "mortally" aggrieving someone, then the obvious candidate is St. Preux rather than her parents: his fascination with and desire for suicide recur throughout the novel, and he has already threatened to kill himself once by the time Julie refuses Bomston (76). Does she think someone as sensitive as her lover will bear the bad news with more aplomb? Even a superficial familiarity with St. Preux's character speaks rather forcibly against this notion: a more drastic or less dignified reaction can scarce be imagined (see esp. 151). What requires emphasis, however, is that Julie has conflicting duties and is going to hurt someone—perhaps "mortally"—no matter what she chooses to do (165). As a consequence, we see that her vivid appeals to the horrors of her parents' suffering do not and cannot decide the matter. Julie herself appears to recognize this when she confesses to Bomston that she "cannot answer" his arguments on behalf of going to England with St. Preux (171). Bomston's account on this score is compelling and Julie's response to him is hardly determinative. She must, then, have other unstated reasons that perhaps she does not wish to disclose to Bomston.

In beginning, to give shape and coherence to these unstated reasons, we should begin by noting Julie's response to Bomston appeals to the interest she has in her own happiness rather than to the duties she owes her parents as an ethical matter. She does *not*, as Shklar's interpretation suggests, argue that her heart carries her to Kent but her duties keep her in Switzerland. Julie is not the deontologist she is often made out to be. Instead, she says she is staying because she will be less *happy* in England than she will be at home: the "shame and regret" of leaving her parents outweigh all other considerations, and the remorse felt for her negligence would poison the rest of her life. The tension she feels is thus not between duty and love, but between competing forms of love; the relevant opposition is not between the heart and the mind but within the heart itself: "Such is the source of the reproaches of a terrified conscience, and of the secret murmurs that *rend my heart*" (*J* 170; emphasis added). As is so often the case in Rousseau, the desires of the heart are couched in the language of conscience. Julie chooses her parents over St. Preux, and does so as a being whose primary concern is, if not exactly the increase of happiness, then at least the reduction of *un*happiness.

The obvious answer is that Julie simply loves her parents more than she loves St. Preux and chooses to stay with them for that reason. This explanation has the virtue of looking for Julie's inner conflict in more or less the right place: rather than search for a tension between "passion" and "duty," the proponent of this view begins by looking at tensions within the passional realm. The evident tension appears to be between pity and love, and it is decided in favor of pity; the prospect of her parents' suffering is simply too awful for Julie to consider, and the anticipation of their suffering is more painful than the loss of her love. This view, however, is also problematic, for Julie often describes herself and her personality as defined by its need for romantic love. Julie's interest in the sexual association is identity-constitutive— "Love," she tells St. Preux, "will be the major business in our lives"—and ceteris paribus it should take priority over her abusive father's emotional bullying (*J* 89). Indeed, the posture Julie strikes in her letter to Bomston rings somewhat hollow because it is inconsistent with everything she has done to that point in the novel: were she as devoted to her parents' happiness as she affects to be in her letter to Bomston—were she consistent in privileging their wishes over those of St. Preux—then she never would have gotten involved with her tutor in the first place. In order to take seriously the proposition that Julie loves her parents more than she does St. Preux, we would need to know why she loves her parents too much to marry St. Preux but not enough to have resisted his advances. This, I think, is a rather tough row to hoe, even if such a case could be made that it is more plausible to take the arguments Julie makes to Bomston as a sincere but incomplete statement of her actual view. What, then, is the unstated source of Julie's hesitance to join St. Preux in England? If neither duty nor overweening guilt can all the way explain why Julie elects to stay home, then what does?

Tanner (1982) finds an answer in Julie's class prejudice. Ever the daddy's girl, Julie shares her father's reservations about St. Preux's social status and, on his interpretation, never intended to wed him in the first place. St. Preux thus becomes a bourgeois Mandingo, a boy toy over whom Julie exercises—often cruelly—an absolute and nonreciprocal empire. Though searching in many ways, Tanner's interpretation is not especially convincing in this regard, for it is difficult to see how Julie could have loved St. Preux as she did if she were as devoted to her father as Tanner's interpretation makes her. Indeed, the very fact that Julie recognized St. Preux as a *semblable* and as worthy of affection speaks forcibly against the notion that her reservations about him are motivated by class differences. An interpretation that narrows Julie's motives thus cannot explain why there is a love story in the first place.

There is, however, a more compelling possibility for explaining Julie's unwillingness to run away to Kent. It is that Julie has quite reasonable reservations about St. Preux in particular, and about male desire more generally, that look very much like Rousseau's own. Part I of the novel gives particularly clear expression to Julie's circumspection about the very love for which her heart is made, confirming the tragic psychology of romantic love articulated in *Emile*. She not only sees the unhappy fate that awaits St. Preux and her with stark and horrid clarity; she also perceives its fundamental cause. Like Rousseau, Julie sees the physicalization of romantic love as both inevitable and destructive, and also like Rousseau she senses that men are inconstant and unreliable romantic partners. Julie's presentiments about the variability of male romantic passion are, Rousseau claims, known to all women but go unperceived by even the best-educated men. One sees this clearly at the end of *Emile*, where Jean-Jacques addresses the young couple and saves for their wedding day the unsettling observation that their love will die. Emile, like St. Preux, cannot conceive the idea: believing his Sophie to be an inexhaustible source of delight, he laughs to himself and at anyone who would follow Jean-Jacques in considering the possibility of his love for Sophie ever waning. The tutor, of course, knows his pupil is simply unable to understand the logic of his own desires, but the impeccably educated Emile hasn't the slightest idea about the mutability of sexual passion. Even the finest and most reflective young men have virtually no comprehension of their own drives and view the romantic situation with an almost shocking lack of foresight. Emile's myopic focus on consummation calls immediately to mind Machiavelli's Callimaco who, after so much ingenious scheming to seduce the married Lucrezia, has absolutely no idea what to do with her after he finally succeeds in doing so.

Sophie, however, cannot hide her "curiosity," and she listens closely to Jean-Jacques's discourse on how to stoke love's first fires. Her anxiety, though felt obscurely, is not unfounded. "Men," Rousseau explains, "are less constant than women. . . . The woman has a presentiment of the man's inconstancy and is uneasy about it" (*E* 476). Julie, for her part, has a far more sophisticated grasp of male inconstancy than does Sophie, and the first part of the novel bearing her name reveals this awareness in striking ways. It tracks the development of Julie and St. Preux's love and its movement, which is both an ascent and a descent, from the spiritual to the physical realm. And as the sentiments of love increasingly require corporeal expression—as the needs of the soul find their ultimate expression in the satisfaction of the body—so, too, do they grow more unstable. The tension of interest here is thus neither between love and duty nor is it between paternal and romantic love; there is, instead, a tension within the bodily and spiritual elements—the "physical" and "moral" parts—of love itself. And *Julie*, like *Emile*, shows that such a tension is not susceptible of resolution. It is perennial and congenital, not provisional and reconcilable.

| He Loves Me, He Loves Me Not: The Limits of Embodied Love

At the novel's beginning, love has virtually no physical dimension. It is almost purely ideational and psychological; it seeks not sex so much as the peculiar form of recognition that attaches to sexual attraction. The desire for this kind of acknowledgment will, of course, ultimately find a specifically sexual expression, but for now the desires of the body are subordinate to those of the psyche. In his confession to Julie, St. Preux claims that he shares with her a unique way of viewing the world and that their suitability for each other consists in this shared distinctiveness. "Not having acquired the uniform prejudices of the world, we have uniform ways of feeling and seeing, and why should I not dare imagine in our hearts the same accord I perceive in our opinions?" (*J* 26). Here and throughout the letter, St. Preux's primary concern is to create a zone of exclusivity for Julie and himself. He wants to keep the homogenous world and its "uniform prejudices" out of sight so he may feel Julie's gaze fixed firmly and exclusively on him. Being *seen* by Julie is, at least for the time being, enough for St. Preux. Bodily desire is nowhere in evidence, and this is, for Rousseau, as it should be: sex isn't especially interesting unless it is joined to exclusive emotional commitment. "Possession," he observes in *Emile*, "which is not reciprocal is nothing." Without the special assurances of one's beloved and the gratification that comes with an intense and exclusive union, a "mule driver is closer to happiness" than a voluptuary (*E* 349). At first blush, then, love seems to live its life not in the dimly lit boudoir (or the musty chalet) but rather in the celestial regions of the mind.

Yet the desires of the body, so quiet in the first letter, are not long in making themselves known. After Julie confesses that she loves St. Preux as he loves her and thereby satisfies his initial desire for recognition, he begins to not-so-subtly hint that a love such as theirs must be physicalized: "What, fair Julie, are the strange caprices of love! My heart has more than it hoped for, and is not content. You love me, you tell me so, and I sigh. This unfair heart dares desire still more, when it has nothing more to desire" (*J* 38).[1] His love for Julie, once an ideational unity, is now a violent compound made up of imaginary and bodily elements; it has been reduced to "warring with itself" and demands a pittance for its struggle. "What then," St. Preux crassly inquires, "will be the reward for so pure an homage if it is not your esteem, and what good to me is perpetual and voluntary abstinence from all that is sweetest in the world if she who demands it is wholly ungrateful to me?" (39). The paradoxical reward for abstinence is its negation. After reaffirming his determination to love Julie as she needs rather than how he likes, he stirs her pity and her too-developed sense of guilt by reminding her of his own needs: "I languish and waste away; fire courses through my veins; nothing can extinguish or damp it, and I stir it up by trying to contain it. . . . I complain not of my fate. . . . Yet a real torment pursues me, I seek in vain to flee it. . . . I would wish to live for you, and it is you who deprive me of life" (43).

Julie's response to St. Preux's coaxing reflects both her lucidity of mind and the depth of her circumspection. She expresses an admirable awareness of the dynamics of romantic love in the very act of submitting to them. She knows St. Preux desires her sexually and that his imagination has been stirred by the prospect of consummation. Indeed, her own imagination has been stirred, and she shares his desires. Yet she insists that the physicalization of their love will lead to its demise:

> Some sad foreboding arises in my breast and cries to me that we are enjoying the only happy times that Heaven may have allotted us. For the future I can glimpse only absence, tempests, troubles, contradictions. *To me the slightest alteration of our present situation can only be for the worse. No, were a sweet bond to unite us forever, I know not whether the surfeit of happiness would not soon be its demise.* The moment of possession is a crisis for love, and any change is dangerous for ours; from now on we can only lose by it. (*J* 41–42; emphasis added)

Julie here considers love's *best* case—a marriage—and can nonetheless see nothing but "tempests" and "contradictions." In doing so, she does more than rearticulate her father's class prejudice. Her concern is not simply political; it is also psychological. She intuits what Rousseau explains theoretically in *Emile*, namely, that the sweetness of love consists most fully in the anticipation of consummation, and that the act itself is bound to disappoint the high expectations to which its antecedent hopes give rise. Julie and St. Preux, like Emile and Sophie, are happiest before consummation because they have everything to expect and nothing to regret. She does not want to alter the "present situation" because she knows that to physicalize love is to push it toward the grave: in saying that the "surfeit of happiness" would soon "become its demise," Julie is calling attention to the limited and tragically compromised character of sexual love. For Julie as for Rousseau, to consummate love is also to destroy it.

She therefore seeks to defer physicalization yet again, telling St. Preux that "we are happy as we are; nothing makes it clearer to me than the vexation I experience at the slightest change of situation" (*J* 49). Ironically, the letter ends with Julie conceding to St. Preux's prodding by proposing the fateful meeting at the bower: "It shall not be said that [St. Preux] must ever show deference and I never generosity . . . I want to make him feel, in spite of vulgar prejudices, how greatly what the heart gives surpasses what insistence seizes" (51).[2] Though Julie, unlike Emile and Sophie, is undeceived about the nature of romantic love, she is nonetheless too susceptible to its sway to resist it. On the one hand, she is acutely aware of her "thirst for love" and of the need for "eternal attachment" that it put in her heart, and she seeks out the *belle âme* St. Preux for his distinctive qualities of mind and heart. These qualities are, of all the virtues, the "least subject to disaffection" and the most conducive to the "eternal attachment" she so desires (50). On the other hand, however, Julie's own language reveals her circumspection about the likelihood that her need for enduring love will be satisfied: note that St. Preux's virtues are not *immune* but rather are "the least subject" to disaffection. In the fullness of time, everyone becomes a tiresome bore. In writing to her lover as she does, Julie is doing little more than yielding to the requirements of her own moralized sexuality. If in her letter she emphasizes how the "moral" elements of love direct and dictate its "physical" expression, the actions that follow show how the needs of the body influence and regulate the moral imagination. The secret of the bower is her recognition of and concession to the inescapably corporeal character of romantic love. If love is a dance between the body and soul, then it is in letter XIII that the body begins to lead.

Physical need, excited rather than exhausted by a kiss under the bower, asserts itself with ever growing strength. St. Preux becomes so unmanageable that Julie banishes him to the Valais country. From this mountainous and secluded region he whines until he is allowed to return, and even threatens suicide in order to shorten the duration of his exile. Julie bears the separation with considerably more dignity, though she is so affected by St. Preux's absence that she becomes ill. Her sickness, of course, is representative of the inner turmoil that her love for St. Preux has caused; it is a physiological expression of the despair created not so much by his absence as by the prospect of his *return*. Banishing him to the Valais was a temporary fix; she knows he is coming back—for she cannot live without him—but she also knows that his reappearance is the reappearance of a bodily need whose satisfaction is, so to speak, the beginning of love's end. Despite her awareness of this she takes advantage of her parents' absence by proposing to St. Preux a rendezvous at a nearby chalet that "serves as a shelter for hunters and should serve only as a sanctuary for lovers" (*J* 92). Their tryst is delayed but finally consummated toward the end of part I.

St. Preux's night with Julie is the signal event in his life. He spends the rest of the novel trying to forget it. His immediate reaction underscores this importance, but it also reveals an important shift in his feelings for her and in the dynamics of their relationship. He understands that things have changed between them without quite understanding what that change means. "Oh let us die, my sweet Friend!" he bellows ecstatically in the letter that follows consummation, "let us die well beloved of my heart! What use can we make from now on of an insipid youth of which we have exhausted all the delights?" (*J* 120). These exclamations are appealing indeed, for St. Preux goes on to explain that he perceives a change within himself, reporting that his feelings for Julie "have somehow have acquired a less impetuous, but sweeter, tenderer, and more enchanting character" (121). This change, he goes out of his way to emphasize, is *qualitative* rather than quantitative: the moment after consummation, St. Preux loves Julie not more or less but differently. His feelings have been altered "in nature" and have become "more affectionate" and "more varied" as the "the frenzies of love" are alloyed with the "gentle pleasures of friendship" (121). St. Preux's new mode of address reflects his more diffuse love for Julie, for he refers to her not only as his "mistress" and "wife" but also as a "sweet friend" and a "sister" (120, 122).

But this same letter provides reason to question the conviction that St. Preux offers so sincerely. As a preliminary matter we must ask: if his love for Julie is undiminished, why does he want to die? If it is true that "the delights" of youth have been "exhausted," it is difficult to understand how St. Preux can tell Julie that his love for her is as intense as it was before. We can begin to understand St. Preux's evolving understanding of his relationship with Julie by noting that, as a general matter, feelings of emptiness and even desperation often follow defining life experiences. To take a mundane example, children commonly enjoy unwrapping their Christmas presents far more than playing with them. To the parent who might say, "But now you can actually play with them. They *belong to you!*" the child might retort that the whole point was to open them. There is something of this attitude, raised to a higher pitch, in St. Preux's postcoital exclamations, for what they reveal above all else is an emergent awareness that there is nothing beyond what was just experienced; the act of possession surpasses the experience of ownership.

If we take St. Preux at his word, his claim that his feelings have not diminished is merely a way of protesting too much; his very need to insist that he does not love Julie less is itself the most telling evidence that he does. It might be, of course, easier to dismiss St. Preux's wish to die with Julie as a peculiar form of pillow talk, an intimate disclosure that, while not exactly insincere, is nonetheless not to be taken literally. But this cannot be done without first acknowledging that this is neither the first nor the last time that St. Preux expresses a wish to die with Julie. To dismiss such language as *mere* rhetoric is also to dismiss the possibility that life after consummation will never attain the felicity of life before it. Rousseau himself was so alive to the connection between love and death that he considered ending the novel at the end of Part IV, with Julie and St. Preux drowning together in a storm. To ignore what St. Preux says on this head would be more justifiable if he repeated it less often. Thus it seems right to say with Shklar (1969, 138) that St. Preux "does not really want to live with [Julie], but to *die* with her." This is precisely what the theory of love articulated in *Emile* would predict.

Perhaps more tellingly, the letter's conclusion, where St. Preux acknowledges that he does not love as deeply as Julie does, is a subtle form of admission that squares with a more literal interpretation of the letter's beginning. When with "self-shame" and "mortification" he acknowledges that she "is better able to love" than he, St. Preux is less praising Julie's seemingly infinite capacity for love than acknowledging that his own feelings are changed. Had they not diminished, he would have nothing to confess and no discernible reason to be ashamed of himself. Thus it is St. Preux's "mortification" that ultimately exposes an ugly truth about sexual love generally but, as we saw earlier, of specifically *male* sexual desire. His confession is not quite buyer's remorse, but it reveals the anxious conscience of a sincere though naïve lover who got more than he bargained for and is now trying to understand—and delicately explain—why, the following day, he finds his feelings so changed.

Even one who believes St. Preux's claims about his new and "more varied" love has reason to be concerned about the stability of the sentiments he expresses. On this score it is very revealing that St. Preux should feel the need for fraternal and familial affection only *after* having consummated his sexual relationship with Julie, for the new variability and diffuseness in his love for her actually indicates a kind of nascent *dissatisfaction* with romantic love proper. Before consummation, all of St. Preux's psychic energy was invested in Julie as a lover and a sex object; he had no family, no friends but Claire (Bomston has not yet appeared), and no evident want of either. Such needs come into being only after love has tried but failed to satisfy his desire for wholeness on its own. The sexual experience, for all the depth of meaning that Rousseau coaxes out of it, is nonetheless characterized by a persistent absence, a nagging dissatisfaction, an obscure but overwhelming awareness of its own insufficiency. The gap between expectation and reality persists not because the reality of love is terribly low, but because the expectations it generates are so incredibly high; love would satisfy us more if it wanted less. But Rousseau knew that eros brooks no compromise, and it is only when St. Preux is confronted with the fact that love qua love cannot satisfy his want of wholeness that he seeks out the supplemental satisfactions of friendship and fraternal love. St. Preux has always wanted Julie to bridge all the divisions and satisfy all the desires in his soul, and this remains true after consummation. Yet he now knows in some vague and inarticulable way that she cannot do so exclusively in her capacity as a lover; she must now also fulfill the roles of "sweet friend" and "sister." It is the dissatisfactions produced by love that create the need for fraternal and familial affection. Rousseau hints at this point when he says that "from the need of a mistress is born the need of a friend" (*E* 215). The disappointment that sets in after consummation—which in St. Preux's case is almost immediate—catalyzes other social needs and requires their harmonious integration into our psychic lives.

We must then ask the question: can it work? Can these derivative forms of affection conjoin to or stand in effectively for love? St. Preux's letter gives us no reason to think so, for though he seeks to supplement his already-flagging romantic passion for Julie with other forms of intimacy it is evident his new expectations of her are entirely unreasonable. No one can sensibly be expected to simultaneously fulfill the roles she is now charged with fulfilling: the absurdity of it all is summed up in his grotesque insistence on calling her his "sister." And yet love demands comprehensive satisfaction: feeling the singular mix of dissatisfaction and ecstasy that characterizes limit experiences—romantic or not—St. Preux sees nothing wrong with or impossible about combining the roles of sex object and sibling, of terrestrial goddess and devoted materfamilias, of carnal seductress and chaste wife. All his emotional energy is still fixed exclusively on a single person, but that energy has lost its some of its concentration and now seeks multiple kinds of social gratification. He wants Julie to be the exclusive source of his consolation and contentment and he seems to believe—very sincerely but very incorrectly—that this is possible.

A less literal but more sympathetic way of interpreting St. Preux's response is to note his growing awareness that the transports of love are of themselves insufficient. For the first time, he clearly sees that romantic passion must be joined to—and eventually replaced by—the intimacy of friendship and mutual esteem in order for a relationship to endure. As we have already seen, this is consistent with the position taken by Jean-Jacques the tutor (if perhaps not by Rousseau the author) in *Emile*, and it is also consistent with what St. Preux says earlier in the text: mulling the prospect of eternal union with Julie, he conjectures that "a long and sweet intoxication would leave us oblivious to the passage of years: and when old age finally slakes our first ardors, the habit of thinking and feeling together would put in the place of their transports a no less tender friendship" (*J* 68). St. Preux believes the transition from love to friendship would be unproblematic, and why should he not? After all, he loves his Julie in all the ways it is possible to love her, and with all the intensity of which his heart is capable. He can imagine that such a love could change its nature but not that it could diminish or disappear. Why, then, should she not join him in Kent under Bomston's protection?

Two answers suggest themselves. First, St. Preux himself appears to have contradictory understandings of the dynamics of romantic love. Though he initially indicates a belief that a specifically romantic passion will eventually expire and turn into something closer to friendship (*J* 68), he claims later that romantic love builds on itself and, far from slackening over time, instead intensifies: "No, Julie, I cannot see you everyday simply as I saw you the day before: my love is bound to increase and grow incessantly with your charms, and you are for me an *inexhaustible* source of new sentiments that I would not even have imagined" (94; emphasis added). St. Preux thus has contradictory theoretical expectations about the effect time has on romantic passion: in one letter he claims that love is slowly replaced by friendship (68), but just a few letters later (94) he insists that love is susceptible of infinite expansion and growth. For all his speechifying about the nature of love, St. Preux does not appear to have a clear idea about whether—or how long—it can last. Even if we are inclined to attribute this latter view to a temporary lack of intellectual lucidity,[3] for St. Preux is not thinking clearly at all at this point in the novel, we are also obliged to note that this is neither the first nor the only time that St. Preux's reason deserts him. His emotional instability is a constituent part of his moral personality. One can certainly imagine that Julie might have concerns about running away with such a person.

Second, and assuming that a lucid St. Preux would recognize the necessity of some type of transition from love to friendship, we find that Julie does not view such a transition with the same optimism that St. Preux does. In fact, she indicates that the memory of expired love would make such a transition unbearable. "I see, my friend," she tells St. Preux, "from the temper of our souls . . . that love will be the major business of our lives . . . for us, the slightest cooling would soon become the languor of death; an invincible distaste, a perpetual tedium, would follow the extinction of love, and *we would scarcely survive long once we had ceased to love*" (*J* 89; emphasis added). To this she later adds, "A love such as ours inspires and sustains the soul as long as it burns; as soon as it goes out the soul lapses into languor and a worn-out heart is no longer good for anything" (185). On Julie's understanding the passing of love, far from being a smooth and natural transition, is instead an acid that erodes the very foundations of the marital union. When one confronts the necessary disproportion between the perfect imaginary model and the decidedly imperfect lover, the present is poisoned by the memory of what the beloved used to be. Memory, or rather nostalgia, induces despair and casts both present and future in a harsh and unflattering light. In so doing, it does for spent love what the imagination does for romantic passion: the one exaggerates the virtue of the beloved and the other his vices.

Lovers never see each other as they are. From Julie's perspective, then, the transition from love to friendship is a dreadful and insoluble problem. It is a source of inevitable disappointments and undignified compromises. Our love for what once was overwhelms and finally crushes our attachment to what is. Shklar (1969, 86) is therefore correct to say that marriage "illustrates the network of insuperable difficulties that society puts in the way of human contentment," but it must be added that it is not simply "society" or the "empire of opinion" that blocks the path to shared happiness. It is, rather, the very structure of romantic desiring that poses the final and decisive difficulty. Love's peculiar psychological dynamics are thus what give true force to Shklar's accurate conclusion that "Julie would not have been happy with Saint Preux, and she was miserable with the excellent Wolmar" (86). Marriage without love is intolerable, and love within marriage is impossible. Julie had already scaled Olympus and walked with the gods. How could the view from Kent hold her interest?

From Friendship to Love? The Marriage That Never Was

Having revealed the difficulties that memory poses for the transition from love to friendship, *Julie* investigates a final possibility: if love does not easily give way to friendship, perhaps friendship might evolve into love. This possibility is explored in the form of Julie's efforts to unite St. Preux and her cousin Claire, but there are at least two compelling prima facie reasons to think her plan would fail. First, we saw in chapter 3 that Rousseau clearly demarcates the psychological foundations of friendship from those of sexual love, and thus builds a relatively impermeable wall of separation between these two largely discrete associational types. Transitioning from one to the other is thus a difficult process fraught with uncertainty; it involves a comprehensive psychic reorientation, a transformation in the way that we "see" the other person. The form of forgetting that this transformation embodies is especially problematic in *Julie*, where the characters have difficulty recognizing each other because they remain so strongly connected to their past experiences and former lives. Second, relationships are for Rousseau path-dependent phenomena. The initial stages of an association are, as Rousseau's emphasis on Emile and Sophie's "first encounter" suggests, decisive for determining the course of its development. One does not simply change the nature of a relationship that, like Claire and St. Preux's, is twelve years in the making (see *J* 629). Love, unlike friendship, tends to arise quickly and spontaneously or not at all; one recognizes a lover immediately but a true friend only over time. These reasons notwithstanding, St. Preux and Claire have developed an intimate and even flirtatious relationship over the course of St. Preux's exile and return, and both confess to having developed a strong physical attraction to the other. Everything, including Julie's blessing, seems to gather in favor of their union. Thus we would seem to have reason to question our initial pessimism about the transition from love to friendship. Yet St. Preux ultimately balks at the prospect (555), and Claire accepts the idea only after expressing some serious reservations (532).

St. Preux's rejection of the idea is unequivocal. His heart, he tells Julie, is spent for love, and though he is physically attracted to Claire he lacks the energy and the disposition necessary for loving her. His reasons are complex—residual feelings for Julie clearly remain—but among the most important is that she does not stir his imagination as Julie did (and continues to do): "Content with her charms, my heart does not lend them its illusion; she is lovelier to my eyes than to my imagination, and I am more apprehensive when she is nearby than when she is far away" (*J* 556). The disturbances Claire introduces are physical but they do not populate the imagination with the illusions love creates. "For all that," St. Preux asks his former lover, "does [attraction] become love? Julie, ah, what a difference! Where is the enthusiasm? Where is the idolatry? Where are those divine distractions of reason, more brilliant, more sublime, more powerful, a hundred times better than reason itself?" (556). Illusion is the source of romantic enthusiasm, and Claire—as her name suggests—cannot inspire it because she does not stir the imagination. St. Preux cannot idolize what he knows to be flawed, and he is too acquainted with Claire to think her perfect in any way. Because no veil hides her there is no temptation to see what the veil hides; her very transparency keeps his imagination quiet. St. Preux goes on to explain that, having experienced the full transports of love, he could never be happy in a relationship that lacked the emotional intensity that seemingly only love can supply: "Grace, beauty, merit, attachment, fortune, all would conspire to my felicity; my heart, my heart alone would poison it all, and make me miserable in the bosom of my happiness" (558). St. Preux's misery would create an intolerable situation both for himself and for Claire. Thus he makes his declaration: "I love [Claire] too well to marry her" (558).

Claire shares many of St. Preux's reservations, and like him she reports that her heart is not capable of the sort of attachment that love requires. Though she confesses she is quite in love with St. Preux, she adds that she would have "driven him crazy" and that she has always thought about a marriage with him "with disdain." Her love for St. Preux ultimately amounts to little more than a refracted form of her love for Julie: Claire tells her cousin, "I derived all my sentiments from you; you alone were everything to me, and I lived only to be your friend" (*J* 526; see Disch 1994). The chief advantage of marrying St. Preux would thus not be the union itself so much as what it would procure for Claire—namely, more and more intimate access to her Julie. Claire's erotic attraction to her cousin is most evident when she defers to her cousin's judgment in the matter of marriage: "Take . . . the responsibility of my conduct, I confide its direction entirely to you. Let us return to our natural state and exchange callings, it will be better for us both. Govern, I will be docile; it is for you to will what I must do. . . . Keep my soul enclosed in yours, why should inseparables have two?" (*J* 532). Prudential concerns and the simulacrum of love make Claire willing to marry St. Preux, but only on the condition that her soul remain in Julie's custody. Friends like Claire and St. Preux may get married, but they will never live for one another.

The concerns voiced both by St. Preux and by Claire speak directly to the paradoxical and ultimately tragic role Rousseau assigns to love. It is man's greatest and most powerful desire, and as such it creates new and exciting social and psychological possibilities that would not otherwise exist. Absent love, there can be no restoration of the Golden Age (see Shklar 1969) or any real happiness in domestic society; life without marriage is undefined and incomplete, and marriage without love is cramped and suffocating. Yet when love expires—as it most assuredly does—it casts a long and dark shadow in the memory; the remembrance of lost love poisons lovers, facilitates resentment between them, and erodes the bonds of esteem that keep a marriage alive once love itself begins to slacken. Thus love forecloses on the very possibilities it creates. We are no more happy with love than we are without it. This is the teaching of *Julie*.

| The Horizon in Every Direction: The Citizens of Clarens

In problematizing the romantic rituals on which the household is based Rousseau also problematizes the idea of the happy household and, with it, the idea of the household *as such*. This problematization clearly has consequences that extend beyond the domestic sphere, but exactly what those consequences are depends on how the relationship between the domestic and political worlds is theorized. On one understanding of this relationship, the family cultivates our basic moral and social dispositions and, in so doing, serves as an important catalyst of political socialization. Politics requires sociability and sociability requires families. Hence the family's role as a socializing agent is on the whole continuous with the needs of the state and not viewed as essentially threatening to its continued health. Were Rousseau to view the relation between the domicile and the polis in this way—as it sometimes appears—then the destabilization of private spaces we have seen in *Emile* and *Julie* would seem to have grave consequences for his political vision, for to the degree that the family structure fails to provide a stable site of moral training the state is robbed of good citizens.

There is, however, a second way of conceiving the relation of household and state, one more typical of classical thought and most fully embodied in Plato's claim that perfect justice requires the abolition of the nuclear family (*Rep.* 449c–d, 457d–61c). The Socratic view posits that the family is not an agent of but rather a rival to the state; far from cultivating strong civic dispositions and ordering the soul in accordance with justice, domestic life encourages an undue attachment to one's own and distracts citizens from the higher and nobler calling of civic engagement. To the degree that Rousseau follows Socrates in viewing the domicile as in some way competing with the state for the scarce psychological and emotional resources that human beings have, the political consequences are less grave, for the instability of the family unit—far from bringing the polity down with it—instead creates a new and bigger space for politics that was not available before.

Though the interpretation of *Emile* and *Julie* advanced in the previous two chapters inclines toward the latter alternative, many readers of *Julie* favor the former, compatibilist view. We have, for instance, already seen that Tony Tanner's politicized reading emphasizes questions of social class and, in so doing, makes it possible to read *Julie* both as an indictment of feudal inequality and as a critique of the emerging bourgeois family and its rigid insistence on sexual monogamy. Nicole Fermon (1997) has also sought to understand the domestic community of Clarens in terms of its social and political importance but argues that *Julie* has not just a negative or critical function but also represents a model of private life that resolves a series of thorny political problems posed by the *Social Contract*. She argues that *Julie* presents a "vision of the 'private worlds' of citizens" that "fleshes out human aspects of the common life left out of *The Social Contract*" and that the presentation of the household in *Julie* helps to mitigate the conflicts that can arise between political society and the various "partial societies" that exist within it. To this she adds that the moral training one receives in a healthy household will prove politically salutary: the "autarkic nature of the household provides the citizens with the material possibilities for free choice while creating an institution that will educate his heart and provide him with sound habits" (119; cf. *SC* II.3, 61–62). The household described in *Julie* is thus precisely the kind required by the regime of the *Social Contract*.

Our analyses of *Emile* and *Julie*, without denying Rousseau's rejection of Socrates's radical collectivism, nonetheless cast serious doubt on arguments like Fermon's for at least three reasons. First, it is rather difficult to see how the stringent demands of the just regime can be unproblematically integrated into the private, introspective, and leisurely lifestyle depicted in the novel. If there is no conflict between politics and the household in *Julie*, it is not because the problem has been resolved but rather because it does not arise: politics make no demands on anyone's time or attention, with Julie's feckless uncle, who is constantly reading the papers and talking about international affairs, being the exception that proves the rule (e.g., *J* 168, 250). And Fermon's characterization of the household as an autarkic social unit only makes things worse, for if the household is truly autarkic then the superaddition of the political is at best gratuitous and at worst harmful to domestic society and the well-being of its members. Clarens is a closed and self-sufficient social system that does nothing to motivate those who live there to engage those who do not. Wolmar's decision to charge St. Preux with the education of his children is telling (to say nothing of its irony), for he is the furthest thing from a citizen and is incapable of providing a public or political education. To the contrary, Wolmar's children will be raised much as Emile was—at a distance from political society and its tumults—and will know Clarens not as a "waystation" to political justice but as a substitute for it. It is their *true* fatherland, their horizon in every direction.

The uncombinability of the political and domestic solutions are indicative of deeper fissures in Rousseau's moral universe, for there seems to be something about the goods themselves that resist joint realization in a space of a single life. The philosopher may comprehend the whole good, but he does so at the cost of enjoying it in the normal fashion. The inward St. Preux will never know the pure "public joy" relished by citizens of Geneva (*LD* n. 136). The Spartan Pedaretus will never feel the individualistic pleasures of deep introspection or the happiness of discovering himself a part of a universal cosmopolitan brotherhood. Our experience with the good we seek is fragmentary, disintegrated, incomplete. Reflections like these are what led Rousseau to say that the educations of "men" and "citizens" must be different and incommensurable, and why he characterizes the process of citizen-craft as a kind of "denaturing." Unlike Socrates, however, Rousseau does not explicitly prioritize political over domestic life. It is not at all clear that he views the way of life embodied by the household as a self-sufficient social unit as lower than or subordinate to the higher calling of political life. For all its drawbacks and difficulties, the vision of the good represented in private society—whether at Clarens, Emile and Sophie's farmhouse, or Rousseau's own fascinating reverie at the end of Book IV of *Emile*—emerges from Rousseau's work as a worthy albeit problematic alternative to its political counterpart.

Second, there is among *les belles âmes* a culture of servility quite at odds with the spirit of self-command characteristic of the Rousseauan citizen. St. Preux is simply unable to give himself direction and wishes only to be governed, first by Julie and later by Wolmar. He is hopelessly and eternally dependent on the powers of others. Claire, as Lisa Disch (1994) has nicely shown, displays a degree of independence not exhibited by St. Preux in her willingness to question the characteristically "masculine" form of power embodied by Wolmar, but in the end she is every bit as subject to Julie's feminine "empire" as is St. Preux. And though Julie undoubtedly displays extraordinary self-command in her heroic struggle against temptation, it must be admitted that her struggle itself is in part a function of an excessive emotional dependence on her father. Julie herself is under the sway of the *maison paternelle* and unable to fully see or act out effectively against its injustice. Her father, the dupe of his own prejudices, knows his daughter well and—like all despots—is more than willing to resort to both emotional and physical abuse in order to impose his will. However, Julie is either unable or unwilling to identify her father's cruelty for what it is, preferring either to make excuses for his behavior or to unfairly condemn her own. Exercising neither voice nor exit, she docilely accepts the husband chosen for her even though she understands all too well that the consequences will quite literally be fatal. Her moral posture toward earthly authority—whether it be her father's despotic rage or Wolmar's distant sangfroid—more closely resembles the gentle resignation of the "true Christian" than it does the proud defiance of the citizen: where the former "knows how to die" but not how to win a battle, the latter seeks victory because informed with "a burning love of glory and homeland" (*SC* IV.8, 129). Julie's submissiveness before her father is thus rather different from the submissiveness of a good citizen before the law. From the perspective of a would-be lawgiver seeking to instill civic-spiritedness through education, the kind of moral instruction utilized at Clarens simply does not fit the bill.

Third, and relatedly, we should hope for the sake of citizens themselves—whoever they turn out to be—that the unstable and unhappy domestic life depicted in *Julie* does not "flesh out" the private lives of citizens, for a quick inventory reveals that there is hardly a single character in the novel who is well-adjusted or content with his lot. We cannot avoid the conclusion that Clarens, for all its virtues as an estate, was nonetheless a failure. It did not succeed in curing either Julie or St. Preux of the psychic devastation wrought by their tragic love: Julie, crushed by the weight of her obligations, is so miserable that she commits suicide as soon it is possible for her to do so, and Claire and St. Preux are ready to follow suit when they learn of Julie's fate. People so invested in their private lives and associations are far better than are the average bourgeois, who does not care about anything enough to contemplate suicide. But they are not to be compared to Cato who, as Bomston reminds St. Preux, killed himself for the sake of his lost republic rather than for the sake of his lost love (*J* 322). There is nothing "civic"—and indeed, something rather *un*civic—about the virtue exhibited by the novel's principal characters.

| Love's Failure: Implications and Conclusions

In both *Emile* and *Julie* we find that elaborate, artificial, and unsustainably fragile imaginative constructions are imposed in order to generate the psychic energy necessary to maintain social affection. Rousseau's turn to the imagination, however questionable prima facie, is made necessary by his insistence on man's natural asociability. He seizes on the promise of the imagination because the act of imagining, whatever else it may be, is a private or solitary activity. If we prefer our imaginings to the objects they represent, we do so not only because images are perfect and people are not but also because our images are *ours* in a way that another person never could be. They, and not others, are immediate expressions of our moral personalities; they create and control us even as we create and control them. The pedagogic project of *Emile* and, to a lesser extent, the romance of *Julie* explore the possibility of establishing this process of reciprocal governance *between* persons; we have seen, however, that the best it can hope to do is establish it *within* them. In the final analysis, then, it is the imagination—not the incorporated other—that is regulative.

An implication of the privateness of imaginary activity is that even when we dream of others we have a tendency to forget them, and to fashion in their stead imaginative re-creations that, by their very perfection, are inaccurate depictions of the flawed objects they represent. Both Emile and St. Preux engage in this process with ultimately unsuccessful results: where the former has difficulty coping with the disappearance of his perfect Sophie and seeks solace in the "too attractive liaisons" of Paris, the latter is denied the opportunity to wed his beloved and is haunted by his perfect image of her for the rest of his life. We are thus led to the somewhat melancholy conclusion that the imaginative re-creations to which Rousseau turns in order to catalyze romantic love mediate and disrupt the relation between I and thou even as they make that relation possible. Imaginary embellishments help to bridge the gap between self and other, but we must remember that Rousseau's purpose was not to bridge this gap but to shorten its distance. Judged by this standard, the educational project of *Emile* cannot be considered a success, and St. Preux's turbulent romance with Julie becomes even more flawed than it appears to be.

Of course, it is necessary to wonder what these failures suggest about Rousseau's more general social and political concerns. Though I will take this question up more thoroughly in the final chapter, I will anticipate that analysis here by simply suggesting that what *Emile* and *Julie* tell us about the attenuated nature of human connectedness has important implications for how we read the *Social Contract* and Rousseau's other political works. For instance, the failure of Emile's education tends to vitiate Frederick Neuhouser's (2008, 23) claim that it is best understood as a blueprint for a new form of "modern" citizenship that supplants and even surpasses the classical conception. If Emile's education is as unsuccessful and his connection to political society as attenuated as my analysis has shown, then it would have been very odd indeed for Rousseau to make it the pedagogic basis for the political project outlined in the *Social Contract*. Any hope of bringing a just and durable regime into being, far from relying on a conception of citizenship as unstable as the "modern" alternative embodied by Emile, would seem to require at least a partial recovery of something like the classical conception of the citizen.

Julie, too, discloses the basic discontinuities between the requirements of the domestic and political spheres. Hardly a word about politics is spoken by any of the novel's hero(in)es, and the virtues and vices on display are not "civic" in any identifiable way. Their identities are formed and expressed by the domestic context in which they subsist and from which they draw their happiness (or lack thereof); their hopes are confined by the horizons of Clarens and carry them back there, at least in St. Preux's case, from the ends of the earth; their emotional and intellectual needs are created and satisfied by each other and do not require the stimulation of the outside world. Their social world is closed and self-sufficient. The family, far from simply being a site of moral habituation that is continuous with state purposes, is instead a site of identity-construction that *rivals* state purposes. Put another way, the family as depicted in *Julie* is precisely the kind of "partial society" that Rousseau seeks to delimit in the regime described in the *Social Contract*; its claim on our identities and as the source of our deepest satisfactions must be neutralized if the sociological preconditions for genuine political justice are to be achieved.

Though the above analyses of *Emile* and *Julie* reveal the domestic solution to the problem of human dividedness to be problematic in decisive respects, they also do much to point up the difficulties with the "political" solution as well. Indeed, the psychological difficulties that attend the realization of the double object in the context of Emile's education would appear to be even more severe in the case of the classical citizen. Public education of the classical sort requires that citizens make virtually no distinction between themselves and the political whole of which they are parts. To effect this unnatural union, the state substitutes the illusions of nationalism for the those of love—patriotism replaces gallantry at the core of human identity. Yet nationalistic fictions would seem even more difficult to sustain than romantic ones because of their remoteness from natural self-love: public education involves not just the redirection and extension of natural desires, as in Emile's education, but a wholesale transformation of human nature (*E* 39; *SC* II.7, 68). If one could imagine a pedagogic enterprise more radical, more ambitious, more difficult, or less likely to succeed than Emile's domestic education, the public education that Rousseau recommends for the citizen is a plausible candidate.

That Rousseau sees decay as inevitable in the domestic world is, it seems, a function of an extraordinarily deep circumspection about the durability of healthy human association. His pessimism reflects a peculiarly modern concern, one in which he participates more reluctantly but perhaps more fully than do any of his predecessors. Rousseau saw clearly that previous modern thinkers had failed to explain the distinctively human desire for wholeness through social connectedness, but his own attempt to generate such an explanation is beset by similar limitations. He thus ultimately distinguishes himself from other moderns less by his successful resolution of the problem of human connectedness than by his acute awareness of and fruitful engagement with it. The effort to reconstruct eros with the materials furnished by modern philosophy is something like trying to build a palace from mud and twigs. Rousseau knew this from the very beginning, and both *Emile* and *Julie* disclose this awareness subtly but unmistakably.

6 | Friendship, Virtue, and Moral Authority

The previous two chapters have sought to locate the limitations of Rousseauan romantic love and, taken together, suggest a somewhat pessimistic vision of social relations. But for all his circumspection, Rousseau was no fatalist, and the tragic teaching concerning love disclosed in his novelistic works does not close but rather opens the question of human connectedness in at least two new ways. First, it helps clarify the meaning of unhappily vague terms like "wholeness" and "dividedness," terms sometimes used by Rousseau and his interpreters with a looseness that betrays their importance. On this head, we see that Rousseau's effort to recapture human wholeness in a social context involves the joint realization of two central human goods: emotional intimacy and moral virtue. Love was attractive to Rousseau in part because he saw in it a unified solution to these distinct but related theoretical problems, for his account shows that exclusive romantic connection gives human beings their greatest experience of intimacy and helps sharpen the aesthetic and ethical criteria relevant to moral decision-making. That it fails in its attempt to realize these goods in an enduring way is certainly disillusioning, but the way in which its failure clarifies the nature of the goods necessary to our happiness is instructive, and perhaps even edifying. Second, the failure of love, while *suggestive* of deeper problems with human connectedness more generally, nonetheless does not *foreclose* on the possibility that human wholeness might be preserved more effectively in other kinds of associational contexts. Indeed, if we momentarily turn our gaze from Rousseau and toward the classical tradition, we will immediately see an alternative form of association through which the twin goods of intimacy and virtue might be realized: friendship.

Friendship has a much longer and more distinguished career in the history of political thought than does love; it was celebrated by Aristotle, Cicero, and Montaigne—thinkers Rousseau knew well—as more rewarding than romantic liaisons. Rousseau himself frequently writes of friendship's emotional importance, characterizing himself as having been "born for friendship" and claiming it to have been one of the "twin idols of [his] heart" (*C* 308, 361). He also puts several extended paeans to friendship in the mouths of the principal characters of *Julie*, providing them with ample space to wax eloquent about the indissoluble bonds that unite them. What is more, friendship appears to be important not only at the domestic but also at the political level, for Rousseau hints at its broader social relevance in both *Emile* and the *First Discourse*: in the former, he calls it "the most sacred" of social exchanges, and in the latter he suggests that the loss of "sincere friendships" is a cause of political instability (*E* 233fn; *DSA* 38). Such remarks at least suggest that friendship might succeed where romantic love failed.

However, it must be conceded that Rousseau never provides the systematic discussion of friendship his own statements invite us to expect, thus forcing scholars to reconstruct his fertile (if scattered) reflections into a unified theory. The surprisingly small number of studies that have undertaken this task focus on Rousseau's curious claim that friendship is a modified expression of pity and seek to understand the degree to which friendship, thus understood, might inculcate virtue (*DI* 131). Critics like Allan Bloom (1993), Clifford Orwin (1997a, 1997b), and Richard Boyd (2004) have charged that pity diminishes moral possibility because it inspires a pessimistic and world-weary outlook, and thus imply that friendship—to the degree it derives from pity—is not a viable catalyst of moral improvement. More recently, however, Jonathan Marks (2007) and Joseph Reisert (2003) have sought to defend Rousseauan friendship by decoupling it from pity and by arguing that it involves a wide range of affective impulses that help counteract the passivity to which compassion might give rise. In his searching analysis, Reisert gives special emphasis to the connection between friendship and moral learning, persuasively arguing that friendship "is the sole relationship within which education to virtue can take place" (80). Such an interpretation ties Rousseau's conception of friendship to the classical tradition deriving from Aristotle, which comprehends the relation between friends as a catalyst of virtue and places it at the very center of man's moral and emotional life.

Below I shall develop an interpretation of Rousseauan friendship that emphasizes its close connection to pity and points to its limitations concerning both the realization of deep intimacy and the inculcation of virtue, but that also identifies for it a new and potentially fruitful, albeit narrower, role. Rousseau's new, aim-inhibited conception of friendship forecloses on the more ambitious possibilities explored by Aristotle and others, but it proves useful in a supporting role: though unable to return us to wholeness, our friends can join and hence console us in our dividedness, thereby softening the inevitable disappointments attending moral and social life.

In bringing out what I take to be the novelty in Rousseau's theory of friendship, it will be necessary to put him into dialog with the tradition in (and against) which he is working. Thus I shall begin by contrasting Rousseauan friendship with relevant competing conceptions (i.e., those of Aristotle, Cicero, and Montaigne) and show that it differs importantly from them in both its psychological origin and its final social function. Against the backdrop provided by Rousseau's engagement with the tradition, I analyze his novelistic portraits of friendship with two central aims: first, to show that, since the form of identification embodied by pity introduces elements both of sameness but also of difference, grounding friendship in pity compromises the emotional intimacy possible between friends; and second, to demonstrate that Rousseauan friendship does not catalyze virtue but is rather designed to provide *consolation* in the face of life's inevitable disappointments. In fact, we find that Rousseau's model friends turn out to be rather inept counselors and that effective moral guidance occurs in hierarchical associations Rousseau himself does not identify as friendships. Though friendship thus conceived proves unable to perform the strong socializing and moralizing functions to which it is assigned by Aristotle and Rousseau's other predecessors, it nonetheless has potentially salutary political applications. I will conclude, then, by seeking to partially rehabilitate Rousseauan friendship, arguing that the ethos of pity on which it is based helps to temper the spirit of impetuosity to which politicized *amour-propre* gives rise, and also that it counteracts the rashness conservative critics often associate with Rousseauan democracy. Once viewed as a *supplemental* motivation rather than the sole spring of political identification, it is possible to view pity as an important psychological support for a genuinely "compassionate conservatism."

I add two provisos in order to clarify what I am—and am not—arguing. First, for expositional reasons I use the terms "pity" and "compassion" somewhat interchangeably. Such usage is already common in the relevant literature, but it is not universally accepted and thus bears explicit mention. Second, Rousseau (much like us) uses the term "friendship" in both broad and narrow senses; the word sometimes comprehends any form of sympathetic association (e.g., a marriage can be a "friendship" in this broad sense) and other times denotes a particular *kind* of sympathetic association. Of interest here is the latter, more specific meaning Rousseau gives to friendship, for it is on this register that he corrects the tradition that preceded him and discloses what he believes its genuine function in human life to be.

Rousseauan Friendship: Revisiting and Revising the Classical Tradition

In approaching the question of friendship, Rousseau inherits a distinguished literary tradition that derives primarily from Aristotle's extended discussion of the topic in the *Nicomachean Ethics* and runs, most notably, through Cicero's *De Amicitia* and Montaigne's "Of Friendship."[1] This tradition views human beings as naturally sociable by way of shared reason, treating friendship in its highest form as a rational partnership dedicated to moral development. It gives to the relation between friends two central characteristics: (1) it views intimacy between friends as a product of a comprehensive *similarity of character*, and (2) it posits the end of friendship is the *pursuit of virtue*. Because Rousseau amends the classical theory on both these counts, a brief look at how the most influential expositors of the tradition characterize friendship along these crucial dimensions will help bring the novelty of his theory of friendship into sharper relief.

Classical treatments of friendship emphasize the importance of similarity of character in catalyzing bonds between friends. Friends qua friends are drawn to each other through the apprehension of shared interests and tastes, and perfect friends hold so much in common that they are able to see in each other idealized versions of themselves. In the *Nicomachean Ethics* Aristotle celebrates this kind of comprehensive identification as a guiding ideal, claiming that friendship is all the more perfect as "both parties get the same things from each other and delight in each other or in the same things" and that friends of the best kind are like second selves (*NE* 1155a20, 1158b1). Cicero follows Aristotle on this point, making Laelius call friendship "an accord in all things" and say that "he who looks upon a true friend looks, as it were, upon a sort of image of himself" (*DA* §§ 5, 7). Montaigne also celebrates the profound similarity he shared with La Boétie in "Of Friendship," albeit in a slightly different way. He uses the language of erotic fusion to characterize the best friendships: friends "mingle and unite one with the other in a blend so perfect that the seam which has joined them together is effaced and can never be found again" (*Es.* 166). The ideal of friendship presupposes and in turn produces such profound similarity in moral disposition that friends may even lose their identities as discrete beings.

Of course, similarity of character by itself is hardly sufficient to produce perfect friendship, for it is easy to imagine that those who share vices (e.g., stubbornness or selfishness) would find it more rather than less difficult to bond as friends. Thus the tradition is also united in theorizing friendship in its highest sense as a rational partnership animated by a very specific shared commitment: love of virtue. On this score Aristotle's analysis of friendship is once again foundational, for it treats the relation between friends as one that "stimulates noble actions," encourages joint rational reflection, and catalyzes superior habits of thought and behavior (*NE* 1155a10). Cicero follows Aristotle in linking friendship to the perfection of character, arguing that a shared concern for moral development is a necessary condition for friendship. He emphasizes in particular the role of practical virtue, claiming through Laelius that the civically oriented virtues of fairness, liberality, and self-control ground friendship more effectively than does wisdom (*DA* §5). Montaigne joins his classical predecessors in linking friendship to the pursuit of human excellence, though in marked contrast to Cicero he gives pride of place to intellectual virtue. Rejecting as incomplete both the civic and the sexual association, Montaigne argues that "truth" is the "nurse of the sacred tie" connecting the best of friends and that its shared pursuit—though unavailable to most—is nonetheless the highest and best thing two human beings can do together (*Es.* 164–65). "Perfect" friendships are perfect because they provide the context in which the conditions for philosophic activity—candor, good faith, and intellectual seriousness—are best realized.

Friends are friends, then, not simply because they share certain character traits but rather because the traits they share are endearing and ennobling, because they seek to strike out together in an ongoing and forward-looking process of moral improvement. Friendship thus understood has a fundamentally *prospective* or aspirational character—it "casts a bright ray of hope into the future" because it encourages friends to share in the process of becoming, to improve each other's characters, to mutually strive toward common purposes (*DA* §7). Friends, whatever else they may do, undertake enterprises and seek good things together; their relation is thus defined by shared hopes.

Rousseau's theory of friendship seeks to correct the classical tradition along both these dimensions, though in order to see why he makes these corrections it is necessary to note a more fundamental disagreement he has with the classical account of human association. Whereas both Cicero and Montaigne follow Aristotle in believing human beings to be naturally social by virtue of common reason or logos, Rousseau begins the *Discourse on Inequality* by forcefully rejecting this assumption. Accusing the Peripatetics of wandering in circles, Rousseau tunnels under Aristotle's account of social identification and, meditating on the "first and simplest principles" of the human soul, finds not a capacity for reason but rather a sentiment that allows human beings to identify sympathetically with unfortunate or suffering beings.[2] Rousseau speaks, of course, of *pity*, which he claims is "anterior to reason" and indeed at the very basis of social identification.

Replacing reason with pity at the ground of sociability leads Rousseau to seek to understand friendship as an expression of pity. This reinterpretation begins in the *Second Discourse*, where Rousseau holds that "all the social virtues" and "even friendship" can be understood as modifications of pity and goes on to define friendship as "constant pity fixed on a particular object" (*DI* 131–32). The intimate if enigmatic connection between pity and friendship is reiterated in *Emile*, where the desire for friendship is described as growing out of the adolescent subject's nascent sense of compassion (*E* 220–22). Rousseau, then, is consistent in emphasizing the psychological importance of pity broadly as well as its special relevance for friendship.

But what sort of friendship does pity make possible? Rousseau's grounding of friendship in pity produces two important changes to the tradition's conception of the relation between friends as a rational partnership devoted to the pursuit of virtue. First, because pity presupposes both likeness *and* dissimilarity of character, Rousseau denies the possibility (and desirability) of comprehensive identification between friends. Second, since friendship is rooted in the capacity to identify especially well with *suffering* beings, its primary end in human life is not the pursuit of virtue but rather consolation in disappointment.

With respect to pity presupposing both likeness and difference, Rousseau's conception of friendship-as-pity prefigures Derrida's critique of the "narcissism" of traditional conceptions (e.g., *C* 361–62). Thus, to the degree that friendship enacts the complex and somewhat paradoxical dynamics embodied by pity—and we shall soon see that it does—it precludes the type of thoroughgoing similarity of character celebrated by the tradition. Now, insofar as pity presupposes some similarity between the observer and the suffering being, it is concordant with traditional accounts of friendship, and indeed Rousseau claims that pity is felt more intensely for our *semblables*—beings who are similar to us in relevant respects—than it is for others (*DI* 95). This idea is more thoroughly articulated in *Emile*, where Rousseau posits that "*one pities in others only those ills from which one does not feel oneself exempt*" (*E* 221). We are able to share in another's sadness only because we recognize that we, too, are subject to the ills that caused it. The sight of an afflicted other is especially moving if we recognize ourselves as susceptible to the sources of his suffering, if we identify with his plight and view it as something that might have been ours. The common vulnerability to the stings of life thus creates a universal community of mutual consolation. But it also makes possible particularly intimate associations centered on the shared awareness of life's hardships, and these associations are what Rousseau calls friendships. In viewing the apprehension of likeness or similitude as a necessary condition for pity and thus for friendship, then, Rousseau is at one with the tradition.

However, pity—as we saw in chapter 3—presupposes not only likeness but also difference between the sufferer and the observer, and the emotional distance built into the pitying relation bounds the kind of emotional intimacy friends may enjoy. Suffering in another and suffering as another are very different things, and it is the disproportion between the two that makes Rousseauan pity such a rewarding psychic experience: pity is "sweet" because "in putting ourselves in the place of the one who suffers, we nevertheless feel the pleasure of not suffering as he does" (*E* 221). The experience of compassion, then, is pleasant precisely *because* our identification with the suffering other is attenuated, and our happiness relies on the fact that the effort to put "ourselves in [his] place" must fall short. We can never fully think or feel as another does, and our best efforts to do so have the paradoxical result of leading us back to ourselves. Thus we share in another's pain as much by choice as by necessity: we elect to "descend" to his condition because it is delightful to do so; our own lot is more bearable when measured against that of the less fortunate (223). To the degree that the estrangement built into pity is reflected in the associations that emerge out of it, the relation between friends is necessarily attenuated.

Because pity makes possible only an incomplete kind of human connection, the *Second Discourse*'s grounding of friendship in pity would seem to preclude the comprehensive identification between friends celebrated by the classical tradition. However, both Joseph Reisert and Jonathan Marks deny the *Second Discourse*'s claim that friendship is strongly informed by pity, arguing instead that Rousseauan friendship is rooted in "a more comprehensive attraction" grounded in shared "moral taste" (Reisert 2003, 90). Though pity enables men to recognize each other as *semblables* primarily through the shared experience of suffering, Marks approvingly cites Reisert's claim that this very specific kind of identification is only "one step on the road" toward friendship, and that pity and friendship are alike only insofar as they "rest on the apprehension of similarities among men" and are "sentiments that draw us out of ourselves" (Reisert 2003, 88; Marks 2007, 732n24). On this view, pity enables only one among many forms of similarity that friends share, but it has no special role in creating the bonds of affection between them.

The effort to distance friendship from pity allows both Reisert and Marks to view Rousseauan friendship as a catalyst for more ambitious moral possibilities and, hence, as far closer to the classical ideal than appearances suggest. Marks, for instance, not only argues that friendship is not derivative of pity but also that it is an *antidote* to the moral "passivity" pity can encourage. Whereas pity encourages resignation and inaction in the face of life's inevitable difficulties, friendship encourages "an uplifting understanding of the world" that promotes virtuous action (Marks 2007, 732). Reisert also finds in Rousseauan friendship a strong moralizing impetus, and on that basis argues that it more closely resembles the tradition deriving from Aristotle than at first may be apparent. Claiming that friendship is for Rousseau "the sole relationship within which education to virtue can take place" and that Rousseauan friends enjoy a comprehensive similarity of moral taste and feeling, Reisert concludes that "Rousseau's account of the friendship of decent people . . . resembles Aristotle's conception of complete friendship" (Reisert 2003, 80, 90, 84).

Though Reisert and Marks both downplay the role of pity, Rousseau himself puts special emphasis on the identity of interests built into the act of shared suffering. In fact, *Emile* develops the *Second Discourse*'s novel suggestion that friendship emerges out of the ability to identify with another's misfortune by more thoroughly explaining the psychological context in which the desire for friendship first develops: "Men are not naturally kings, or lords, or courtiers, or rich men. All are born naked and poor; all are subject to the miseries of life, to sorrows, ills, needs, and pains of every kind. Finally, all are condemned to death. This is what truly belongs to man. This is what no mortal is exempt from. Begin, therefore, by studying in human nature what is most inseparable from it, what best characterizes humanity" (*E* 222). Being human is *hard*, and this realization lies at the very basis of social identification. The first bonds that unite human beings do not connect them as competitors in a race for preeminence (as malignant *amour-propre* would have it) or as aspirants to virtue (as the classical tradition holds), but rather as *victims* who require consolation and care. It is on the basis of this particular form of identification that both the capacity and the desire for friendship emerge: once we are able to identify with the needfulness of others, we are prepared to meet them as fellow sufferers and, hence, as friends. This, of course, is not to deny that forms of similarity not underwritten by pity (e.g., aesthetic and moral taste) contribute to Rousseauan friendship. It is, rather, to follow Rousseau himself in emphasizing the importance of the initial conditions in which friendship comes to be: Rousseau views human association as a path-dependent phenomenon and is consistent in arguing that a relationship's beginning has a disproportionate impact on the course of its development. With this in mind, we may easily see how significant it is that the conditions in which friendship emerges are characterized primarily by privation, for if bonds between friends are forged by the recognition of the other's misfortune, then the centrality of consolation for friendship becomes clear.

Rousseau discloses the connection between friendship and suffering even more directly in his epistolary novel *Julie*, where he has multiple characters identify not virtue but *consolation* as the chief function of friendship.

"Are you not aware," the novel's eponymous heroine asks her "inseparable" cousin Claire, "that the communion of hearts imbues sadness with a sweet and touching something that contentment does not know? *And was friendship not specially given to the unhappy to relieve their woes and comfort their sorrows?*" (*J* 332; emphasis added). Echoing Julie is the affably bumbling Englishman Edward Bomston, who gravely intones, "Sadness and silence are the true language of friendship" (157). Though Rousseau does not make these claims in his own voice, they are nonetheless consistent with what he himself says about both the human condition and friendship's place within it. Across his philosophical and novelistic works, then, Rousseau consistently maintains that there is a close connection between pity and friendship and points to consolation—not the pursuit of virtue—as the end of friendship. Thus, without denying the presence of "traditional elements" in Rousseau's portrayals of friendship, it appears reasonable to deny their salience for his theory as a whole.

| Rousseau's Novel Theory of Friendship

Though questions of friendship figure prominently in *Emile* and the *Discourse on Inequality*, Rousseau himself regarded his epistolary novel *Julie* as an important and even definitive statement of his theory. He reports in his *Confessions* that the work's thorough and varied depictions of the lives of friends are central both to its internal meaning and to his broader understanding of the phenomenon of friendship: *Julie*, according to Rousseau, is first and foremost an elegy to love *and* friendship, those "twin idols of [his] heart" (*C* 361). The thematic importance of friendship for *Julie* is evinced further by the fact that, as Rousseau began sketching his "plan" for what would become one of the best-selling books of the eighteenth century, the first letters he wrote were not between the two lovers but rather between two friends (*C* 365–67). Thus, though the serene transports of friendship are at times obscured by the Sturm und Drang of the romance, Rousseau himself persisted in believing that *Julie* contained portraits of friendship that were, however imperfect, nonetheless worthy of admiration and attention (*J* 9).

Among the scenes contained in the novel, perhaps none reveals the activity most characteristic of friendship more effectively than an event St. Preux describes to his friend Edward Bomston as a "morning spent in the English manner" (*J* 456). This episode, which depicts St. Preux sharing a leisurely breakfast with his former lover Julie and her husband and children, would at first glance seem fairly unremarkable. Yet Reisert perceptively notes that it depicts a limit experience in the kind of intimacy that belongs especially to friends, and adds that it contains importantly novel elements of Rousseau's teaching on friendship (Reisert 2003, 94–95). Rousseau himself signals the importance of this particular episode by having St. Preux react in an extraordinarily enthusiastic (even for him) way to the seemingly pedestrian morning. "But friendship, Milord, friendship!" he exclaims, "powerful and heavenly sentiment, what words are worthy of thee? . . . Oh God! How many things a clasped hand, a spirited look, a warm embrace, the sigh that follows it say" (*J* 456). Something, it seems, has happened during this breakfast that has turned St. Preux's mind toward friendship. It is not only the substance but also the placement of his exclamations that underscores their importance: St. Preux *begins* the letter—the novel's longest—by recounting the details of his morning with Julie and Wolmar, thus suggesting its priority over the other matters he discusses. Still more important, this letter is written late in the novel and by an increasingly self-aware St. Preux, who at the ripe age of thirty-one is finally beginning to comprehend the requirements of adult friendship. His mature reflections, born of hard and humiliating experience, are among the novel's most serious, and are certainly worthy of close attention in the attempt to understand Rousseauan friendship.

Unsurprisingly, this discussion both invokes and inverts elements of the classical tradition. St. Preux—like Cicero and Montaigne—seeks to distinguish the affection he feels for friends from the "mediocre attachments" so common to social life. However, the temperamental Swiss reforms the traditional conception by claiming that true friendship reveals itself not through speech but rather through *silence*. Whereas Montaigne in particular emphasized the role of logos in effecting intimacy, the prolix St. Preux sees in the shared silence of friendship a way to combine the solitary satisfaction of "daydreaming" with the social pleasure of passing the time with like-minded persons. In downplaying the role of reason in the creation of sympathetic community, St. Preux is seeking to understand and be understood by others without needing recourse to the cold mediation of speech. Words, for all their usefulness, can be a kind of insult to genuine friends, for to use them presupposes they cannot understand other and more natural efforts to make one's needs and feelings known. The very need to resort to words thus implies that the relation between I and thou is compromised (*DI* 122–23). Shared understandings, and the shared ways of perceiving and feeling on which they are built, are limited as much as they are empowered by language. They are all the deeper for their being understood by everyone without having to be explained by anyone.

If silence is the language of friendship, then it is well equipped to communicate the sentiment of *pity*. On this score we see that the shared silence to which St. Preux refers is induced, ironically, by a revealing bit of speech: Wolmar brings conversation to a screeching halt by telling his wife not to envy kings their absolute power because "we have all long been your subjects." The "we" in question is, of course, St. Preux and himself, and the subjection he mentions refers to Julie's having inspired intense feelings of love in both men. This remark seems insensitive, as it calls to mind St. Preux's failed efforts to wed Julie and forces the former lovers to revisit a past full of heartache. It is, however, precisely this shared remembrance of misfortune that serves as the affective basis for community among the three friends. Wolmar's remark, as St. Preux explains, did not offend or embarrass the former lovers so much as unite them all the more closely through the bonds of pity: he notes the "touching" and "tender" look Julie gave her husband, and he goes on to claim that all three friends were "caught up in the same emotion" (*J* 457). Friends qua friends suffer together.

Because Rousseauan pity presupposes similarity of character, it may be wondered how two men as different as the composed Wolmar and the mercurial St. Preux could make claims on each other's sympathy. Wolmar's use of the word "subject," however, points to something the two men share and thus establishes the ground for mutual sympathy. To be a "subject" is to be an instrument of an external will and an agent of alien designs. It is to vacate one's powers of self-determination and to employ one's capacities with the aim of benefiting an outside other. In becoming Julie's "subjects," then, Wolmar and St. Preux have both ceded to her some portion of the capacity for free and rational self-creation. This similarity points to a still deeper one, for the experience of subjection is all the more costly for men like St. Preux and Wolmar, who both view detachment from the world and its tumults as a condition of their freedom. Their relation to Julie embeds them in and subjects them to the influence of the social world and its potentially corrupting structures. The transformation of identity Wolmar and St. Preux have undergone in order to love and be loved by Julie is therefore fraught with danger, and the happiness they consequently enjoy is fragile. The two men are united, then, by a shared awareness of the costs and risks of intimacy as well as a shared willingness to pay those costs and run those risks.

Yet, if an awareness of the transformative impact of love unites Wolmar and St. Preux, then different degrees of success with love itself place necessary limits on that union. Indeed, Wolmar's efforts to empathize with St. Preux are and must be incomplete, for underneath the shared awareness of love's power is the knowledge that St. Preux has suffered deeply for that understanding while Wolmar has benefited from it. The "living eye" sees that he has been spared the pains of frustrated love while St. Preux suffers under them every day. Thus Wolmar makes himself St. Preux's superior in the very act of claiming an equality with him, for though both have suffered for Julie, there can be no question about who has suffered more. Wolmar is Julie's "subject" but he is also her husband, which means that the process of subjection is reciprocal and even empowering. St. Preux, on the other hand, is caught in an asymmetric and nonreciprocal form of dependence, for, though he loves Julie, fate has forced him to cede to Wolmar the much-desired dual standing of lover/beloved. It is therefore possible for Wolmar to imagine the difficulty of being Julie's subject without also being her husband, but the extent of his identification is necessarily limited (and indeed even *sweetened*) by the simultaneous awareness that he himself does not suffer such bad luck. Wolmar's comment thus simultaneously assuages and magnifies St. Preux's unhappiness, for while it shows him that others identify with his suffering it also magnifies that suffering by forcing him to recall a disappointing past and face a hopeless present. Wolmar's remark thus enacts the complex and somewhat paradoxical interplay of conceptual opposites embodied by pity.

Indeed, the dramatic context of Wolmar's remark suggests that its immediate emotional effect would be to reinforce rather than ameliorate St. Preux's feelings of isolation and inferiority, for when he claims to be Julie's subject he is surrounded by countless reminders of his own power. He has no need to assert that power explicitly, for the setting in which he makes his remark—in his well-run estate, surrounded by his well-behaved children and doted on by his ravishing wife—says everything for him. Thus, though Wolmar's comment about subjection establishes a sympathetic connection between himself and St. Preux, the dramatic setting in which the remark is made weakens that connection. It is therefore unsurprising that though St.

Preux describes his morning with Julie and her husband in an enthusiastic tone, the letter as a whole shows that Wolmar's comment deeply wounded his pride: he confesses that the sight of his former lover raising another man's children induced in him an "indolence," one that he attributes to the apparent lack of attention that Julie and Wolmar paid their children (*J* 460). But this is subterfuge, and it is easy to see that St. Preux is upset because, having just been reminded of his romantic interest in Julie and of everything he has suffered for its sake, he now must look on the children his former lover bore another man. Such a humbling experience could well dispose anyone to resentment and petty faultfinding, so it is unsurprising to find the touchy St. Preux, who has just suffered a dreadful blow to his *amour-propre*, looking for flaws in Wolmar and Julie's domestic procedures.

The "morning spent in the English manner" thus depicts in narrative action the deep conceptual affinity between friendship and pity established in both the *Second Discourse* and *Emile* by (1) highlighting the distinctive and central role that *consolation* plays in the activity of friendship, and (2) underscoring the emotional separation that exists between friends united primarily through shared suffering. Taken together, these summary considerations reveal an attempt on Rousseau's behalf to reinterpret the function of friendship in human life and help to point up the distance between his conception of friendship and that found in the classical tradition.

| The Sound of Silence: Memory and Illusion

If analysis of the events of the "morning spent in the English manner" helps illustrate the emotional distance between friends, then closer examination of the "language of shared silence" mentioned there only reinforces the point. The language that the friends use to communicate that morning, far from showing how well they understand each other, instead shows quite the opposite. We can begin to see how Rousseau's friends differently interpret the silence they share by recalling St. Preux's claim that he, Julie, and Wolmar were all "caught up in the same emotion" after Wolmar says that he and St. Preux had long been Julie's "subjects" (*J* 456). Though the analysis above makes clear that all three friends recalled the same *events*—St. Preux's failed attempt to wed Julie, and so on—it also makes clear that they did not have the same *feelings* about those events. Though we can only speculate about the specifics of Julie and Wolmar's emotional reactions to Wolmar's curious remark, it is clear enough they did not share the "indolence" it occasioned in St. Preux who, quietly brooding on his past failures, seeks to even the score with Wolmar by questioning his parenting strategies. The language of shared silence, then, seems to say different things to each.

The unhappy ambiguity in the language of friendship rears its ugly head yet again in the same letter, where St. Preux—warmed by the prospect of emotional togetherness—is reminded of other instances in which shared silence seemed to catalyze intimacy. Writing to Bomston, he reminds his friend of the time immediately following his intensely painful separation from Julie, wherein Milord Edward took him away to Besançon and watched over him while he grieved. There, the two men spent several nights in a pregnant silence comparable to that enjoyed over breakfast with Julie and Wolmar. "O the late evenings of Besançon!" bellows an ecstatic St. Preux. "Moments devoted to silence and treasured up by friendship! O Bomston! Great soul, sublime friend! No, I have not belittled what you did for me, and my lips have never said a word of it to you" (*J* 456). Bomston, too, refers to their shared silences earlier in the novel and, like St. Preux in the later letter, thinks them evidence of a strong connection between the two men. He attributes St. Preux's unwillingness to speak as a function of compromised pride, an unwillingness to risk the esteem of a friend by disclosing the extent of his emotional injury. "He is ashamed of his condition," Bomston writes to Claire, "and controls himself carefully in my presence" (157). He goes on to explain that St. Preux "was quite downcast on the first day [of traveling]" and that both men stayed silent out of unspoken mutual respect. "He did not speak to me, nor I to him; indiscreet consolations can only irritate violent afflictions. Indifference and reserve easily find words; but sadness and silence are the true language of friendship." It would appear, then, that in the registers of Bomston and St. Preux's respective memories lie experiences—once again, experiences of *misfortune*—that serve to maintain and intensify their affection for each other. Consistent, then, with St. Preux's ex post panegyrics, Bomston assumes that considerations of respect and a deep familiarity with each other's characters formed the foundation for the shared silences at Besançon.

Yet St. Preux's recollection of his quiet nights with Bomston at Besançon is a self-serving misremembrance of what actually happened there. In fact, he remembers those days, and his feelings toward Bomston, very inaccurately indeed. Earlier in the novel St. Preux gives a very different account of his reticence to speak to Bomston, telling Claire that the reason for his own silence was his *distrust* of the Englishman, whom he suspected of trying to wed Julie himself. "I thought," he confesses, "I detected a premeditated design, and I had the gall to impute it to the most virtuous of men" (*J* 179). St. Preux discovered that Bomston was writing Julie in secret, concluded that he was seeking to ingratiate himself with her and her family in the hopes of marrying her, and fell into sullen silence. Believing he had caught Bomston with his hand in the cookie jar, St. Preux burst into his study and accused him of betrayal. Thus it was deep distrust—not deep affection—that motivated St. Preux's silence; he did not speak because he was too angry, too depressed, and too concerned that his friend sought to deceive him. Upon learning that Bomston had been working in secret to reunite his friend with Julie, St. Preux was predictably contrite. But it was *then* that he began to develop genuine feelings of trust and affection for Bomston, feelings he proceeded to retroactively and inaccurately project on their entire time at Besançon. St. Preux, who spends the entire novel trying to forget his lover, has no difficulty forgetting that he ever mistrusted as good a friend as Milord Edward. Yet again, the unspoken language of friendship leads to misunderstanding rather than to deep understanding. The two men do not know each other nearly as well as their shared silences permit them to believe.

St. Preux's effusive praise of the peculiar language of friendship thus discloses some of the difficulties to which that language is subject, for the friends who employ this language often misunderstand each other because of it. The shared recollections that enable intimacy between friends often turn out, upon close examination to be falsely nostalgic, self-serving, or simply inaccurate accounts of the events being remembered. Friendship, too, has its illusions, and these illusions show the ways in which men—however much they seek unity—remain estranged.

| Bad Education: Moral Learning and the Virtue of Friendship

Rousseau's emphasis on the importance of consolation certainly distinguishes his view of friendship from classical conceptions, but it does not preclude the possibility of Rousseauan friends helping each other become more virtuous. Indeed, because consolation might prove useful as one among many techniques that friends deploy in order to inspire each other to reach for ever-greater moral heights, it may appear that Reisert is correct to say Rousseauan friendship remains "traditional" at least insofar as it an association in which human beings raise each other to virtue. Yet a revisitation of Rousseau's novelistic portrayals of what friends do as friends shows that they, for all their sensitivity, are distinguished not by their ability to catalyze morality but rather by their tendency to re-create the conditions under which ethical failure is inevitable. They exhort each other to virtue without knowing what it is or how it best expresses itself in common life. Thus their intercourse proves to be a study in unintended consequences: the counsel *les belles âmes* offer one another, while always well-intentioned and often perceptive, nonetheless proves ineffective and sometimes quite destructive. Thus they perpetuate and even magnify the sense of moral confusion they seek to resolve.

If Rousseauan friends were effective stewards of one another's moral development then they should show gradual improvement under one another's tutelage. *Julie*, however, shows precisely the opposite: when the omniscient Wolmar weds Julie in Part III, he inherits a moral community in complete disarray. His new wife has suffered a nasty bout with smallpox, has endured at least one vicious beating (and an equally vicious shaming) from her despotic father, and continues to grieve the death of her mother and her forced separation from St. Preux. This physical and emotional exhaustion results in moral exhaustion. She continues to carry on an illicit correspondence she had promised to break off, and she strongly considers resuming a secret relationship with her former lover. "Nature, O sweet nature," a resigned Julie exclaims in inviting St. Preux to reprise his previous role, "take back all thy rights! I abjure the heartless virtues that obliterate thee" (*J* 275). A disconsolate and desperate St. Preux heartily commends his lover's resolution: "Why should we alone . . . subscribe with childlike simplicity to illusory virtues that everyone talks about and no one practices?" After all, examples of adultery "are not scandalous; they cannot even be criticized, and all the honorable people here [in Paris] would chuckle at the man who out of respect for marriage resisted his heart's penchant" (277). St. Preux's time in Paris has compromised both his resolve to do the right thing and his understanding of what that right thing is, and his transparently self-serving appeal to Parisian *moeurs* reveals just how far he and Julie have fallen. We must ask: how did it get to this point?

While the exhaustion afflicting the two lovers is partially a product of a necessarily difficult situation, it is clear their friends do not make matters easier. Neither Bomston nor Claire exhibits a satisfactory awareness of what the good is or of how to effect it in their friends' lives, and absent this awareness they magnify the very problems they seek to alleviate. Bomston, the putative sage of the group, proves a zealous but injudicious advocate of St. Preux's best interests. By the time he intercedes on St. Preux's behalf—first to propose the marriage to Julie and then to assist his friend after Julie's father rejected that proposal—we have good reason to question the extent of his self-knowledge and moral vision (e.g., *J* 103, 135, 167). Bomston's limitations show themselves in the way he looks to rehabilitate his friend: following his separation from Julie, Bomston takes a wounded St. Preux to Paris and sets him up with a generous annuity. Any reader of Rousseau knows the City of Light is the last place a depressed and vulnerable St. Preux needs to go, and the effects on his weary soul are predictably destructive: after repeatedly expressing concern about the kind of person he is becoming in Paris, St. Preux's moral decline is consummated by his solicitation of a prostitute. The choice to bring his morally exhausted friend to a city distinguished for its capacity to corrupt reflects Bomston's incomplete understanding of how to help, and this lack of knowledge has direct and serious consequences for St. Preux's moral fate. He does not *understand* the conditions under which his friend might be rehabilitated, and his ignorance leads him to put St. Preux in an environment that, in the context of Rousseau's moral universe, is singularly destructive to moral health.

Claire, too, fails to provide helpful moral counsel either to Julie or to St. Preux. She imprudently puts herself in the difficult position of serving as a sounding board for both her cousin and her friend, but like Bomston she does not know the good or how to best effect it in her friends' lives. To be sure, she occasionally provides thoughtful and even searching advice, but her indiscretion harms the very friends she seeks to assist. Her incomplete grasp on the principles of human character show themselves most readily when she advises St. Preux to terminate his correspondence with Julie: "The sacrifice you have made to Julie's honor by leaving the country is a token to me of the one you will make to her peace of mind by breaking off a pointless relationship" (*J* 253–54). This is sound counsel. Yet she undoes her own work in her very next letter by implying that Julie's mother wishes to see St. Preux and Julie married: "This tender mother . . . is beginning to understand thanks to everything she sees how greatly your two hearts surpass the common rule, and how much your love bears the natural character of sympathy that neither time nor human efforts could ever destroy. She who has such need of comfort would gladly comfort her daughter if propriety did not hold her back. . . . She forgot herself yesterday to the point of saying in her presence, perhaps somewhat indiscreetly, 'Ah if it were only up to me'" (257). If Julie's mother is guilty of indiscretion in telling the truth to her aggrieved daughter then Claire is doubly guilty for communicating the story to the desperate St. Preux, who is all too willing to believe in any possibility that keeps him connected to his lover and all too eager to interpret any gesture of sympathy from Julie's family as evidence of a willingness to accept him as a son-in-law. Claire's telling St. Preux that he has gained the favor of Julie's mother, of course, has the effect of encouraging him to believe in precisely the possibility of which she sought to disabuse him. How can St. Preux be expected to follow Claire's advice and forget Julie when Claire herself continues to remind him of her?

Rousseau, in his editorial capacity, cannot resist calling attention to Claire's failure to understand the impact her letter will have on the desperately credulous St. Preux. "Claire," he says, "are you less indiscreet here? Is this the last time you will be?" (*J* 257n). Rousseau thus notes in his own voice that Claire's mistake is not an isolated error in judgment but rather a reflection of her general habit of saying things she should keep to herself. Claire's failure to understand what St. Preux is (and is not) in a condition to hear multiplies rather than reduces the difficulties he faces in attempting to honor his responsibility to Julie. The first half of the novel thus presents us with a picture of friends who love virtue but who clearly lack the necessary knowledge to give effective expression to their moral energy. Left to their own clumsy devices, they lead each other in circles rather than forward. It will take the appearance of an authoritative moral guide—the puppet master Wolmar—to provide some semblance of moral order.

| Moral Marionettes: Equality, Hierarchy, and Ethical Learning

The moral incapacity of Rousseauan friends is reflected not only by their inability to independently create conditions conducive to moral growth but also by their need of a strong moral guide. In an important letter to St. Preux, Julie speaks to the need for an authoritative figure by sounding a familiar Rousseauan theme, namely, the fragility of human happiness: "One strays for a single moment in life, deviates by a single step from the straight path. At once an ineluctable slope drags him down to his ruin" (*J* 291).

Because friends lack the judgment to protect each other from this sad fate, the search for virtue remains unsuccessful until Wolmar appears to guide it. His emergence is key for the moral stability of the entire group, for he is the only figure in the novel with the knowledge required of an effective moral counselor. Wolmar gives form to matter; he reinvigorates and then redirects the will to be good, which had exhausted itself in the culture of moral failure *les belles âmes* had created. He does so by claiming control both of his new wife and her friends, because he knows the entire social context in which his wife exists must be shaped anew if she is to be cured of her self-destructive attraction to St. Preux. The inseparables are knotted together so closely that the sickness of one is inevitably the sickness of all.

Thus Wolmar, as Claire explains to St. Preux early in Book IV, seeks not only to rehabilitate his wife but his wife's friends as well. "Monsieur de Wolmar wishes to see you," she tells her world-weary friend. "He goes farther, he means to cure you, and says that neither Julie, nor he, nor you, nor I, can be perfectly happy failing that." The health of the entire group depends on St. Preux's return and rehabilitation. With her invitation to return to Clarens, however, Claire sounds a note of circumspection about Wolmar's plan: "Although I expect much from his wisdom and more from your virtue, I do not know how this undertaking will turn out" (*J* 342). Though this is not the last time Claire will challenge Wolmar's new power over the group, Wolmar is undoubtedly more successful in his efforts to rehabilitate St. Preux and his wife than Claire or Bomston were (cf. Disch 1994). His foresightedness, knowledge of human nature, and capacity for environmental manipulation make him an excellent manager of the domestic economy at Clarens and an effective steward of the group's interests. Under Wolmar's paternalistic authority St. Preux reports some decisive progress in his quest to understand himself and his illness. Explaining the circumstances under which he and Julie were able to resist the temptation they posed to each other, St. Preux tells Bomston that "the scene at Meillerie was the crisis of my folly and my ills" but adds that "Monsieur de Wolmar's explanations have entirely reassured me as to my heart's true condition. This too frail heart is cured insofar as it can be." Though St. Preux pronounces himself cured several times in the novel, we see here a reasonable circumspection not present in previous self-diagnoses: he does not say he is cured simply but that he is cured "insofar as [he] can be." St. Preux's new measure is owing to "Monsieur de Wolmar's explanations," which have given him the strength to resist "the terror of being constantly besieged by crime." He feels himself "the child of the house" and, finding his place within the harmonious whole that Wolmar has constructed at Clarens, reports that it is in a child's capacity that his "heart is gradually coming into unison with theirs" (432). St. Preux's voluntary submission to Wolmar has given him peace, unity, and increased moral fortitude. If it has not made him "perfectly happy," then it has reduced his suffering considerably by showing him his place within the whole. Paradoxically, it is in his role as the "child" of Clarens that St. Preux begins to learn the requirements of adult friendship. Before being taken in by Wolmar, St. Preux was undoubtedly a "high maintenance" friend: he dwelled constantly on the fact of his own misfortune, and his attempts to console others inevitably led him back to a consideration of his own pain. It is only under Wolmar's careful guidance that St. Preux is able to dissuade Bomston from a dishonorable marriage and thus give *active* expression to the sentiments of friendship he eulogizes throughout the novel.

As Judith Shklar (1969) has shown, the distinctive social world depicted in *Julie* is hardly the only context in which the emergence of "figures of authority" proves necessary for ethical growth. Indeed, the education described in *Emile* also requires the existence of an authoritative moral guide who can negotiate the many hidden pitfalls in Rousseau's moral universe. Joseph Reisert (2003), however, does not view this as evidence that friends do not learn from each other, arguing instead that the relationship between Emile and his tutor is a qualified kind of friendship. Insofar as Rousseau—much as we do—uses the term "friendship" in both wide and narrow senses, such a suggestion is perfectly plausible, but it is very difficult to see how Emile and Jean-Jacques's relationship satisfies Rousseau's technical definition of the term:[3] "Attachment can exist without being returned, but friendship never can. It is an exchange or contract like others, but it is the most sacred of all. The word *friend* has no correlative other than itself. Any man who is not his friend's friend is most assuredly a cheat, for it is only in returning or feigning to return friendship that one can obtain it" (*E* 233n). Friendship is an "exchange" or "contract," and as such it is a *voluntary* association into which rational persons freely select. Friends do not hold each other hostage or employ deceptive tactics in order to win affection and regard. Indeed, one who only pretends to return the honest goodwill and concern characteristic of friendship is a "cheat" rather than a true friend. Friendship, then, is not something imposed on us or that we are tricked into, but rather something that requires our free and reasonably informed consent.

Friendship is also a *reciprocal* institution, which means friends must share the pleasures and burdens of their association in a roughly equal way. This does not mean friends must be equal along every dimension of life, for Rousseau's own examples show that friends may have different aims and excellences: Bomston's immense personal fortune does not undermine his friendship with St. Preux, nor does Claire's jealousy of Julie's superior beauty and magnetism prevent genuine love and affection. It would, however, be quite unusual for the overall distribution of excellences between friends to be profoundly inegalitarian, since the mutual respect necessary for friendship is satisfied only where both friends are capable of giving to and receiving from each other. One who needs little or nothing from others might be a benefactor, but he cannot be a friend on Rousseau's understanding of the term. Thus, though friends may possess distinct excellences, those excellences must be distributed in at least a roughly egalitarian way.

When, however, we look at Emile's relationship with his tutor, we see an association that fails to satisfy both the conditions of voluntariness and reciprocity. These conditions begin to hold when Emile reaches sexual maturity, for at this "critical moment" it becomes essential to recognize him not as a child but as a friend and an equal: "He is still your disciple but he is no longer your pupil. He is your friend, he is a man. From now on treat him as such" (*E* 316). Emile now shares with his species and his tutor that desire that will give him access to distinctively human pleasures. After its birth all the aspects of his being will be active: he possesses will, judgment, reason, and a libido, and it is by way of these possessions that he acquires the right to decide how to live his own life. The first decision he must make as "a man" is whether to continue living under his tutor's watchful eye.

Jean-Jacques recognizes Emile's new moral status and knows that his own authority must be explicitly authorized by his pupil in order to be legitimate. To force an adult Emile to continue in an education he believes to be onerous is to deny him the use of the very capacities he is now entitled to employ, and if Emile is to make an informed decision about whether to stay under Jean-Jacques's tutelage he must know the truth about how he has been raised. Jean-Jacques therefore discloses to his pupil the unique nature of his education, for part of what it is to be respected as a friend and equal is to be treated with honesty. Indeed, if complete candor were *ever* called for, it would be in a situation in which a presumptive equal asks another to consent to be governed by him. Yet Jean-Jacques continues to interfere with the exercise of the very freedom that Rousseau himself has insisted Emile is entitled to employ, for when he comes to ask his pupil to remain under his tutelage he utilizes all his old tricks. He manipulates all the circumstances around the choice situation in order to elicit Emile's consent, and harangues the young man with a guilt trip worthy of the Dominican Order: "You are my property, my child, my work. It is from your happiness that I expect my own. If you frustrate my hopes you are robbing me of twenty years of my life, and you are causing the unhappiness of my old age" (*E* 323). Jean-Jacques is laying it on thick. We might expect such manipulative talk from Julie's father, but is this the way that one deals with a friend?

I submit that it is not, and for reasons Rousseau himself recognized. First, the tutor's mode of address—*my* property, *my* child, *my* work—is not only inegalitarian but also demeaningly proprietary. The choice to address Emile in this way is clearly calculated to remind the boy of his continued dependence on the tutor and to make him feel like a child at the very moment he is to choose like a man. To be sure, the tutor does what he does because he desires what is best for his Emile, because he suspects (and is *right* to suspect) that his pupil lacks the wherewithal to preserve his fragile happiness and that he will make destructive choices if left to his own devices. It might be reasonably urged that such lack of faith is itself inconsistent with the spirit of friendship itself—especially if we select our friends because we respect not only their right to choose but also their ability to choose *rightly*—but the point here is not about the validity of Jean-Jacques's concerns but rather about the underhanded way in which he resolves them. The manipulative measures he takes, coupled with the sense of distrust that motivates them, seem manifestly inconsistent with the respect Rousseau himself claims friends owe each other.

It is, however, fair to wonder whether respect always entails perfect honesty. Bomston and St. Preux—friends if there ever were any—intercede on each other's behalf without explicit permission, and Rousseau seems to think that such behavior is the mark of an especially distinguished kind of friendship. It is hasty, then, to conclude that Jean-Jacques's unsolicited interventions are somehow necessarily at odds with the requirements of adult friendship. It is, however, essential to remember that St. Preux and Bomston are *both* engaged in such behavior. They intercede on each other's behalf because both lack self-command; it is, in fact, this common character *deficiency* that opens the emotional space in which the bonds of their friendship are strengthened. Far from disproving the rule, then, St. Preux and Bomston's example instead confirms it, for they show us that unrequested interventions must be *mutual* in order to be consistent with the requirements of Rousseauan friendship. One sees immediately that this mutuality fails to obtain between Jean-Jacques and Emile. The pupil simply does not have occasion to assist the self-sufficient and quasi-divine tutor, who is needed by others without ever needing others himself. The student-teacher relationship is for Rousseau many wonderful things, but it is not a friendship in the strict sense.

Conclusions: Rousseau's Compassionate Conservatism?

Though friendship has a long and distinguished history in the history of political thought, and though Rousseau is undoubtedly a canonical political thinker, very little work has been done to understand Rousseau's treatment of friendship. The work that does exist obscures the originality of his conception and moors him to a classical tradition he sought to correct as much as to follow. Far from cleaving to the traditional understanding of friendship as a catalyst of ethical perfection between same selves, Rousseau instead emphasizes the contrast between remedial pedagogic relationships, which can inculcate virtue because they are hierarchical, and friendship proper, which cannot inculcate virtue because it is not. This central finding is significant in its own right, for it not only draws attention to an interesting and neglected aspect of Rousseau's thinking but also advances an original and somewhat subversive interpretation of it. Yet because it raises questions about friendship's ability to both catalyze comprehensive intimacy and inculcate virtue—matters central to Rousseau's broader social and political concerns—it may be helpful to conclude by touching on Rousseau's understanding of the relationship between friendship and politics.

On this head, I should like to suggest that Rousseau's theory of friendship is for at least two reasons unpromising as a template for civic concord. The first is that Rousseau's portraits of friendship emphasize features of human connection that would seem especially problematic in the context of his own political project. Whereas Rousseau's ideal political society requires thick community founded on an egalitarian ethos, his theory of friendship-as-pity shows the association between friends to be an attenuated and even hierarchical relation in which a fortunate observer consoles a suffering other. The distancing, inegalitarian features built into the experience of pity strain emotional bonds between friends even as they make those bonds possible; to the degree that civic connection is grounded in compassion, we should expect to see the same troubling dynamics at work between citizens. The point deserves special emphasis because many influential interpreters of Rousseau have claimed that his theory of political identification *is* based on compassion: John Charvet (1973, 19) calls pity "the solution to the social problem," Allan Bloom (1979, 19) "the glue binding men together," and Martha Nussbaum (2001, 385) "the basis for . . . democratic-egalitarian thinking." The present analysis problematizes that line of interpretation, for it points up the difficulty of making a sentiment so deeply imbued with inegalitarian elements be the psychological basis for egalitarian fraternity.

There is still another reason to wonder about the political effectiveness of Rousseauan friendship, namely, its manifest inability to inculcate virtue. Though Joseph Reisert and Jonathan Marks have both emphasized the moralizing potential of friendship, we have seen that the problems on this head are both cognitive and conative: Rousseau's friends not only lack the wisdom—both practical and theoretical—required to serve as effective moral counselors for one another, but they are also united through a pessimistic view of the moral world that emphasizes the limits of the human condition and the ineliminability of suffering. The spirit of resignation that helps unite friends, as both Rousseau and his critics have noted, can be politically destructive: Clifford Orwin (1997a, 7) and Richard Boyd (2004) have both argued that the melancholy ethos attached to Rousseauan compassion promotes ethical fatalism, and Rousseau himself worries in the *Preface to Narcisse* (25) that "so many reflections on the weakness of our nature" might be so dispiriting as to "turn us away from generous undertakings."

It is therefore unsurprising that Rousseau's citizens, far from displaying the gloominess and spirit of inaction so often exhibited by his friends, instead exhibit the moral enthusiasm and active, engaged habits of mind that help them fulfill their moral and civic duties. Among the most telling examples Rousseau provides on this score is found in the *Letter to D'Alembert*, where Rousseau opposes the institution of a theater in Republican Geneva because he believes it would inculcate the very moral passivity so prevalent in his own models of friendship: the "afflicting images of servitude" required by dramatic performance induce in theatergoers a "gloomy" mentality that, in its turn, inspires narcissism and habits of "inaction" (*LD* 124–25). Such habits are uniquely inappropriate for the citizens of a free republic, who must be enthusiastic and active in the discharge of their civic obligations. Thus Rousseau rejects the dour self-absorption of the theater in favor of public events—balls, festivals, and civic competitions—designed to promote cheerful fraternization among citizens. Of these events, the various forms of public competition appear to be especially important in catalyzing civic virtue, for they provide strong incentives for citizens to develop and display those forms of individual excellence that best facilitate social concord.

Though the preceding analysis points up the political limitations and potential dangers of Rousseauan friendship, it is necessary to acknowledge that its effects on the polity need not be entirely damaging. On this score, it is easy to imagine how the spirit of inaction and the resigned, almost tragic view of the social world exhibited by Rousseau's friends could actually play a salutary *preventive* role in a political society, restraining some of the nastier expressions of self-love and helping prevent healthy *amour-propre* from sliding into delusional forms of antisociability—forms that range from the disillusioned drift of the bourgeois to the domineering cruelty of the tyrant. The somewhat resigned spirit of Rousseauan friendship might also help counteract the impulsiveness many critics associate with both democratic decision-making generally and Rousseau's political philosophy in particular, for it expresses an ethos that encourages circumspection about the human capacity to eliminate contingency and counsels inaction in the face of uncertainty (*E* 445). Such a worldview, though not unproblematic, is also not without its advantages, for it facilitates a generalized awareness of the human susceptibility to error and, in so doing, provides reminders about the limits of political action. Insofar, then, as Rousseau's theory of friendship facilitates a spirit of restraint, it may also provide some resources for responding to a criticism of his political thought dating back to Burke, namely, that it encourages rash, radical, and detrimental forms of political change.

With that said, it is difficult to view Rousseau's retheorization of friendship as anything other than a significant diminution of its power. Indeed, Rousseau consigns what was once viewed to be the highest and best human relationship to the margins of man's moral life, showing it to be an ameliorative rather than a remedial association. It may console us in our dividedness, but it cannot return us to wholeness.

7 The Ecology of Justice

> Everything that destroys social unity is worthless. All institutions that put man in contradiction with himself are worthless.
>
> —ROUSSEAU, *Social Contract*

In the previous three chapters we have looked at romantic love and friendship and have seen that neither succeeds in preserving human wholeness. Though the failure of each is due to a combination of psychological and environmental conditions, the explanatory emphasis thus far has been on the former: the shortcomings of love and friendship are attributable to limitations inherent in the imagination and in pity, respectively. Yet it is time to acknowledge that Rousseau's heroes and heroines do not pursue their respective goods in a social or political vacuum. Their actions and interactions are embedded in particular sociopolitical contexts which exert an inevitable and a destructive influence on the course of their lives. In *Julie*, the eponymous heroine and her lover take the first and most decisive steps down their tragic path in the profoundly dysfunctional social world shaped by the "gothic maxims" of her violent and despotic father. In *Emile* and its sequel, the happy couple must preserve their union in a city teeming with infidelity and moral corruption. In both cases Rousseau's heroes complain of the external world's corrupting forces, which punish sympathy, undermine trust, and frustrate the desire for transparent human relations. Such considerations tempt us to pronounce the "domestic" healing strategy explored in *Emile* and *Julie*—namely, the effort to be *in* society without also being *of* it—a failure.

Though the socially embedded character of human action problematizes the rehabilitative possibilities explored thus far, so, too, might it allow us to explore new and more promising ones, for, though those seeking to heal themselves from within a corrupt social environment cannot reasonably expect to succeed, they might still find the satisfaction they seek in a well-ordered society. It is, then, not as lovers or friends but rather as *citizens* of a just political community that we may at last find the comprehensive satisfaction we seek.

In order to find this comprehensive satisfaction, however, we must answer a number of difficult questions about what Rousseau's well-ordered society looks like and what ends it seeks to realize. I interpret Rousseau's political works as an attempt to identify the general institutional and sociological situation in which man's inner unity is most effectively realized and make two broad arguments in support of this general claim. The first is that the fundamental standard for assessing social institutions is not freedom—as so many interpreters have argued—but unity. The inner unity that characterizes man's life in the state of nature is predicated on a harmonious relationship to the natural environment in which he is embedded, and it is the disruption of this harmonious relation that generates all the ruinous psychological consequences about which Rousseau complains. At its most basic level, then, Rousseau's political philosophy is about creating a social environment in which humans might live in harmony with themselves and with one another. To the degree this is true, freedom, however conceived, cannot serve as the end either of human nature or of social institutions; it is valuable, then, because it contributes to social and psychological unity and not because it provides an evaluative standard somehow beyond it.

The second argument is about the particular type of harmony that must obtain between man and his environment. On this head, I use the metaphor of an ecology to identify the key features of the unity Rousseau seeks to effect between citizen and society. Though unavailable to Rousseau, ecological systems theory (Bronfenbrenner 1979) helps bring into focus how deeply one's identity is influenced by surrounding structures and provides a useful framework for understanding how unity within is predicated on unity without. So, too, does it clarify how *fragile* the unity between self and environment is, for in conceiving of political society as a set of nested social structures and of citizens as the possessors of multiple social roles, it highlights the possibility of identity conflict. As conceived here, then, citizens are not just bearers of specifically political rights and responsibilities—they are also friends, lovers, parents, producers, consumers, and the like. Yet these various social roles are not always consistent with one another, and in the absence of a principle of identity that resolves role conflicts citizens inevitably fall into the passive drift of bourgeois dividedness.

The interpretation I shall develop in this chapter and the next has at least three controversial implications. The first is its privileging of unity or harmony over freedom as the basis of Rousseau's political thought. Though freedom in some form is widely considered to be the central concern motivating Rousseau in the *Social Contract* and perhaps beyond (e.g., Levine 1976; Cassirer 1989; Cullen 1993; Simpson 2006), I argue that freedom is only one of many characteristics of human nature, and that it deserves protection in a just regime only because it is contributory to the still more fundamental end of wholeness. Second, though I reject efforts to turn Rousseau into a liberal individualist, I will also show the "totalitarian" readings of Isaiah Berlin and Lester Crocker (among others) to be decisively flawed. Finally, and consistent with the argumentation provided in chapters 4 and 5, I emphasize the basic disjuncture between the respective educations of "men" and "citizens" and resist the temptation to read the individualistic educational program of *Emile* into the social and political context of the *Social Contract*. I do so by showing that the sociological supports necessary to the regime in the *Social Contract* are supportive of a public-spirited ethos quite at odds with the domestic individualism cultivated in *Emile*.

| To Be or Not to Be Free? Is *That* Rousseau's Question?

The literature on Rousseau's political theory in general and on the *Social Contract* in particular is as fragmented as it is vast. Scholars have long disputed whether Rousseau's analysis of the principles of political right is coherent or confused, classical or modern, liberal or authoritarian, progressive or conservative, nostalgic or foresighted, utopian or fatalistic. Despite such disagreements, however, many scholars do seem able to agree on the work's central theme: freedom. This is not without reason. Indeed, it is almost indecently obvious to say that a concern for freedom figures prominently in

Rousseau's political and social theory. It was his treatment of this theme—by turns illuminating and obscure—that drew both the admiration and the ire of his earliest readers: Robespierre was said to have kept a dog-eared copy of the *Social Contract* with him at all times, but Constant—mindful of all the trouble caused by Robespierre's love of Rousseau—famously criticized the great Genevan for misunderstanding the true character of modern liberty. Burke (*RRF* 270) was especially violent in his denunciation of that "insane Socrates of the National Assembly," believing his radical conception of freedom to be utterly at odds with the demands of civilization itself.[1]

Such controversies were rehearsed anew in the twentieth century, with critics finding in Rousseau's oeuvre either many of the necessary resources for combating the rise of "totalitarianism" (e.g., Kateb 1961; Shklar 1969) or, alternatively, one of its most appalling theoretical instantiations (e.g., Nisbet 1943; Talmon 1952; Crocker 1995). The broad disputes concerning Rousseau's liberal credentials began to take more specific shape in Isaiah Berlin's famous "Two Concepts of Liberty" essay, in which he distinguishes "negative" and "positive" forms of freedom and claims that Rousseau's "positive" conception gives his political thought an illiberal character. Implicit in the assimilation of liberty and sovereignty, Berlin argues, is a perfectionistic moral doctrine that imposes on citizens a conception of a "higher" or "autonomous" self to be realized in and through the activity of self-governance. The understanding of freedom as "self-mastery" denies citizens the right "not to be interfered with in a defined area" and thus represents a "monstrous impersonation" of true political liberty (Berlin 1990, 133). More recently, contemporary democratic theorists like Cohen (1986, 2010) and Rawls (2007) have followed Berlin in characterizing Rousseauan freedom as "positive" but have forcefully disputed the claim that there is anything authoritarian in it. Cohen's (2010, 11) revealingly titled "social autonomy" interpretation claims on Rousseau's behalf that "freedom is the basis of humanity's special worth, and is the basis of our standing as responsible, moral agents," and Rawls (2007, 247–48) argues that the regime of the *Social Contract* effectively cultivates the individuality of citizens through the provision of self-respect.

Both Rawls's and Cohen's accounts show that the authoritarian regimes of the twentieth century have little if anything in common with Rousseau's republican model and that the exercise of Rousseauan sovereignty is limited in ways that Berlin and others fail to grasp (see also Strong 1994, 79–85; Simpson 2006, 52–56). While they, like Berlin, emphasize the importance of Rousseau's claim that submission to the state involves the exchange of "natural freedom" for "moral freedom" and thus implicates the emergence of a "higher self," they also argue that this exchange is not disrespectful to individuality but is rather the basis for its preservation. The acceptance of the terms of the social compact is nothing but the renunciation of "the right to everything that tempts [you]" and the realization that submission to the general will makes sense only because it is ultimately more empowering and possibility enhancing than the freedom of the state of nature (SC I.8, 56). Citizens deliberately realize their sense of self and the capacities that attach to that realization through the exercise of political sovereignty. And since the act of replacing natural freedom with moral freedom and its subjectivity-enhancing tendencies is "the most voluntary thing in the world"—because free and informed consent is an ongoing condition of membership in a just political society—it is inaccurate and unfair to say with Berlin that Rousseau's positive conception of liberty produces institutional arrangements unfriendly to liberty.

Neither Cohen nor Rawls stops here, however. Both follow Ernst Cassirer (1989) in finding embodied in Rousseau's concept of "moral freedom" an uncommonly deep commitment to and productive way of thinking about individual liberty. Rousseau defines moral freedom as "obedience to the law one has prescribed for oneself" and claims that it alone "makes man truly the master of himself." It is contrasted with "the impulse of appetite alone" (*l'impulsion de seul appétit*), which is characterized as a form of "slavery" that is transcended once we learn to act not just in accordance with the law but out of respect for it and it alone (SC I.8, 56). The passage clearly evokes the shade of Kant, and Rawls in particular views the form of self-legislation embodied by moral freedom as both central to Rousseau's political project and as a prefiguration of Kantian autonomy: "The society of the social compact achieves in its basic political and social institutions both civil and moral freedom" (Rawls 2007, 235).

Though neither Rawls nor Cohen emphasizes Rousseau's proto-Kantianism quite so much as Cassirer does, their assimilation of "civil" and "moral" freedom nonetheless generates a highly individualistic interpretation of Rousseauan citizenship, one in which the morally free citizen views himself as a self-originating source of valid claims, and the laws he authors as expressions of his individual identity. On their view, the legislative impulse emerges from the deepest recesses of the self qua self, is the unifying force in the moral personality, and is an immediate motivation for lawfulness. The law as such requires respect because it is an articulation of one's own deepest rational commitments and an expression of each citizen's capacity to create—rather than be created by—his surrounding environment. To disrespect the law is therefore to disrespect oneself, and to obey it is to understand that lawfulness and moral dignity are mutually constitutive and complementary concepts. Citizens of a just regime must therefore develop their capacity for moral freedom both in order to realize their nature as free beings as well as to effectively discharge their civic duty. Connection to the state is established not at the cost of individuality, as Nisbet or Berlin would have it, but rather is premised precisely on its proper development.

Though correct to locate a kind of developmental imperative in Rousseau's political thought and useful as a corrective to the superficial authoritarian view, the "social autonomy" interpretation exaggerates Rousseau's concern for the development of autonomy in the civil sphere and, in so doing, misunderstands the relationship between moral freedom and the just regime. Indeed, it is clear that the privileged status given to moral freedom by Rawls and others is based on an inaccurate reading of the passage in which the concept is introduced. The first indication of this is Rousseau's paragraphing: after contrasting "natural" and "civil" freedom in the same paragraph, Rousseau breaks his discussion off and introduces his treatment of moral freedom in a new paragraph, thus indicating its distinctness from the concepts that came before. Moreover, the way moral freedom is introduced hardly suggests that its emergence is necessary (cf. Simpson 2006, 94–100). After noting that civil freedom and property are gained only in society, Rousseau claims that "to the foregoing acquisitions *could be added* moral freedom, which alone makes man truly the master of himself" (*SC* I.8, 56; emphasis added).[2] The distinctness of moral and civil freedom is underscored not only by the fact that the former "could be" (*on pourrait*)—and thus need not be—attached to the latter, but also by Rousseau's use of the verb *ajouter* (to add), which suggests that civil and moral freedom are distinct but related, as icing is distinct from cake or sauce from meat. Perhaps most revealingly, after defining moral freedom in a brief two sentences Rousseau simply drops the matter entirely, claiming that he has "already said too much about this topic" and stating flatly that "the philosophical meaning of the word freedom is not my subject" (I.8, 56). The character of moral freedom is patently *not* the subject of the *Social Contract*, and Rousseau raises the topic not to show its importance but instead to point to its marginality.

If the priority that Rawls and Cohen give to moral freedom is not established on the basis of the very passage in which the concept is introduced, then it is made even more questionable when viewed in light of Rousseau's other remarks about civic education. We have already seen *Emile* sternly insist that the education most appropriate for citizens is a form of "denaturing" in which the political subject's sense of self, far from being the psychological ground of his love of the state, is instead compromised by it. We have also seen that the hero of that work, who supposedly establishes the historical possibility of an individualistic form of modern citizenship based on something like moral freedom—has far too attenuated a relation to his country to be called a "citizen" of any particular community. But Rousseau reiterates the basic incommensurability of the individualistic educative program of "men" and the desubjectivizing civic pedagogy of "citizens" in *Considerations on the Government of Poland*, where he claims that every Polish child, upon opening his eyes, "should see the fatherland, and see *only it* until his dying day" (*CGP* 189; emphasis added).[3] "This love [of fatherland]," Rousseau continues, "makes up his *whole* existence; he sees *only* his fatherland, he lives *only* for it; when he is alone, he is nothing: when he no longer has a fatherland, *he no longer is*, and if he is not dead, he is worse than dead" (emphasis added). In the Polish context, incorporation into the social union comes at the cost of developing anything resembling an autonomous self. The *moi*, far from the establishing the ground of robust citizenship, is instead sacrificed to the *patrie*, which becomes the source of being. The contrast to the modern individual Emile, who can leave his home country without losing his identity, is stark: the citizen of Poland, once removed from his homeland, is not only no longer a citizen—he no longer *is*.

Such advice is not specific to the nonideal circumstances of Poland. Indeed, Rousseau anticipates the advice he gives to Count Wielhorski in his *Discourse on Political Economy*, where he avers that if citizens "are taught from sufficiently early on never to look upon their individual [self] except in its relations with the body of the State, and to perceive their own existence as, so to speak, only a part of its existence, they will at last succeed in somehow identifying with this larger whole, to feel themselves members of the fatherland" (*DPE* 20).[4] Once again, love of the fatherland does not emerge out of selfhood but is rather purchased at the cost of selfhood. The precondition and initial purpose of public education—the task to which it sets itself "from the first moments of life"—is to replace the sense we have of ourselves *as* selves with the "exquisite sentiment" that attaches to love of the fatherland

(20–21). One's self-understanding is at its deepest level informed and even constituted by the association to the political community. Utterances like this occur far too frequently in Rousseau's political works to simply be set to the side. If there is any interesting developmental dynamic in Rousseau's political thought, it would not appear to have much to do with the sense of moral freedom.

Seizing on these and other arguments, a different group of scholars have rescued Rousseau from Berlin's association of positive liberty and authoritarianism by simply denying that his conception of freedom is "positive" in any meaningful way. Shklar (1969, 165, 182) provides the classical exposition of this view, characterizing Rousseauan politics as a "politics of prevention" and claiming that sovereignty "is a condition free from personal oppression, but it is not self-determination in a politically active sense." On her accounting, the general will is fundamentally *negative* and has as its aim not the advancement of some developmental imperative but rather the *prevention* of those forms of inequality that would systematically subject some citizens to others (185). Consistent with Shklar, Cullen (1993, 8) argues that Rousseauan "freedom consists in avoiding the domination, even the assistance, of others." This negative interpretation corresponds more closely to Rousseau's own language, for in his characterization of the social compact Rousseau indicates that members must remain "as free *as before*" but does not make any strong claims about enlarging the sphere of freedom through the development of rational autonomy (*SC* I.6, 53; emphasis added). Contractors need not be and indeed are not *more* free than they would have been in the state of nature, for all it means to be free in the political or civil sense is to remain unsubjected to the whims of another's private will or—what amounts to the same thing—to a law that is not general in its "object" and its "essence" (II.4, 62). It is, then, to be free *from* the scourge of specifically personal dependence. Each citizen must will the law to which he is bound less because such activity expresses and deepens the sense he has of himself as an autonomous being than because his presence in the assembly is necessary to prevent the incursions of others. Indeed, Cullen (1993, 61–64) has decisively shown that the exchange of "natural" for "civil" and "moral" forms of freedom does not undermine but instead supports the authoritative status of the original, natural standard.

Though the more restricted or "negative" understanding of Rousseauan liberty improves on the "social autonomy" interpretation in important respects, it does so at the cost of obscuring the active, identity-constitutive element of Rousseau's political thought. To say that a citizen is free in the negative sense is to say he is protected from a whole series of destructive social forces. But this is to define him by what he is *not* rather than by what, exactly, he *is*. However helpful this may be as a point of departure, it is not an adequately precise description of the end of political life or of the subject's relation to his political community. The nonexistence of destructive social forces implies the existence of nondestructive social forces, and the effect of these latter forces on the human personality is not just negative or preservative but also positive and developmental. As a way of beginning to see how public life requires the activation and extension of human capacities, we should remember that the subject does not enter the polity as a finished moral and social product but rather "just as he currently is—both himself and all his force" (*SC* I.9, 56). Underneath politics, then, is a self in the possession of certain natural interests and "forces." However, political life does quite a bit more than protect its native integrity from others. Indeed, this integrity must be taken away and reconstituted anew from the materials and forces created by human interdependence: every political community takes "away man's own forces in order to give him forces that are foreign to him and that he cannot make use of without the help of others" (*SC* II.7, 68). It is important to note that the forms of power to which we gain access upon entrance into the civil state require deep interdependence for their emergence and useful application. The right kind of social cooperation assuredly prevents the onset of destructive and malignant forms of personal dependence, but it activates new psychic capacities that enrich and deepen the lives of individual citizens. What is at stake in the creation of political community, then, is not simply the avoidance of the pernicious and mutually destructive forms of interdependence described in the *Discourse on Inequality* but also the *realization* of an alternative and more salutary form of dependence—dependence on the law and all the sociological structures that make law possible.

If the new form of dependence engendered by the social compact has transformative consequences that remain unexplained by proponents of the "negative freedom" thesis but are mischaracterized by the theorists of "positive freedom," then in light of what end or aim can we understand the Rousseauan polis? The alternative I shall argue for is already familiar to, though often deemphasized by, those who attribute to Rousseau a negative conception of liberty: it is *unity* or *wholeness*. For instance, while Cullen's central theoretical interest is freedom he nonetheless notes (1993, 8) that its realization "depends on a carefully structured environment, for which the pure state of nature constitutes the paradigm. By associating freedom with the natural condition, Rousseau ends up with a conception of freedom that is as stripped bare as his notion of natural man." We should note an important gloss here, namely, that freedom is "associated" with the natural condition but is not *definitive* of it. To say man is naturally free is not to say that he is not also other things as well (e.g., self-loving, pitying, perfectible). Freedom is thus one among many native human traits. But it is the harmonious coexistence of all these traits—not the special importance of one in particular—that truly defines the state of nature and makes it morally and politically meaningful. Indeed, a freedom that is "stripped bare" is an existential vacuum, not an end. Thus, though Cullen's own chief concern is freedom, his analysis here points to the still more fundamental importance of the "carefully structured environment" that makes freedom possible in the first place. Shklar, too, occasionally vacillates between freedom and unity in her characterizations of the basis of Rousseau's political theory: though calling Rousseauan politics a "politics of prevention," she declares that its "end" is much more than prevention—it is the establishment of "unity . . . within each man. Social peace," she adds, "is merely the reflection of that inner harmony which had marked natural men in contrast to the civilized" (1969, 167). Once again, then, it would seem that the truly *fundamental* natural standard to be reproduced by good social institutions is not freedom per se but harmony within one's soul and with one's environment.

| Dividedness Revisited

Though it is now clear that freedom points beyond itself and toward unity as the end of social institutions, it remains less than obvious how Rousseau conceived of unity or why he believed it had priority over other and perhaps more familiar goods (e.g., civil liberty or material prosperity). Intuition supplies part of the answer, for when we describe others as having a "unity of purpose" or as being "centered" we generally intend to commend them, and when we call them "divided" we mean quite the opposite. Yet Rousseau does not say that dividedness is merely undesirable; he says that it is the condition to be avoided at all costs (*E* 38–40; *SC* IV.8). To understand why he says this is to take a big step toward understanding the problem that politics is intended to solve; it is also, however, to go well beyond what our intuitions suggest. It may, then, be helpful to return to the question of dividedness and to recall why Rousseau believed that condition so singularly destructive to human well-being.

As a way of beginning this analysis, we would do well to note that the language of dividedness is Rousseau's way of talking about a general internal condition, not the occurrence of particular psychological events. Though we might describe ourselves as "divided" if we experience the co-presence of two uncombinable desires (coffee or tea? Mexican or Thai?), or—perhaps more significantly—if we feel desire and duty pulling in different directions, Rousseau has something else in mind. What defines a life as divided for Rousseau is not isolated experiences of internal conflict, for these are inevitable, but rather the lack of a principle of *identity* that can resolve such conflicts when they emerge. To be a unity is to have an identity, and to have an identity is to have a principle that generates coherent patterns of thought and behavior. Human life is full of difficult choices about who and what matters most, and in order to resolve them in a psychologically tolerable and reasonably consistent way we need regulative principles that govern our choices. Such principles help us set priorities, distinguish permissible from impermissible behaviors, and select a particular plan of life; in so doing, they stabilize our moral and social lives, giving them a continuity and consistency through time they would otherwise lack. Those who exhibit such continuity can be said to have a moral identity.

Rousseau's discussion of unity early in *Emile* is in fact about unity in the sense explained above, and the diagnosis of the modern bourgeois as the exemplar of "dividedness" does not—as the reader of the *Discourse on Inequality* might expect—emphasize his avariciousness or insatiable greed but rather his *passivity*, his aimlessness and basic lack of purpose. On this score, Rousseau contrasts the bourgeois with those who are "something" and "one" on the ground that, whereas the former spends his life "in conflict and floating" between unrealized possibilities, the latter follows a set of coherent impulses that give his life continuity. Unified beings make decisions "in a lofty style" and stick to them, but the bourgeois is defined by his lack of sound principles in accordance with which he can organize a rewarding life. He does not think any difficult choices have to be made, preferring instead to persist in the erroneous belief that the human good is realized most fully through the successful pursuit of narrow self-interest. He accepts in some vague way the view that all or even most goods are jointly realizable, that simply by consulting his own interest he may reconcile the perennial tensions between private passion and public good, wealth and taste, science and virtue, liberty and equality, citizenship and cosmopolitanism. This attitude is summed up by D'Alembert's belief that Geneva could unite "the prudence of Lacedaemon" with "the urbanity of Athens" through the institution of a theater (in *LD* 4).

For Rousseau such a view is not only deluded but also destructive. Human goods are not laid out buffet-style, to be mixed and matched at the whim of the chooser, and the platitudinous belief in a unity of goods realizable by raw self-interest does not lead to comprehensive satisfaction but rather to a kind of developmental purgatory. The attempt to have everything prevents one from being anything. We exist wholly in life's interstices, and our perpetual in-betweenness—our inability to commit to the requirements of any particular plan of life—culminates in the halfhearted pursuit of a series of disjointed pleasures. The condition of dividedness is, in the precise sense, a condition of nothingness—hence Rousseau's profoundly damning characterization of the bourgeois as a *rien*. To be a bourgeois is to be a nonentity, a site of undeveloped possibility (*E* 40–41).

The costs of bourgeois dividedness are not just psychological but also social and political. The complacent selfishness, cowardly obsession with self-preservation, and blithe disregard for virtue that characterize the empty life of the modern bourgeois are damaging to the city as well as the soul. The culprit, once again, is self-interest badly understood: Rousseau notes in *Emile* that modern social institutions reduce all sentiment and social affection to a "secret egoism" that "prevents [men] from being born by . . . detaching them from their species" (312n), and in the *Social Contract* he adds that this "secret egoism" prompts us to systematically neglect our public obligations. The passive and indifferent selfishness of the bourgeois leads to free-riding, making "him view what he owes the common cause as a free contribution, the loss of which will harm others less than its payment burdens him" (I.7, 55). Thus the political evils of apathy and disengagement are a direct consequence of our internal dividedness, our inability to fully commit ourselves to the requirements of social and political life.

In order to ameliorate the internal and external tensions that define bourgeois life, it is important to recall that Rousseau views the phenomenon of dividedness not as a natural fact but an institutional consequence, a mutable product of an anemic political sociology rather than an expression of ineliminable human tendencies. How, then, to remedy the disease? If the bourgeois is divided because he cannot accept the tradeoffs that moral and social life require, then the path to unity begins, perhaps paradoxically, by accepting the incommensurability of human goods. One must squarely face contradictions in order to avoid becoming one. Thus Rousseau's insistence that it is possible to make a "man"—a private self who is a "numerical unity" and an "absolute whole" unto himself—*or* a "citizen"—who has a "relative" existence defined by his participation "within the whole" political community—but that it is impossible to make both at the same time. For, from "these *necessarily opposed* objects," there emerge "two contrary forms of instruction—the one, public and common; the other, individual and domestic" (*E* 39–40; emphasis added). Thus, in our quest to create a healthy human type, we are faced with a difficult decision. We can make a man or a citizen, but we cannot make both at the same time. We have a choice, but not a choice of choices.

The tragic choice between making a man and a citizen is not a false dichotomy but is rather is forced on us by the incommensurability of human goods. This reading gains plausibility when we see that the choice between citizenship and cosmopolitanism is far from the only costly decision we must make in Rousseau's moral universe, which constantly confronts us with the tough reality that the enjoyment of one good precludes the enjoyment of others. There is doubtless a rhetorical component to Rousseau's presentations of moral conflict, which often lend seemingly cosmic significance to the everyday difficulties faced by everyday people. But the rather grandiose presentation he gives to familiar problems is not mere rhetorical posturing. Rousseau's intellectual career is marked by his tendency to point out value conflicts and his inability to accept cheap resolutions. Where others saw complementarity and continuity, Rousseau saw contradiction and incoherence in germinal form. It is therefore not surprising that in both the private and public contexts, Rousseau's moral exemplars are exemplary largely because of their willingness to face and resolve precisely the kinds of tragic choices the bourgeois spends his life avoiding.

In the private realm, Julie's example springs immediately to mind, for her personal fate—indeed, the fate of all her friends and intimates—turns on her decision to obey her father rather than wed St. Preux. Her life is defined by role conflict, by the choice she must make between being a good daughter and being a good lover. This choice, it is worth adding, has social—or if one likes, "political"—effects, for it ultimately determines the shape of the social structure at Clarens. Later in the novel she must decide between honoring her marital commitment to Wolmar and following her heart back to St. Preux. Though it is perhaps fair to wonder whether Julie is perhaps *too* willing to suffer, whether her eagerness on this head is as much a cautionary tale as an example to be imitated, there is no denying the intrinsic difficulty of her situation. She is caught in and crushed by the crosscutting demands of contradictory social obligations, defined and destroyed by her perpetual in-betweenness. However, she does not act as a *rien*. To the contrary, she is obedient to the logic of identity: she makes her choice and sticks to it in a "lofty" style. That her struggles are never rewarded with happiness is disconcerting but not fatal to the theory, for Rousseau's claim is that maintaining unity is a necessary but not a sufficient condition for attaining the happiness that is the end of human life.

Emile's example also points up the inevitable presence of value conflicts and the importance of decisively resolving them. After learning of Sophie's infidelity Emile, like Julie, is faced with a difficult choice. He is a cuckolded husband but also a father; thus he must decide whether to raise his child or leave his wife. To stay with Sophie is to demean himself, but to abandon his offspring is surely to do the same, as well as to neglect his paternal and civic obligations. Emile's obligations do not conflict as dramatically as Julie's, but neither are they immediately continuous with each other: what he owes his child as a father is care and concern, but what he owes his unfaithful spouse is, strictly speaking, nothing at all. The choice he makes—sneaking out in the middle of the night and abandoning his family—may fairly be questioned, but only after acknowledging that he, like Julie, must choose between two decidedly imperfect options. Being a something is hard.

Rousseau's domestic heroes are not the only figures who understand that the best and most human—that is, the most *unified*—life is full of conflicts that must be stared down. Indeed, the ideal of citizenship provides a very different principle for resolving the difficult choices social life forces on us. Of the many exemplars of classical citizenship that Rousseau wields in order to humiliate modern readers, perhaps none better points up the conflict between private and public attachments than that "tender father" Junius Brutus, who presided over the trial and execution of his own sons in order to save a fragile Roman Republic. Rousseau treats Brutus's example at some length in his *Final Reply* to the critics of the *First Discourse*, in which he enters into dialogue with a hypothetical interlocutor who confesses to admiring Brutus but would nonetheless "*admire even more a powerful and well-governed state*" where "*citizens would not be condemned to such cruel virtues*" (123).[5] The objection, important because characteristic of Rousseau's century, is that Brutus's sacrifice, however noble, was made necessary only by the

Romans' primitive political culture and inadequate understanding of institutional design. A "powerful and well-governed state" would have kept Brutus from having to make such a terrible choice in the first place. The modern interlocutor in effect denies the necessity of tragic tradeoffs; he believes it would have been possible to reason one's way out of Brutus's problem and that it would not have been prejudicial to civic virtue to do so. Freedom does not require the "cruel virtues," and it is only the ignorance of the ancients that led them to insist on their necessity.

Though Rousseau does not entirely disagree with the objection he has his interlocutor raise—the ancients *were* deficient in their understanding of political institutions—his initial response points up the inescapability of moral conflict and the necessity of Brutus's actions. For Rousseau it is "certain" the Republic would not have survived long had he pardoned his sons' crimes against the state, for such partiality would have created a very troublesome precedent and fatally undermined the idea of the rule of law. The structure of the social situation required that Brutus make a choice, and he made the choice most in keeping with his identity as a citizen. If being a good citizen is anything, it is putting the good of the polity before everything else and accepting the consequences, even and indeed especially when they are onerous. It is, then, wrong to simply assume with Rousseau's interlocutor that Brutus's public and private obligations could be reconciled: "There is no middle ground. Either Brutus had to be an infamous person or the heads of Titus and Tiberinus had to fall by his order to the axe of the Lictors" (123). There is no other way to slice it: Brutus had to choose between the death of the Republic and the death of his sons, and he made the choice most befitting a citizen.

Brutus's is not the only case in which profound love of state is accompanied by astounding hardness toward one's own offspring. In *Emile*, Rousseau relates from Plutarch the story of a Spartan woman who, upon being informed that her five sons were killed in war, ran to the temple to thank the gods for the military victory rather than collapsing in agony for the loss of her children. "This," he exclaims with evident relish, "is the female citizen" (40). Though this anonymous Spartan woman was not, like Brutus, forced by an external necessity to undertake active violence against her own progeny, note that Rousseau takes her willingness to suffer almost unthinkable personal losses on behalf of the state to be exemplary of citizenship *as such*. The conflicts that arise in our associational lives are inevitable, requiring some form of resolution, and what defines the citizen is a disposition to resolve them on behalf of the state. For citizens, the public good becomes internalized and serves as the unifying principle by which they organize moral and social life. The example of the anonymous Spartan woman is particularly telling when compared to Sophie, her modern counterpart and wife of the presumptive "man-citizen" Emile. Sophie, far from bearing the death of her offspring with such chilling aplomb, sinks into deep depression. Her response is that of a mother who loves her family more than anything else; the Spartan woman's response is that of a citizen who loves the state even more than her own children. If more evidence of the enormous psychological distance between "men" and "citizens" were needed, surely this example provides it.

This, however, is only half the argument. As even a casual reader of the *Social Contract* knows, Rousseau is not an unqualified admirer of the ancients nor does he simply demand that citizens sacrifice everything to the state without being compensated. Indeed, there are limits to human nature that good regimes are obliged to respect, and Rousseau would be among the first to censure a regime that exacted needless sacrifices from citizens or perpetuated itself at the expense of its inhabitants. Just societies acculturate citizens to the necessity of sacrificing for the common good, but they are organized to prevent the need for gratuitous privation: "[A] citizen owes the State all the services he can render it as soon as the sovereign requests them. But the sovereign, for its part, cannot impose on the subjects any burden that is useless to the community" (*SC* II.4, 62). Though even the best regime cannot eliminate all the sources of conflict and contradiction in human life—to suffer is our estate—it can at the very least be expected not to multiply them and, to the degree possible, be responsible for neutralizing them. So, while it is incumbent on the citizen to discharge his public obligations even when he finds them onerous, it is nonetheless true that such obedience is justified if and only if political institutions are basically consistent with the demands of human nature, rightly developed. All citizens have "duties . . . as subjects," but they are only obligated to fulfill them if the environment in which they are embedded is conformable to their nature (II.5, 62). Thus conceiving of the political problem in terms of "unity," far from authorizing states to exact limitless sacrifices from citizens, in fact provides a way of distinguishing between modes of social organization that create unnecessary burdens for citizens and those that do not.

Le Tout Est Bien: "A Complete Return to Political Unity"

Though Rousseau's account of dividedness is in many ways the center of his critique of modern political thought and the impoverished human type it brought into being, he is one with other modern thinkers in believing Christianity to be an important institutional cause of that dividedness. Rousseau was concerned that the "true religion" had destroyed the psychology necessary for political freedom by encouraging a disengaged political quietism, introducing profoundly destructive contradictions into social life by insisting on a division of spiritual and temporal powers. In addressing himself to the social friction caused by institutions answering to different authorities, Rousseau follows Machiavelli, Spinoza, Locke, and many others in seeking to weaken the political influence of the church. Yet he credits Hobbes with being the sole "Christian author" to see that the only way to solve the problem of divided allegiances is to grant to the sovereign final authority on *all* matters of fundamental import, including and especially those concerning religion. Thus he follows his bête noire in insisting that the union of church and state—or rather the subordination of church to state—is the indispensable condition of a much-needed "return to political unity" (*SC* IV.8, 127).

It is in this context that Levine (1976, 54) emphasizes Rousseau's debt to Hobbes, claiming that the Hobbesian thesis of "complete alienation" is "taken for granted" by Rousseau and that it is adopted in the *Social Contract* "virtually without argument." Yet the account of human dividedness provided above shows that Rousseau has his own theoretical reasons for emphasizing the theme of unity, reasons that, far from their being a product of an uncritical acceptance of Hobbes, are instead suggestive of a deep *dis*agreement with Hobbes's understanding of the social problem. If Rousseau not only disagrees with Hobbes about what "dividedness" means but also believes Hobbes's philosophy to be a primary *cause* of that dividedness, then it is highly unlikely that the kind of institutional unity he seeks will have much in common with Hobbes's theory. The unity Rousseau sought was far different, and far deeper, than that posited by Hobbes. It is therefore necessary to tunnel under Levine's claim and to articulate a more satisfying account of the theoretical features of unity.

On this head, I would like to suggest that the particular form of institutional unity Rousseau sought is best comprehended by way of naturalistic metaphor: an *ecology*. Ecosystems are self-sustaining and self-regulating environments in which all living beings are embedded, and the concept has recently been applied to social and political institutions in order to understand both how those institutions fit together as well as how their fit (or *lack* of fit) affects the individuals within the system (e.g., Bronfenbrenner 1979). Though unavailable to Rousseau—who uses the traditional metaphor of a "body politic" in order to talk about the interdependence of social systems—ecological systems theory provides at least three considerable advantages in seeking to understand Rousseau's political thought. The first is its emphasis on the idea of *embeddedness*. Individual subjects are conceived not as autonomous, free-floating units but rather as necessarily situated in a series of nested structures. Though such a conception may initially appear unpromising as a way of explaining a theory like Rousseau's, it helps reveal the way in which the subject's internal or psychological unity relies on the structure of the environment. Harmony within is predicated on harmony without. Second, an "ecological" interpretation allows us to attain a comprehensiveness of explanation that eludes many alternative approaches. While we shall be able to account for both Rousseau's philosophical and sociological commitments, we have already seen that other approaches tend to explain the one at the expense of the other. The "social autonomy" interpretation, for instance, provides a sophisticated analysis of Rousseau's philosophy of freedom but rejects as distasteful the political sociology attached to it; "totalitarian" readings, on the other hand, often focus so intently on the ugliest sociological particulars of Rousseau's theory that one forgets "liberty" was even of interest to Rousseau. Our approach, however, is able to account for both sides of the coin. Finally, the dynamic unity exemplified by ecological systems possesses three structural features—harmoniousness, comprehensiveness, and fragility—that are reflected in and help explain Rousseau's political thought. In what follows, I shall show how these three features map onto both the natural order depicted in the *Discourse on Inequality* and the social order envisioned in the *Social Contract*.

The unity of any system is manifested in the equilibrium it produces, and the equilibria that emerge within ecological systems have a *harmonious* character. This, of course, is not to say there is no conflict within the system but rather to say that the continued life of each species is predicated on the health of the system itself. An example may clarify. Let us assume a simply ecological system in which antelope (A) graze on grass (G) and lions (L) prey on antelope. These patterned interactions produce a system-level equilibrium that facilitates the continued life of all three species: (1) the presence of G contributes to the survival of A, (2) the presence of A contributes to the survival of L, and (3) the presence of L contributes to the survival of G by thinning out the population of A, thus allowing G to replenish. The web of interdependence linking these three life forms is far from frictionless, but it can nonetheless be broadly characterized as harmonious because the emergent ecological equilibrium preserves the continued life and development of all the organisms within it. The isolated particulars may be ugly, but *le tout est bien*.

Embeddedness in an environment ordered to be broadly conducive to the requirements of self-preservation is an essential element in Rousseau's argument for natural goodness. Indeed, though man in the state of nature is said to be good because his two most basic passions—self-love and pity—are organized in a salutary way, it is clear that this salutary organization owes much to the environment in which the passions express themselves. We see this with especial clarity in the *Discourse on Inequality*'s famous depiction of natural man, whom Rousseau sees "satisfying his hunger under an oak, quenching his thirst at the first stream, finding his bed at the foot of the same tree that furnished his meal; and therewith his needs are satisfied" (*DI* 105). The autarchic contentment described here is predicated on both psychological and environmental factors. The psychological claim is that human beings have very limited natural needs and that nothing could disturb the equilibrium between power and desire so long as food, shelter, protection, and sexual partners are sufficiently plentiful. But what if the environment in which we were embedded were less hospitable to us? What if food were scare? It is when the environment ceases to meet our natural needs that we begin to have to reflect on how to meet those needs ourselves (116). No longer able to thoughtlessly rely for our subsistence on our surroundings, we find it necessary to attempt to shape those surroundings in accordance with our needs. In so doing, however, we acquire *new* needs, and once this happens the spontaneous and prediscursive harmony between self and environment that characterized life in the pure state of nature is gone forever. When the environment changes, our passions follow.

This becomes still more clear once Rousseau sets himself to explaining why human beings would have ever left a condition so hospitable as the state of nature for one so deplorable as civil society. At a early but important juncture in Rousseau's account man finds himself back under a tree—perhaps the very one under which he had contentedly lived for so long—but suddenly finds it too tall to reach its fruit. The scarcity this new condition imposes—in conjunction with droughts, floods, and other natural disasters

Rousseau imagines to have been inevitable—brings natural man into competition with other animals and quickly teaches him the use of tools, which in turn produce in him "the first stirrings of pride" (*DI* 143–44). Man's environment, then, is decisive in determining both what passions he has and how they are able to express themselves. Thus the unity that characterizes his life in the state of nature owes as much to the broadly hospitable environment in which he is embedded as to his native disposition.

Though the type of dependence required by the civil association is "moral" as well as "physical," and is thus different from that which exists in an actual ecological system, citizens of the just regime must nonetheless be embedded in a harmonious and self-sustaining environment that allows for the preservation and extension of being. Good social institutions are like laws of nature insofar as they do not work at cross-purposes or embody uncombinable visions of the good, since to do so would be to disrupt the equilibrium of the moral and social environment and thus to undermine the health of those who exist within it. We have already glimpsed the importance Rousseau places on inducing through institutional design the harmony inherent in the state of nature—of rendering harmonious and hospitable the environment in which citizens act and interact—in his praise of Hobbes's effort to eliminate the conflict between church and state.

But church and state are not the only social institutions that must exist harmoniously, and if we wish to understand the harmony Rousseau sought for each citizen it is perhaps best to consider things from the citizen's point of view. In so doing we immediately see that citizens in the context of Rousseau's political project are sovereign-subjects, bearers of particular entitlements and obligations that attach to the "citizen" role. But the citizen is and must be more than that. He occupies other roles and serves other functions: in addition to being a citizen he is also a parent, a friend, a lover, a spouse, a churchgoer, a consumer, a producer, and so on. He is embedded in a complex of nested social structures. This is his inescapable condition. The problem that emerges from this multiplicity is that these structures are in an ongoing struggle for his scarce psychological and emotional resources, and when they make different and contradictory claims on his identity he falls into identity conflict and all the trappings of dividedness. In order to create a social environment in which psychic unity can be achieved and maintained, the citizen's various conflicting social obligations must be somehow reconciled. His needs are more numerous and more complex than are natural man's; their reconciliation is therefore a more difficult problem.

Second, Rousseauan social institutions mimic ecosystems in their *identity-constitutive* character. In ecosystems, the interdependence of one species on another, and of every species on the shared environment, is complete and comprehensive. Strict ecologists like Charles Darwin maintain that *everything* about the natures of living beings—their physical appearances, needs, habits, instincts, and drives—is ultimately explicable in terms of the physical environment in which they act and interact. While Rousseau at least seems to reject this radical view in his disavowal of the protoevolutionary notion that "man's elongated nails were at first hooked claws"— a thesis he rather strangely attributes to Aristotle—he is quite clear that the change in man's environment had produced fundamental changes in the nature of his being (*DI* 104).[6]

These changes, as every reader of Rousseau knows, had been ruinous, and the *Social Contract* is Rousseau's attempt to set things aright by specifying the social and moral conditions in which human beings can through self-conscious rational reflection recapture the harmony they had with the natural world. The Rousseauan citizen's dependence on the moral environment of the just regime mirrors the comprehensive dependence that living beings in an ecological system have on their physical environment: in order to be protected from the alienating and mutually destructive forms of personal dependence embodied by the bourgeois, the citizen must divest himself of all his natural rights and give his entire self to the political community as a whole. Indeed, the complete identification with and dependence on the state is underscored by Rousseau's description of the social compact, which involves "the *total* alienation of each associate, with *all* his rights, to the *whole* community." Only a *complete* divestiture of rights—a giving of one's "*entire* self"—will suffice, since "if some rights were left to private individuals, there would be no common superior who could judge between them and the public," and thus "the association would necessarily become tyrannical or ineffectual" (*SC* I.6, 53; emphasis added). Human identity is utterly transformed by the new moral and social environment in which it is embedded. The political subject must adapt to the logic of his new environment, and this adaptation requires a reconception of his fundamental interests and, hence, his basic identity.

The comprehensive dependence of the citizen on his environment is reflected again, and with especial clarity, in the *Social Contract* (II.4), where Rousseau treats the vexed question of the limits of sovereign power. In this chapter he stakes out a radicalized version of the Hobbesian view that the establishment of genuine sovereignty requires a divestiture of all the subject's rights, save the "right of nature," which allows subjects to resist in the event that they are sentenced to death (*Lev.* XIV, 79–80). The crucial point about the Hobbesian covenant is that no transformation of moral identity or fundamental reinterpretation of self-interest is required; contracting agents will seek within the context of the association the same goods they sought outside of it. Thus, because individuals consent to social order primarily in order to enhance the likelihood of preserving themselves, and because the sovereign can do nothing to make them divest themselves of this overriding natural imperative, they may fairly resist the sovereign if it seeks to destroy them. Even the "absolutist" Hobbes allows the political subject to carry into civil society a portion of his natural powers.

The reconciliation between self and society that Rousseau seeks is far deeper than that sought by Hobbes, and this is reflected in his insistence that a citizen may not reasonably resist the sovereign even when his individual preservation is threatened. Consenting to the terms of the social compact means handing control over everything—even a right as deeply particularized as that to self-preservation—to the sovereign: "When the prince has said to him, 'It is expedient to the State that you should die,' he ought to die. Because it is only under this condition that he has lived in safety up to that point, and because his life is no longer only a favor of nature, but a conditional gift of the State" (*SC* II.V, 64). Here as elsewhere, Rousseau has radicalized the already radical Hobbesian view: rather than follow Locke in expanding the set of rights that subjects bring with them into political life and thereby circumscribing the sphere of sovereign action, Rousseau responds to Hobbes by insisting even more sternly on the discontinuity of the natural and civil states and by requiring an even more complete divestiture of the contracting agent's natural powers. This utter divestiture is necessary because in order to harmonize man's relation to his environment, he must be fundamentally reshaped to exist entirely within and depend entirely on an environment for which he is not naturally suited. This harmonization requires an exchange of "natural freedom" for "civil freedom," which in its turn requires the "total alienation" of all one's natural rights and the attendant reorientation of the motivational field: politicized man is "forced to act upon other principles [than private desire] and to consult his reason before heeding his inclinations" (I.8, 55–56; I.6, 53). Thus are the moral identities and interests of citizens made and remade in the polity in the same way that the habits, drives, and instincts of living organisms are shaped by their ecological systems.

From a moral point of view, the citizen's identity is solely a function of his environment.

Finally, ecological equilibria—like so many of the goods Rousseau describes—are often characterized by their *fragility*. Though the emergent balance of forces in ecological systems have self-regulating and self-correcting mechanisms that can absorb some degree of disruption, they can be thrown into disequilibrium by even slight alterations. Scientists have, for instance, called attention to how the introduction of even a single non-native species into an ecosystem—for example, kudzu in the American South or Asian carp in the Mississippi River—can have drastic and destructive effects on the habitats of hundreds of other life forms and on the stability of the system as a whole (e.g., Hickman et al. 2010; Freedman, Butler, and Wahl 2012). What is more, the effects of these environmental disturbances are often irreversible; once done, they cannot be undone. We have in the previous chapters seen just how fragile human happiness is for Rousseau, how difficult it is to establish and maintain the delicate balance of environmental forces necessary for its realization. To see the significance of this in the present context we need only recall what Julie tells St. Preux when reflecting on their star-crossed relationship. "One strays for a single moment in life, deviates by a single step from the straight path," she tells her lover. "At once an ineluctable slope drags him down to his ruin" (*J* 291). The unanticipated consequences of even the most seemingly insignificant mistakes can have ruinous psychological and social consequences. Goodness and happiness are delicate; their enabling conditions are nearly impossible to create and even more difficult to sustain. This is evinced by the fact that even Wolmar and Jean-Jacques—the most authoritative remedial figures that could be imagined—had in their remedial endeavors only a partial and limited form of success.

The fragility of human things makes the presence of authoritative moral teachers as necessary in the political realm as in the domestic. Thus we should not be surprised to see Rousseau introduce Wolmar's and Jean-Jacques' political equivalent—the "Legislator"—who is charged with the task of creating a people by persuading them to accept good social institutions (*SC* II.7, 67–70). It is at present impossible to say whether his institutional creation will endure longer or meet with any more success than Wolmar's or Jean-Jacques' pedagogic projects, but the crucial role he plays at the founding points up the extreme delicacy of the social enterprise by revealing a people's incapacity to assemble and constitute itself. Rousseau took it for granted that common people were unable to independently fashion their own environment or provide the institutional conditions for their own happiness. He asked not whether a people may raise itself up through a process of organic historical development, but rather whether it was capable of operating with tolerable effectiveness the machine constructed by a beneficent wise man. The present purpose is not to answer the question so much as to show that we cannot answer it in a serious way without remembering Julie's warning about the tenuous position of virtue or Rousseau's belief in the fragility of even the best human institutions. This fragility is glimpsed yet again in Rousseau's formulation of the social compact, whose terms are "so completely determined by the nature of the act" of consenting to be governed that even "the slightest modification" would destabilize the civil association to the point of nullifying the original agreement (*SC* I.6, 53). Even the slightest deviation from the strictest terms of justice would seem to explode the entire social and political enterprise. Here and everywhere in Rousseau's moral universe, the margin for error is razor thin.

| Conclusions

Rousseauan man requires unity, and unity of a particular—and particularly deep—kind with his environment. Yet life in political society is necessarily something complex and differentiated; it forces us into roles that can and do conflict and, thereby, exerts a centrifugal, decentering effect on the human personality. Modern social institutions unnecessarily magnify this destructive tendency by imposing on men obligations that are not only different but *inconsistent*: by instantiating in the soul conflicts between public and private forms of life and between spiritual and temporal forms of power, modernity had put us at odds with ourselves and one another. So long as we live within an institutional order at odds with itself, we are doomed to dividedness and its aimless, disempowered drift. Rousseau seeks to correct this situation by organizing social institutions in such a way as to mimic the ordered harmony of the state of nature and, in so doing, to mitigate the destructive effects of the conflicts that characterize social life.

But what, practically speaking, does this solution look like? This preceding discussion has tried to identify the broad contours of the problem Rousseau seeks to solve through politics, but it has not given us a sense of *how* or *to what extent* Rousseau believed that problem could be resolved. We need, then, to look more closely at what life looks like in a Rousseauan regime, at how society's basic institutions ought to fit together and how living within a coherent institutional order empowers the human soul. After having done so, we will be in a better position to see whether the political path to wholeness is any more satisfactory than the domestic alternatives we have examined in previous chapters. If Rousseau is critical of modernity for imposing contradictory obligations on men, then his constructive alternative ought to prove successful where modernity failed. It is therefore necessary to look more closely at Rousseau's analysis of society's basic institutions and the way they ought to fit with one another.

8 | The Sociology of Wholeness

In the previous chapter we saw that social life is complex and comprehends multiple forms of obligation. We also saw that, in order to have the wholeness Rousseau seeks, these obligations must be in harmony with one another. Because this harmony cannot be expected to spontaneously emerge, it is the job of political institutions to create and sustain it. How and to what extent they do so is the subject of this chapter.

Among the structural social conflicts Rousseau diagnosed as damaging to human wholeness, he identified those obtaining among state, household, and church to be especially destructive and hence most in need of resolution. He believed this to be true because all three institutions make incommensurable claims on the identities of individuals and, taken together, create a social environment in which it is impossible to fulfill any of our obligations. We have, for instance, already seen that the model of the domestic society Rousseau develops in *Emile* and *Julie*, far from catalyzing citizenship, is instead developed at the cost of citizenship. Christianity, too, is ultimately inconsistent with the requirements of political freedom, both because it insists on the church being recognized as the state's equal and because it cultivates an ethos of passivity and meekness at odds with the proactive spirit of the republican citizen. These institutional conflicts reproduce themselves in the soul and are the root cause of the dividedness that both defines and destroys modern life. In order, then, to bring the citizen into a lasting harmony with himself and with others, these tensions must be resolved.

Setting out to create a social environment in which occasions for institutional and psychological conflict are minimized, Rousseau unifies all major social institutions and forms of association under the aegis of the *one* authority that is able to provide a basis for a legitimate and enduring union: the sovereign. A social union grounded on the doctrine of popular sovereignty gathers power in a single source—the people—and confers on it the authority to make authoritative and binding decrees about the basic terms of social cooperation. In its capacity as the sovereign, the people trumps the rights of fathers and of the church; it draws the boundaries between the private and public domains and is the court of final appeal. The claims that our private associations and beliefs make on our identities must therefore be consistent with the requirements of citizenship.

In arguing thus I shall show that Rousseau's solution to the problem of political unity is a kind of halfway point between the extreme collectivism of Socrates and the extreme individualism of Hobbes and Locke. Socrates, of course, seeks to resolve the political problems created by the existence of religion and the family by eliminating the private realm altogether and instituting a collectivistic program of civic education that unites all citizens through devotion to the common good. Hobbes and Locke, on the other hand, insist on the ineliminability of narrow selfishness and make it the basis for a politics of private acquisition. Rousseau rejects both the Socratic attempt to annihilate the private self and the Hobbesian effort to understand political life in terms of narrow private interest. He must chart a course between these two unacceptable alternatives and show that the claims of the individuated self can be accommodated without also being exaggerated.

Though this may sound reasonably uncontroversial as a characterization of Rousseau's political project, I believe that at least two contestable propositions follow from it. The first concerns the relationship of Rousseau's domestic theory and his political theory. If, as I will argue, the household's crucial function in the just regime is political socialization, it must differ fundamentally in its priorities and structure from the households depicted in *Emile* and *Julie*. Friendship, too, undergoes a kind of redefinition intended to cultivate good civic habits. These should hardly be unexpected results—since both love and friendship have been shown to be intrinsically unstable and generally ineffective as catalysts of civic identity—but they may nonetheless continue to meet with resistance from a number of quarters. The second regards the vexed question of Rousseau's relationship to Christianity. Though I shall not follow some interpreters in insisting on Rousseau's complete irreligiosity, I will argue that his analysis of civil religion in the *Social Contract* more than demonstrates his infidelity to some rather basic points of Christian doctrine.

In focusing primarily on public, domestic, and religious associations, I exclude others (e.g., economic relations) that are no less a part of the basic structure of society and about which Rousseau has much to say. However, the forms of association I have selected for analysis are both necessary to and sufficient for our limited purposes: they are necessary insofar as they are clearly central sources of human identity, and sufficient insofar as their reconciliation would provide the social conditions necessary for the preservation of psychological unity. In addition, though Rousseau clearly recognizes the importance of industry and material abundance (indeed, he praises Geneva for both) and is—despite some rhetorical posturing to the contrary—supportive of private property rights, he is also suspicious of commercial activity and does not view economic activity as directly contributory to the preservation of human wholeness. Thus, for the time being, it is enough to say that markets may operate freely in a Rousseauan society subject to the constraints imposed by those relations that *do* contribute directly to wholeness.

Public Assemblies and Citizen Identity

Rousseau does not believe that his much sought-after "complete return to political unity" could develop spontaneously, or that it could emerge as the unplanned result of self-interested behavior. Social equilibria are too fragile to entrust to an invisible hand. The harmonious coexistence of society's basic institutions requires a structural center that gives all social bodies specific shape and direction. This center is the locus of authority in any political society; it is the seat of power and the institutional core around which the other parts revolve. It provides citizens with the most fundamental principles they need for resolving conflicts both between and within themselves. Rousseau believes that the structural center of every political society is the office of *sovereignty*, and that society's other institutions must fulfill their distinct purposes in ways consistent with the sovereign's requirements. These "requirements" go beyond the demand for mere lawfulness, for though *all* political societies require that private aims be pursued within the constraints of law Rousseau demands further that the citizen's role as a sovereign/subject take psychological precedence over his other social roles and responsibilities. The political dimension of identity must have priority in the minds of citizens, and the institutional and sociological structures in which citizens are embedded must be supportive of that priority.

The first and most important of these structures is the public institution par excellence: the sovereign assembly. Rousseau emphasizes the identity-constitutive importance of public assemblies by electing to place his discussion of them in Book III's extended treatment of political decline and regeneration, where he seeks to identify those forces that may forestall or at least delay the inevitable death of the state. He begins his consideration of political stability by identifying the fundamental obstacle to it, namely, that the private wills acts "incessantly" (*sans cesse*) against the general will until the former extinguishes the latter (III.10, 96). States degenerate, Rousseau claims, either when the government shrinks (e.g., from an aristocracy to a monarchy) or when the sovereign authority is usurped, either by an individual or by a group (III.10, 97–98). This process of decline is described as "natural" and "inevitable" in the following chapter, but we are not told why this is so until Rousseau essays to show how the forces of degeneration might be combated. In these chapters (III.12–15, 99–104) he emphasizes the importance of "regular, periodical" popular assemblies that are established by law and that "nothing can abolish or postpone" (III.13, 100). Such assemblies stabilize just institutions in two ways. First, they establish a mechanism of accountability that tends to restrain the prince from usurping the sovereign authority. Popular assemblies "have always terrified" the established government because its continued existence is often at stake. The existence of such assemblies, then, encourages responsible governance by providing the government with predictable and powerful reminders that it is the sovereign's subordinate and will be unseated if it reaches beyond its trust. An agent accountable to its principal in this way is far less likely to attempt to usurp the sovereign power of lawmaking (III.14, 101).

Second, and for our purposes more important, popular assemblies provide powerful reminders of the people's sovereignty not only to overreaching magistrates but also to the *people itself*. After pointing to the concerns that incumbent governments have with the congress of whole peoples (*SC* III.14), Rousseau goes on to explain how assemblies reinforce the psychological salience of citizen identity as well as how the maintenance of that identity is necessary to social stability. He begins the chapter by drawing the connection between good citizens and good institutions: "As soon as public service ceases to be the main business of the citizens, and they prefer to serve with their pocketbooks rather than with their persons, the State is already close to ruin" (III.15, 101). He elaborates on this connection by explaining that the attentions of citizens in a well-constituted state must be attuned to public rather than private affairs: "The better constituted the State, the more public affairs dominate *the minds* of the citizens. There is even less private business, because since the sum of the common happiness furnishes a larger portion of each individual's happiness, the individual has less to seek through private efforts" (III.15, 102; emphasis added). In order for a good state to survive, then, individuals must think of themselves preeminently *as citizens* and have "public rather than private affairs" at the forefronts of their minds. The associational life conducive to the construction and the maintenance of citizen identity, and the self-conception that is its consequence, is correspondingly public and political. And though Rousseau believes it impossible to formulate precise rules about exactly how often such assemblies should be called, he is clear about their identity-constitutive function. The more we gather and associate as citizens qua citizens, the more likely it is that we will place a high subjective value on the fulfillment of our public obligations and that their discharge will inform our identity in meaningful ways. Neither commerce nor contemplation nor domestic life should furnish the "larger portion of each individual's happiness" in a just society, for good citizens live for and through one another more than for themselves. No citizen of the just regime should join Emile in saying "Give me Sophie and my field, and I shall be rich" (*E* 457). Rather, the opportunities they have to gather as equal citizens and act in a legislative capacity are those for which citizens qua citizens live. When the people gathers in its specifically legislative capacity, the psychological effect on each citizen ought to be profound. All should be reminded of the salience of public affairs, of the importance of subordinating the *moi particulière* to the *moi commun*. The legislative assembly, then, is not important only because it enables an institutionalized expression of a people's corporate will but also because it is an agent of political socialization and a catalyst of citizen identity. It, above all, maintains a people *as* a people.

It is, of course, not the mere fact but also the *purpose* of the people's congress that sustains political identity in the appropriate mode, for it is easy to imagine a people assembled under circumstances Rousseau would find distasteful (e.g., under Mussolini's balcony). It is essential that such assemblies reinforce each citizen's idea of himself as a free and equal participant in the lawmaking process. The condition of political equality deserves special emphasis in this connection, both because it is the defining feature of Rousseau's social compact and because the structure of the assemblies themselves provide much-needed reminders to citizens of their equal moral worth. On this head, Rousseau concludes Book I by emphasizing how important the equal distribution of rights and obligations is in any healthy society, claiming that the substitution of "a moral and legitimate equality for . . . physical inequality" that makes all citizens "equal through convention and right" is so crucial that it "ought to serve as the basis for the whole social system" (*SC* I.9, 58). By giving to each citizen the same rights and obligations, by making no one demand of another what he would not do himself, Rousseau makes mutual respect the condition of self-respect.

Equality is the essence of the social compact because it connects the individual citizen's pride to political participation without inspiring in him the tyrannical ambitions and delusions of grandeur to which malignant *amour-propre* is so susceptible. All civil-social men have a fundamental interest in attaining rewarding forms of social recognition, and the political process in a Rousseauan republic gratifies this wish by indicating at every point the equal importance of all citizens. In formal public assemblies, for instance, each may justly feel he is a part (indeed, an *important* part) of a grand spectacle—so important, in fact, that if he and he *alone* is excluded from public deliberations then the results of those deliberations are not general and therefore illegitimate (*SC* II.4, 62). Each, then, becomes indispensable without becoming more important than anyone else.

This rather extreme case not only illustrates how an institutional commitment to equality can reinforce one's own sense of importance and power, but also how each citizen's sense of self-worth is predicated on and hence constrained by his profound dependence on the social body. This is important for two reasons. First, it tightens the identification between the citizen and his regime, for one is far more likely to be civic-spirited where political practices affirm his dignity by giving him equal voice. Maintaining the closeness of this identification, as we have already seen, is absolutely essential to Rousseau's political program. Second, the institution of political equality contributes to social stability by discouraging the onset of malignant forms of *amour-propre*. On this head, it is important to remember that citizens ennoble and are in turn ennobled by their roles *as* citizens, as members of an egalitarian brotherhood. And because one's sense of self-worth is so closely tied to the discharge of civic duty, the individual and collective good tend to converge. Those, however, who choose to follow the misguided path of malignant *amour-propre* and seek preeminence over others also choose to leave that social position from which one's dignity and moral standing derive. That form of self-destructive striving, far from winning approbation, will instead be frowned on and, in extreme cases (e.g., an aspiring tyrant), will be punishable by law. An egalitarian social compact thus stimulates *amour-propre* by making the discharge of civic duty a point of personal pride, but it also delimits some of the problems to which this problematic passion gives rise by encouraging citizens to view the state as the source of their equality and hence of their dignity. To attack the social body is to attack the ground of one's own worth.

Private Lives, Public Ends: Friends and Factions in Rousseau's Geneva

Given Rousseau's strong emphasis on the importance of constructing a robust sense of patriotism, it is hardly surprising to see him emphasize the identity-constitutive effects of legislative assemblies or other specifically civic gatherings. However, he knows that the associational life in a political community is complex and multidimensional. Citizens act and interact in subpolitical as well as political capacities, and such associations have a unique pull on our hearts. Indeed, it is precisely this tendency that is so concerning from the "the political point of view," for since time and emotional resources are scarce, devotion to one's family and friends often comes at the expense of devotion to the common good. If the particularistic concern for one's own takes regular priority over the general concern for the good of the social whole, Rousseau's moral ecology collapses. He must therefore find a way to resolve the tension between the devotion to the common good that public life requires with the particularistic attachments that private desire necessarily seeks.

In the *Social Contract* this problem manifests itself most clearly at II.3, which treats the question of whether the general will could err in its pronouncements regarding a political community's common good. In seeking to determine the conditions under which citizens might correctly identify the common good, Rousseau notes the singularly corrupting influence of "partial societies," which lead us to identify our fundamental interests with subpolitical groups (our "particular wills") rather than with the political society as a whole:

> But when factions, partial associations formed at the expense of the whole, are formed, the will of each of these associations becomes general with reference to its members and particular with reference to the State. One can say, then, that there are no longer as many voters as there are men, but merely as many as there are associations. The differences become less numerous and produce a result that is less general. Finally, when one of these associations is so big that it prevails over all the others, the result is no longer a sum of small differences, but a single difference. Then there is no longer a general will, and the opinion that prevails is merely a private opinion. In order for the general will to be well expressed, it is therefore important that there be no partial society in the State, and that each citizen give only his own opinion. (II.3, 61)

This passage speaks to many but says different things to each. Plamenatz (see Gildin 1983, 55) simply finds it incomprehensible; Parry (1995) sees its emphasis on "expressing one's own opinion" as evidence of a commitment to a form of autonomy; Crocker (1995) interprets its suspicion of private groups as a manifestation of Rousseau's authoritarian tendencies; Grofman and Feld (1988) view its misgivings about reducing the number of voters as sufficient to support a proto-Condorcetian reading.

This last interpretation is of particular interest, for it draws on Condorcet's "jury theorem" in order to identify the conditions under which the general will and the will of a legislative majority might coincide.[1] Condorcet demonstrated that, under the right circumstances, the likelihood of a majority opinion being correct increases as a function of the number of voters. What is more, according to Grofman and Feld (1988, 570), these arguments were known to Rousseau: "It seems virtually certain that ideas similar to those later to be formally developed by Condorcet were 'in the wind,' and influenced both Rousseau and, later, Condorcet." If a large pool of voters is more likely to make correct judgments than a small one is, Grofman and Feld reason, then Rousseau could well be concerned about "partial societies" because their emergence shrinks the number of voters and, thereby, decreases the likelihood that the will of the majority will be expressive the true general will: "As the *effective* size of the assembly is reduced—because people vote as a herd (part of a faction) and not as separately thinking and independently acting individuals—the Condorcet jury theorem tells us that group accuracy will be reduced" (571). Grofman and Feld's reading of Rousseau's analysis of "partial societies" thus seems to capture at least part of what is at issue in this puzzling passage.

Though the Condorcetian interpretation helpfully shows that the emergence of bloc voting drives down average voter competence by decreasing the number of voters, it fails to explain the emergence of bloc voting itself. Why would citizens be disposed to make political decisions based on their subpolitical group affiliations in the first place? One explanation is that—due to a host of psychological, pedagogic, and institutional factors—citizens identify more closely with their private affiliations than with the public good. Though Grofman and Feld are far from denying this possibility, it is clear that once we explicitly acknowledge its plausibility, the nature of the problem posed by partial societies changes from one about sustaining a sufficiently large pool of voters into one about identifying the cultural and institutional catalysts of citizen identity. If civic competence varies primarily as a function of individual citizens caring enough about public affairs to inform themselves about issues and participate in public assemblies, then the emergence of partial societies is alarming not simply because they reduce the effective size of the sovereign assembly but also because they cultivate in citizens attitudes and priorities that are inconsistent with the requirements of civic life. Without denying the usefulness of the Condorcetian interpretation of the *Social Contract*, then, we must remember both that there are many other determinants of civic competence beside the sheer number of voters and that Rousseau devoted far more time to discussing these other determinants than to formal probabilistic analysis.[2]

Indeed, when we read the passage concerning "partial associations" in light of others from the *Social Contract* it becomes clear that Rousseau dislikes the mediation of private groups between individual and state not simply because it decreases the effective size of the assembly but also because it substitutes a narrow and particularizing form of self-love—the *moi particulière*—for the appropriately generalized and expanded *moi commun*. We see this more traditional republican concern at work particularly in Book III's treatment of political decline and regeneration, where Rousseau again discusses the obstacles impeding the effective expression of the general will. Here, however, his concern is not the sheer number of voters but rather that citizens give their personal interests priority over public affairs: when social conditions have reached a point when it is predictable "that the general will won't predominate," the reason given for this decline is that "domestic concerns absorb everything" rather than because the pool of voters has shrunk. Rousseau goes on to claim that good regimes depend decisively on citizens having politically centered self-conceptions, on their tendency to think of themselves first and foremost as citizens: "The better constituted the State, the more public affairs dominate the minds of citizens. There is even less private business because since the sum of common happiness furnishes a larger portion of each individual's happiness, the individual has less to seek through private efforts. In a well-run City, everyone rushes to assemblies" (*SC* III.15, 102). In a good regime men can and do have both private and public obligations, but are disposed to view their public obligations as having priority. The role of citizen is and must be central to the self-conceptions of the inhabitants of a free regime.

Against this backdrop we gain a fuller sense of Rousseau's concern about "partial societies" than the Condorcetian reading allows, for we see that the existence of factions prevents the expression of the general will not only because they shrink the pool of voters but also (and primarily) because they undermine the citizen-centered self-conceptions necessary to civic life. Those who cast votes on the basis of their private group affiliations do so because they view those affiliations as more rewarding and more central to their self-concepts than they do political life, because their identity interest in being a "citizen"—in being the kind of person who cares preeminently about the good of the city—contradicts the private identity interest they have in representing the corporate wills of their respective "partial societies." The problem posed by factions, then, is more psychological than aggregative. They erode civic competence by eroding citizen identity.

Rousseau's solution to this problem is a kind of halfway point between the radical collectivism of Socrates and the radical individualism of Hobbes. Like Socrates, Rousseau denies that narrow self-love can solve the political problems it creates and thus affirms the necessity of a robust, deindividualizing form of civic education. Like Hobbes, however, Rousseau makes (a certain form of) self-love the basis of the political association and rejects as both unrealistic and undesirable Socrates's proscription of the private realm. He neither annihilates the domain of particularity nor gives it complete priority. Instead, he recruits that domain and the associations within it into the process of citizen identity formation, arguing that properly structured private associations can catalyze connection to the regime by instilling in citizens affective habits that facilitate mutual respect and fraternity.

This may sound somewhat surprising since I have heretofore emphasized the discontinuities between the domestic and political realms, but it is important to add that the isolated households depicted in *Emile* and *Julie* are patently not the ones Rousseau has in mind when he identifies the domicile as a site of politicization. Those households, as was argued in chapters 4 and 5, remain largely independent from the tumults of the public world and do not generate the habits of mind appropriate to good citizenship. We need, then, a fully politicized conception of the household and the private realm. Rousseau's attempt to flesh out the private lives of good citizens is seen less in *Emile* or *Julie* than in *Letter to D'Alembert*, in which the great Genevan seeks to protect his fatherland from the scourge of the theater. Rousseau's *Letter* gives the most detailed picture of the kind of social life appropriate to a good political society and, in so doing, fills in many of the sociological details that the *Social Contract* can and must leave out. What we find there are models of marriage and friendship very different from those we examined in earlier chapters. They are different insofar as they are not direct instantiations of the human good but are instead provisional and preparatory—they ready men for the good of citizenship and for the particular kind of social connectedness that good requires.

Unsurprisingly, Rousseau emphasizes the civic unity of Genevan society, and chief among the intentions of the *Letter* is to show how the introduction of the theater will upset the complex and fragile equilibrium on which that unity is based. In arguing that the introduction of the theater is inappropriate for his homeland, Rousseau claims that the act of joint observation is intrinsically divisive and that sharing the shared spectacle of a play does not unite but rather separates viewers from one another. Rousseau's highly interesting discussion of the effects of drama on the emotions acknowledges that the theater inevitably stirs in the audience feelings that in other circumstances might catalyze social togetherness, but it also claims that theatergoers are led to a consideration of their *own* troubles rather than those of others. Far, then, from being led by sympathetic feelings to the actual *practice* of beneficence, they instead leave the play feeling self-satisfied and emotionally exhausted.

The theater, Rousseau explains by interrogating the emotional responses of a hypothetical theatergoer, indulges our cheapest moral instincts: "Is he not satisfied with himself? Does he not applaud his fine soul? Has he not acquitted himself of all that owes to virtue by the homage he has just rendered it? What more could one want of him? That he practice it himself? He has no role to play; he is no actor" (*LD* 25). The theater does not catalyze virtue but rather encourages moral escape; like the philosophers who love the Tartars in order to ignore his neighbors, we weep over the ills of fictional characters so that we may forget the unfortunate who surround us in real life. The "fleeting and vain" form of pity produced by the drama thus fails to generate virtuous action, but it also encourages a type of isolating inwardness that is anathema to a good republic. Disunited by the dramatic spectacle, citizens turn inward after seeing depicted before the world the conflicts they feel within themselves. The result for self-loving beings is predictable: they learn to pity themselves rather than to assist their fellows. Thus, those who come together to share in theatrical performances will leave all the more divided, for though each "loves virtue" as it is presented in the drama, so, too, is it loved for the least virtuous of reasons: "He wants none of [virtue] for himself because it would be costly to him. What then does he go to see at the theater? Precisely what he wants to find everywhere: lessons of virtue for the public, from which he excepts himself, and people sacrificing everything to their duty while nothing is exacted from him" (24). We scrupulously fail to practice all the virtues we preach. In observing actors we become them, and all the destructive internal and external conflicts characteristic of modernity attend this fateful development. And thus does the argument from virtue collapse: the theater does not contribute to good public morality but rather destroys it by encouraging each citizen to view himself as separate from and more unfortunate than his fellows.

Though observing spectacles inspires neither virtue nor unity, citizens of a good regime may cultivate both by *enacting* them. Republican performances catalyze citizen identity, and thereby allay the conflicts between the public and private world, far more effectively than does the cold isolation of a dark theater. Indeed, Rousseau concludes his *Letter* by recommending that Geneva eschew the theater in favor of public festivals, games, and events that would feature the citizens themselves. He makes the civic usefulness of such spectacles clear from the outset: "What! Ought there to be no entertainments in a republic? On the contrary, there ought to be many. It is in republics that they were born, it is in their bosom that they are seen to flourish with a truly festive air. To what peoples is it more fitting to assemble often and form among themselves sweet bonds of pleasure and joy than to those who have so many reasons to like one another remain forever united?" (*LD* 125). Republics above all regimes require shared diversions, for common pleasures help to forge the thick civic ties necessary to sustain political freedom. The politicized and politicizing character of republican divertissements becomes more explicit in the following paragraph, where Rousseau argues that theaters are unnecessary in a city where citizens are free to "plant a stake crowned with flowers in the middle of the square" and enjoy an impromptu festival. The happy result, in direct contrast to the isolation of the theater, is that "each sees and loves himself in the others so that all will be better united" (126). Here as elsewhere the model is Sparta, for it was there "that the citizens, *constantly assembled*, consecrated the whole of life to amusements which were the great business of the state and to games from which they relaxed only for war" (133; emphasis added). Formal legislative assemblies are, then, not the only way that citizens qua citizens may gather. Indeed, it would seem that citizen identity is constituted best when citizens themselves do not realize that their identities are being constituted.

Rousseau does not stop at public games and festivals in his attempt to mold sub-political associations in a way that reinforces the salience of citizen identity. He also brings friendship into accord with the demands of civic life by vigorously defending "the circles" (*cercles*)—informal social groups with no explicitly political aims or ends—from critics both within and outside of Geneva. These nominally private associations, though perhaps not friendships in the specific, technical sense which we gave the term in chapter 6, nonetheless surely qualify as friendships in the broad sense, for membership in a *cercle* allows men to enjoy intimate association through the shared activities and values of the group. That some of these activities (e.g., drinking and gambling) are rather unsavory is of less concern to Rousseau than the crucial identity-constitutive function these institutions serve. The *cercles* are a bulwark against the destructive "revolution in morals [*moeurs*]" that the establishment of a theater would bring about in a "simple and innocent" republic like Geneva, for they shape the associational life of citizens in ways that reinforce the public dimension of identity (*LD* 100).

Rousseau begins his account of the political importance of the *cercles* by announcing that he is writing to a new audience: rather than address D'Alembert and other "philosophers"—whose interests are not implicated—he directly addresses "the people" *as* the people, for it is the entire civic way of life that is at stake in this discussion (*LD* 100). Despite their undesirable consequences, the *cercles* ought to be preserved because they have two related sociological effects that help preserve the civic identity of Genevans. The first benefit is negative: by separating men and women into different social groups the *cercles* prevent a too-frequent intermingling of the sexes, which in its turn would lead to an increase in adulterous practices and would make men too soft to fulfill their martial duties (100–104). Though inter-gender social mixing is perfectly appropriate for, even necessary to, the gentle domestic societies of Clarens or Emile and Sophie's farmhouse, it is entirely unsuitable for a free republic that needs men to be citizen-soldiers. Such men cannot be what they must be if they are constantly among women, whose company softens and intoxicates. The *cercles* are therefore an excellent republican substitute for the delicate social charms of private retreat, for through them men can enjoy meaningful social companionship but in a way that reinforces rather than undermines their civic identity. The good republic is and must be gendered, and the *cercles*' segregation of men and women both protects conjugal fidelity and prevents male citizen-soldiers from acquiring a politically destructive "feminine" softness.

The *cercles* do more than prevent the onset of social evils. Indeed, they remind both men and women of their respective social roles and thus help to reinforce the connection between personal identity and politics. On this score, Rousseau notes that the *cercles* have a largely political origin: they grew out of the celebrations that followed military festivals and drilling exercises and were purified by "civil discords" that led their members out of raucous taverns and into places more suited to reasoned discussion of public affairs (*LD* 99). It is, he says, in the *cercles* as much as the agora that members learned not only how to fulfill their civic duties but also how to be the kinds of people who care about such duties in the first place: "These decent and innocent institutions combine everything which can contribute to making friends, citizens, and soldiers out of the same men, and, in consequence, everything which is most appropriate for a free people" (105). Thus the *cercles*, though nominally private associations, nonetheless turn individuals toward their role as citizens and reinforce the salience of that role. They have been recruited into the process of citizen-craft.

With this in mind, it is easy to see that the *cercles* Rousseau celebrates in the *Letter to D'Alembert* are not the kind of private groups that would be disallowed even under ideal conditions, as they do not narrow the boundaries of the self or invite the kind of identity confusion that such narrowing inevitably involves. Indeed, they reinforce rather than weaken the subjective importance of public affairs by providing reminders of the state's unifying power even in the context of our private associational life. The members of *cercles* are not defined by their association with that group; to the contrary, both the individual member and the private group to which he belongs are defined in important ways by their integration into the larger political community.

Though the *cercles* institutionalize friendship in a civically salutary way, perhaps the more serious threat to citizen identity is the household. And since Rousseau rejects the Socratic attempt to eliminate the nuclear family, he must provide a model of the household suitable for his political society. We have already seen, of course, that the models of the family life developed in *Emile* and *Julie* are inappropriate to a good political society for at least two reasons. First, they both prove entirely too unstable to serve as a basis for a sound political project. Second, they shape the identities of their inhabitants in ways that are inconsistent with the requirements of civic life. Therefore we need an alternative conception of the family, one that more effectively catalyzes good civic habits and dispositions.

Rousseau provides at least the beginnings of such a conception in the *Letter*, which through the proposal of a series of dances and balls for persons of marrying age specifies the conditions under which properly politicized family life is best inaugurated. These dances introduce young men and women to one another and to the mysteries of sexual experience, and do so in a way that politicizes the sexual relationship from the outset. Before descending into the particulars of Rousseau's account of these balls, however, it is important to recall the extreme importance he places on the earliest stages of a romantic relationship: *Emile* teaches the circumstances under which young people are introduced have "distant effects whose links are not perceived in the progress of the years but do not cease to act until death" (415). We saw in chapter 4 how the specific circumstances under which Emile and Sophie met foretold their tragic end. Rousseau himself, then, gives us especially good reason to look closely at the conditions in which civically salutary marriages are inaugurated, for he has already told us that these conditions have a disproportionate impact on the development of a relationship.

With this in mind, it is clear that Rousseau has the preservation of republican freedom in mind while recommending these balls. The institution of state-sponsored dances, he holds, would forestall political corruption by combating economic inequality and would give an important assist to public festivals and legislative assemblies in the constitution of citizen identity. This argument is predicated on the assumption that they would be open to *all* marriageable young people, and on the belief that exposure to more suitors than parents might permit would allow young people to follow the dispositions of their hearts rather than the directives of their parents. Left to mingle freely with one another, Geneva's next generation of citizens would form attachments which their fathers—often more concerned about dowries than compatibility—could never have envisaged. Whereas arranged marriages tend to centralize economic and political influence in ways that vitiate political liberty, voluntary unions strengthen republican values: young people, Rousseau reasons, will consult their moral tastes rather than their pocketbooks, and thus would tend to form unions "less circumscribed by rank." Chosen attachments are also said to "prevent the emergence of parties, temper excessive inequality, and maintain the body of the people better in the spirit of its constitution" (*LD* 131). Here, and here alone, the marriages of citizens resemble that of Emile and Sophie, for in both cases Rousseau makes the union voluntary. Political freedom is inaugurated through the choice of a spouse.

In arguing thus, Rousseau departs from rather than reiterates the conventional wisdom of his homeland, for many Genevans believed the dances Rousseau recommended would undermine the authority of fathers and give public sanction to the untoward desires of youth. Rousseau, however, answers that there is nothing untoward about sexual desire itself, and he adds that it becomes socially dangerous only when consigned to the private realm. The political recognition of emergent sexual desire does not corrupt society; rather, it purifies sexuality. It does so by transforming that most intimately private of things into a social performance, a republican spectacle that, well executed, would serve as "an important component of the training in law and order and good morals" (*LD* 130). Rousseau's mise-en-scène is striking: young people dance under the proud and watchful gaze of their parents, with parent and child alike watched from above by Geneva's oldest and most distinguished citizens, who are to be saluted by all those entering or exiting the hall. Of all the things that might be said about the observational situation and its effects on the nascent *amour-propre* of the dancers, perhaps the most important is the way in which the grand and gallant setting reinforces and even helps to constitute the political identities of the young. It is easy to imagine the effect of Rousseau's proposed surroundings on the anxious young dancers, whose first tentative steps in the sexual realm are made under the gaze not only of parents but also of the city's great citizens. And it should be noted that it is in a specifically *political* capacity that the elders seated in the panoptic spectators' box preside over the ball. It is thus in a politically charged atmosphere, with reminders of the homeland everywhere, that young people experience their sexual awakening.

It is tempting to say that these events are structured to make young people think of everything *but* the inclinations of their own hearts, and that, though many may leave the dance without romantic prospects, no one will go home without a fatherland. But we may certainly say that the household to be created through marriage, far from the independent retreat sought by Emile and Sophie, is from its very inception thoroughly political and politicized. Its primary function is not to instantiate the human good, for this would make the household a rival to the state and turn it into a "partial society," but rather to serve the state—much as Roman households did—through the production of virtuous citizens. The household in a just or approximately just political community cannot itself embody the good; it must *orient* young citizens toward the good to be found in the public realm.

| Religion and Social Unity

The *Letter to D'Alembert* seeks to show that the theater is a poor fit within the institutional and social framework of Genevan society, for drama requires taste that Geneva does not have and undermines the virtue that it needs. Yet, in the thorough analysis of Genevan social life that occupies him for a full third of the work, Rousseau devotes very little attention to the role of specifically religious customs and practices. He does not provide the vivid portraits of religious ceremonies that he does of state-sponsored dances and festivals, and he chooses to not discuss directly the civic effects of state-sponsored Calvinism. Thus we are left to wonder whether Genevan freedom flourishes because or in spite of its official religious doctrine.

What Rousseau *does* say about religion in the *Letter* redoubles rather than resolves this ambiguity, for though he thinks the question of the relationship of religion to politics so important that he begins the work by addressing it, what he says raises more questions than it answers. Before addressing the merits of D'Alembert's case for the institution of a theater Rousseau finds it necessary to correct his adversary's claim that many of Geneva's religious ministers privately profess Socinianism. Reminding D'Alembert that to attribute to civil authorities a belief in an officially condemned albeit intellectually serious doctrine is quite literally to damn through faint praise, Rousseau takes the posture of a traditionalist pushing back against the foolish indiscretions of a book-learned outsider: he claims to "not know what [Socinianism] is," that he has a "disinclination" for what he does understand of it, and that he has nothing but "love and respect" for the revealed truth of the Gospel (*LD* 11–13). In arguing thus he allies himself with religious conservative opposition to the theater and indicates that the city's traditional Calvinism needs no help from some newfangled natural religion to sustain Genevan freedom.

But this is hardly Rousseau's last word on the matter, for though respectful of Geneva's religious authorities and careful not to put heretical dogmas in their mouths he makes pronouncements in his own voice radical enough to suggest he may be further away from his homeland's official religion than from D'Alembert. For instance, he steadfastly declines to follow Geneva's church fathers in condemning the Socinian dogma, denies that reason can justify belief in an afterlife or in extra-temporal consequences, and—though claiming to "love and respect" holy scripture—refuses to affirm its inerrancy. After confessing so much he is understandably eager to drop the topic of religion altogether, and he does so satisfied he has said "nothing in general that is not honorable to the church of Geneva and useful to men in all lands" (*LD* n. 14).

Much more might be said about Rousseau's extraordinary caginess in the first section of the *Letter*, but for our purposes it suffices to show that the analysis there is far from the philosopher's last word on the question of the relationship of religion and politics. To the contrary, the topic figured prominently into the most important works he wrote afterward and is related directly to his analysis of modern man's dividedness. *Emile* somewhat surreptitiously implicates Christianity in this analysis by claiming that political freedom and the unifying "public education" necessary to it are no longer possible in modern times: "Public instruction no longer exists and can no longer exist, because where there is no longer fatherland, there can no longer be citizens. These two words, *fatherland* and *citizen*, should be effaced from modern languages. I know well the reason why this is so, but I do not want to tell it. It has nothing to do with my subject" (*E* 40). Because Emile's own education bears little resemblance to that of the "citizen" there is a limited sense in which a full treatment of public education has "nothing to do" with the specifics of the prescriptive agenda of *Emile*. However, to the degree that the anonymous force that had crushed the possibility of civic education had also helped create the world in which fragmented modern man and his "laughable" education emerged, then it is far from irrelevant to Rousseau's broader philosophic enterprise to disclose "the reason" why the language of citizenship is no longer understood (40).

Rousseau's refusal to name the enemy is itself a fairly strong hint about what it is. In a footnote to his translation of *Emile*, Allan Bloom directs the reader to chapter 8 of Book IV of the *Social Contract*, believing that it identifies the cause *Emile* demurely elects not to name: Christianity. And indeed, Rousseau argues there that Christianity has divided man's allegiances between heaven and earth in a way that undermined human relations both within and between political communities: the separation of "the theological system and the political system" brought about "the end of the Unity of the State, and caused internal divisions that have never ceased to stir up Christian peoples" (*SC* IV.8, 126). It is, of course, not obvious that Rousseau blames Christianity per se for the disunity and unsociability characteristic of modern regimes, for he distinguishes between "the religion of man"—which he associates with the religion of the Gospel or Christianity rightly understood—and "the religion of the priest," which gives men "two legislative systems, two leaders, and two homelands" and thus "subjects them to contradictory duties" and obligations. Where the former "is the pure and simple religion of the Gospel" that is "devoted to the eternal duties of morality," the latter is "a mixed and unsocial" doctrine that "is so manifestly bad that it is a waste of time to amuse oneself by proving it" (IV.8, 127–28). Thus Rousseau, like his republican predecessor Machiavelli, distinguishes between Christianity and its institutionalized expression, seeming to blame the latter for its grotesque interpretation of the former.

Also like Machiavelli, however, Rousseau makes a distinction between Christianity and "the priests" only in order to drain it of any real significance. After calling the Christianity of the Gospel "saintly" and "true religion," he goes on to analyze it from a "political point of view" and finds that it does not have the salutary civil effects so many attribute to it.[3] Viewed from the appropriate perspective, one sees that Christianity fails to catalyze allegiance to the political regime, for it has "no particular relation to the body politic" and thus "leaves laws only with their intrinsic force, without adding any force to them." Because the true church neither derives its authority from the state nor relies on state power for enforcement of its commands, it is unable to affect the content of the laws or directly motivate citizens to love and endorse them. It would seem, then, that the neutrality of the church with respect to the polis is guaranteed by its institutional independence from it and that Christianity in its purest form has a null effect on the political identities of citizens.

This alone would be sufficient for Rousseau to reject the Christian teaching concerning the relation of church and state, since any religion that does not actively aid in cultivating civic virtue is failing in its essential function, but Rousseau goes a good deal further. In fact, the apparently null effect created by an institutional separation of church and state undermines the sovereign's authority in precisely the same way that the pernicious "religion of the priests" does, for its very insistence on institutional autonomy is the functional equivalent of refusing to cede its spiritual authority to the sovereign. This refusal is enough to make Christianity unworkable as a civil religion, for in seeking to establish its own independent domain of authority within a political community that must be absolute in order to be anything at all, it necessarily sets itself up in opposition to the political community: to allow the kind of independence sought by the Christian church is to restrict the sovereign's ability to act within its rightful sphere. The church becomes, in Locke's phrase, a kind of "foreign Jurisdiction" within a political community that undermines sovereignty by claiming to be exempt from it (*LCT* 52).[4] If the church may claim in the name of God an exemption from political authority, what would prevent any private person from doing the same?

Though no genuine sovereign could countenance the introduction of any independent "spiritual" authority into the political community, Rousseau insists with astonishing explicitness that the substantive specifics of Christian doctrine make it a peculiarly destructive social force in a republic. All religions make claims on the moral identities of believers, and Christianity is no exception. However, Rousseau makes clear that the individualistic and transcendental vision of the good expressed in the Gospel is discontinuous with the civic sociability required by a free way of life. Indeed, he charges that "far from attaching the citizens' hearts to the State, [Christianity] detaches them from it as from all worldly things. I know of nothing more contrary to the social spirit" (*SC* IV.8, 128). The ultimate effect of Christianity on civic engagement is thus not null—as Rousseau initially suggested—but *negative*. Its otherworldliness makes it politically pernicious, for it creates a psychology of quietistic disengagement that is simply inconsistent with "the social spirit" of republicanism. The indifferent obedience the good Christian owes to the regime in which he happens to live cannot be combined with the enthusiastic partiality the citizen qua citizen has for his *patrie*. Christianity thus not only claims to be exempt from sovereign control but also introduces into the republic a particular conception of the good that is harmful to its continued preservation. So, too, does it sap civic engagement by orienting the identities of citizens away from the polis and toward individual salvation. In its political effects, then, there is no meaningful difference between "the religion of the priests" and "true" Christianity. Both necessarily divide the allegiances of citizens and create all the social and psychological disorders that attach to that dividedness.

Rousseau's concern with Christianity's effect on "the social spirit" is telling, for the unfitness of the religion of man as a civil creed stems not only from its tendency to divide the moral allegiances of citizens but also because of its contemplative and unsocial nature. Indeed, Rousseau believes that the transcendental individualism of Christianity militates against the thick social unity needed in a republic and that reconciliation between the two will prove impossible (*SC* IV.8, 129). On his analysis even a "society of true Christians" existing "in all its perfection" would "be neither the strongest nor the longest lasting" because it would "lack cohesion" (IV.8, 128–29). The lack of social togetherness is a function of the true Christian's indifference to worldly things and the preeminent care he places on the salvation of his individual soul: "Christianity is a purely spiritual religion, uniquely concerned with heavenly matters" such as one's eternal salvation. Thus the "Christian's homeland is not of this world" and the attachment he has to his fellows is in the final analysis a matter of "profound indifference." The "essential thing" is to worry about the condition of one's own soul and "to go to heaven," not to love and glory in one's political community, befriend one's fellows, or enact the "sentiments of sociability" without which freedom cannot subsist (IV.8, 129). Citizens of a republic must be at home in the world, and Christians must view it as a way station.

Doubtless the contemplative individualism of the true Christian is at the individual level more salutary than the alienated selfishness of the bourgeois, but it nonetheless creates serious political and social problems that cannot be dismissed as mere inconveniences. Rousseau is especially concerned that the true Christian's ultimate indifference to temporal authority will leave his state susceptible to the domineering impulses of tyrants: "If there is a single ambitious man, a single hypocrite . . . he will very certainly get the best of his pious neighbors" (*SC* IV.8, 129). He goes on to say not only that Christian societies are vulnerable to tyrannical persons but also that Christianity itself is inimical to the cause of political freedom. His discussion is shockingly candid: "Suppose that your Christian republic is face to face with Sparta or Rome. The pious Christians will be beaten, crushed, destroyed before they have had time to look around, or they will owe their salvation only to the scorn their enemies will conceive for them" (IV.8, 129). He continues: "But I am mistaken when I speak of a Christian republic; these two words are mutually exclusive. Christianity preaches nothing but servitude and dependence. Its spirit is so favorable to tyranny that tyranny always profits from it. True Christians are made to be slaves" (IV.8, 130). "The religion of man" sacrifices freedom and unity in this life for salvation in the next. No citizen can tolerate this contradiction, and no good regime would ask him to do so.

It may be fairly wondered why Rousseau, if his reservations concerning Christianity are this strong, might not turn away from transcendental appeal altogether and seek to found a regime on a purely rational, secular basis. We, however, have already seen at least two reasons why he rejected this alternative as impracticable. First, he believed men on the whole too credulous and prone to superstition to ever do away completely with their need for religion. We crave consolations that reason cannot provide, and the Enlightenment promise to deliver salvation through reason was based on an irrational faith in rationality itself. Second, and more centrally, religion is a singularly powerful catalyst of those expansive passions necessary to civic virtue. Only in the rarest cases does reason move men to virtue, and its simulacrum more commonly directs them to vice. Religion, properly constrained, makes virtue the object of the passions; it inspires a passionate love of the standards of morality and bids us treat others with the good faith, mutual respect, and sympathy those standards enjoin.

What, then, might religion properly constrained look like? A full answer is, I fear, a book to itself, but if Christianity's lack of fitness as a civil religion stems from its (1) insistence on dividing the allegiances of citizens, (2) general inability to discipline the fanatical passions it foments, and (3) tendency to encourage social disengagement, then a more salutary alternative must succeed on all these scores. With regard to the first, we have already seen that Rousseau solves this problem as Hobbes did, by putting religious forms of social control under the aegis of the sovereign and making religious and political duties more or less synonymous. He believes that a salutary civil religion cannot follow Jesus's imperative to separate the theological and political systems, and must instead combine "the divine cult and the love of the laws" (IV.8, 125–26). Success on this point will have removed one of the great sources of contradiction in human life and have taken a large step toward making men more at home in the world.

Though the idea of political control over religious belief quite justifiably conjures the specter of authoritarianism, Rousseau understands—perhaps better than we do—how destructive the combination of religious fervor and state power can be and seeks to avoid its terrible excesses. Thus, though he argues for the union of religious and political systems, he also insists that union can reach no further than "the limits of public utility." Consequently, the "dogmas of civil religion" that all citizens must profess are extremely limited. The positive articles of faith give divine sanction to a few simple, precise, and reasonable beliefs centered on those "sentiments of sociability without which it is impossible to be a good citizen or a faithful subject" (*SC* IV.8, 130). Christianity's demand for anything more has proven both philosophically misguided and practically destructive: because reason is incapable of determining the truth or falsity of many questions of dogma, only that portion of belief that bears directly on the ability to discharge civic duty should be susceptible to social control. Everything else is left to the domain of private conscience, and since "the sovereign has no competence in the [transcendental] world" it is obliged to tolerate what it is not competent to judge (IV.8, 130).

In addition to demanding that subjects believe what their reason resists, Christianity had on Rousseau's accounting inculcated a socially destructive ethos of disengagement that led subjects to devalue worldly things and focus on the private goal of individual salvation. Civic duty may be discharged but it is done without relish or joy, and this is much the same as saying that it is done badly. Citizens who march into battle with the enthusiasm of a child eating his broccoli are not likely to return victorious. So, although the civil religion Rousseau proposes does posit an afterlife and hence in some way calls on a realm beyond, it makes extra-temporal rewards contingent on love of country and of one's fellows. Far from devaluing this life by comparing it to the eternal felicity that awaits in the next, it makes that eternal felicity available only to those who value their relations to and within the state above all else.

| Can the Center Hold? The Fragility of the *Moi Commun*

Through the last two chapters we have sought to understand Rousseau's political philosophy as a particular manifestation of his generalized philosophical quest for human unity. It has the character of a balancing act, one intended to reconcile the seemingly competing demands of justice and utility, of private and public, of self and other. This balancing act is indicative of Rousseau's hybridized solution to the political problem: rather than follow Socrates in attempting to destroy the domain of particularity altogether, Rousseau seeks to recruit it into the process of citizen-craft, for it is through this process that members of a political community learn to associate their own first-order interests with the good of the state. Of course, given Rousseau's understanding of the human soul and his insistence on the centrality of self-love, it should hardly be a surprise that he would reject the Socratic route and seek to strike some kind of balance between the public and private worlds. Political life must realize the unity it seeks without imposing a false unidimensionality on the lives of citizens; it must respect and accommodate the existence of private associations (e.g., marriage and friendship) without compromising the political association.

However, the balance of forces Rousseau provides for is as fragile as it is essential: like Machiavelli, he knows that all the things of men are in motion, that it is one thing to persuade men to become citizens and quite another to keep them in that persuasion. The political problem thus conceived is not—as a social contract framework sometimes implies—static or essentially captured in a particular moment, but rather is inherently dynamic and concerned with the psychological tendencies that multiple institutions, working in conjunction, create in and over time. Thus, in seeking to understand just how stable Rousseau believes his own solution to the social problem to be, we must look beyond the *Social Contract* and to his portrayals of political life *in action*. The *Letter to D'Alembert* has proved helpful in this regard, as it depicts in idealized form the daily life of Genevan citizens and, in so doing, points to the way in which an approximately just regime might ameliorate those tensions that affect all regimes.

Rousseau is, of course, quite explicit (*SC* III.11, 98) that political unions cannot sustain themselves in perpetuity: "The body politic, like the human body, begins to die at the moment of its birth, and carries within itself the causes of its destruction." The question, then, is not if but when good regimes devolve, and Rousseau's analysis of the Genevan case suggests that he believes the equilibrium of forces required in a just society is intrinsically unstable. At least three reasons gather in support of this conclusion. First, the strength of his opposition to the institution of a theater in Geneva is telling: that he would think the introduction of a single playhouse could have such drastic cascading social and psychological consequences indicates just how delicate he believed social harmony is. One might attribute Rousseau's stern critique of the theater to other causes (e.g., to a generalized social paranoia or his dislike of Voltaire's meddling with his homeland), but it seems that his suspicions are motivated by a more comprehensive pessimism about the stability of social unity. On this head it is instructive to note that Rousseau opposes the institution of a theater on a specifically republican basis. He might have built a very different case, for instance, arguing on the classical liberal basis that publicly funded entertainments are an illegitimate use of the state apparatus. But Rousseau prioritizes institutional and social unity over the claims of individual liberty: without forgetting the short-term fiscal consequences—a decline in industry, an increase in public expenditure, and the introduction of luxury are among the most serious—Rousseau focuses on the long-term moral and social effects a theater will have. The introduction of refined entertainments will not only empty Geneva's treasury but also destroy the city's institutional integrity, disrupt its social equilibria, and undermine the civic-mindedness of its citizens. Ever sensitive to the profound effects produced by the smallest changes, Rousseau claims that by the time the subterranean effects of a theater are felt, it will be too late to control them: men will have already turned into sycophants and wits, women into temptresses or worse, and all will have acquired "a soft disposition and a spirit of inaction" at odds with both the commercial industriousness and the martial discipline that characterize Geneva (*LD* 64–65).

Second, Rousseau points to the fragility of Genevan social order by noting it is based on a peculiar balance of martial spirit and commercial activity that relies for its continuance on the moderation of its inhabitants and the existence of sumptuary laws. Geneva is neither Sparta nor England, neither the small military republic of the classical world valorized by Rousseau nor the extended commercial republic preferred by Montesquieu. It is itself a hybrid. Its distinctiveness lies in its ability to fuse the public spirit of the former to the bustling industriousness and ingenuity of the latter. The fragility of this balance is signaled by the very existence of sumptuary laws, made necessary to temper the greediness that attends commercialism but which Rousseau recognizes in *Poland* as a sign not of political health but rather of corruption: "Luxury does not get rooted out with sumptuary laws," which stimulate rather than extinguish the desire for wealth (*CGP* 189). Though Rousseau is conspicuously silent in the *Letter* on the conditions that make sumptuary laws necessary, what he says in *Poland* suggests that Geneva is in a more advanced state of decline than initial appearances suggest.

Finally, Rousseau includes in a footnote late in the *Letter* an image of a "dance" that suggests the intrinsically unstable balance between the public and private realms. In it, he recalls having as a young boy witnessed "a simple entertainment" enjoyed by a regiment of Genevan troops after drilling exercises. These troops, cheered by wine and a long supper, gathered in the town square and began playing music and dancing together. Such a spectacle struck the young Rousseau, who was moved by "the harmony of five or six hundred men in uniform, holding one another by the hand and forming a long ribbon which wound around, serpent-like, in cadence and without confusion." The display stirred Rousseau's passionate father, Isaac, to address his young son. "Do you see," he intoned, "these good Genevans? They are all friends, they are all brothers; joy and concord reign in their midst" (*LD* 135n). The basis of this "joy and concord" is, as Rousseau's depiction attests, a shared vision of the human good as realized through political and martial solidarity, and the dance reflects and reinforces that solidarity through its total inclusiveness and its unity of purpose. It exists in contrast to the exclusive and romantically charged form of dancing that takes place at Rousseau's public balls, for in this case all the soldiers were joined together in a "single ribbon" that spontaneously negotiated a series of complex maneuvers and reflected their oneness of mind. Warmed by the memory of his Genevan fellows in the town square both expressing and reproducing their unity, Rousseau exclaims, "The only pure joy is public joy."

Like its private counterpart, however, "public joy" can and must expire, and the way in which Rousseau explains the termination of the spontaneous dance points up the ineliminable contradiction between the private and public realms. After emphasizing the unity of mind and heart with which the dancing was animated, Rousseau notes that city's women were awoken by the noisy men and came down to join them: "The wives came to their husbands, the servants brought wine; even the children, awakened by the noise, ran half-clothed amidst their mothers and fathers." The gathering of citizens qua citizens has now become a gathering of fathers, mothers, children, and servants; the "pure joy" of the civic association has been admixed with the particularistic pleasures of the household. The disruptive effect on the "dance" is clear, for when the men tried "to pick up the dance again" they found it "impossible; *they did not know what they were doing anymore; all heads were spinning with a drunkenness sweeter than that of wine*" (*LD* 135–36n; emphasis added). After some friendly chatting, each citizen "withdrew peaceably with his family," retired to his home, and resumed his private domestic life. The effort to combine the rapture of citizenship with the pleasures of the household results not in successful reconciliation but in disruption and confusion. Even in the favorable sociological circumstances of Geneva, the roles of father, husband, and citizen are difficult to integrate and, assuming this integration achieved, even more difficult to sustain.

| Conclusions

Rousseau's political theory has a peculiar dynamic. It invokes as its basis a self in the possession of particular interests that require special protection. Indeed, the protection of these interests is the foundation of political legitimacy, and the theory of sovereignty for which Rousseau is so (in)famous only embodies and expresses his more fundamental concern to protect the integrity of the selves that make up the sovereign body. Yet the very self that serves as the foundation of Rousseau's theory is simultaneously transformed by it, and transformed in such a way that the sense one has of himself *as* himself is obscured by the comprehensive way in which he identifies with the social institutions that constitute his personhood. The integrity of the moral person is imperiled by the very theory that claims to secure it. In the just regime, the particularized self is both coming into and falling out of being at the very same time. It is Rousseau's belief in the necessity of circumscribing the domain of particularity that allowed him to admire regimes as institutionally and culturally diverse as commercial Geneva, expansionist Rome, and virtuous Sparta. These political societies not only were able to direct the psychic forces of individual citizens toward the good of the community, but all did so with the understanding that creating citizens comes at the cost creating individuals with robust self-conceptions. The tension between the embeddedness and the discreteness of the self is managed and controlled through a strategy of mutual accommodation, but it is never resolved at a theoretical level. This, I think, means at least two things.

First, both the radically collectivistic and radically individualistic interpretations of Rousseau are mistaken. The claims that Berlin, Talmon, Nisbet, and Crocker make concerning the "totalitarian" character of Rousseau's thought ignore his rejection of Socratic communism, his recognition of formal limitations on the exercise of sovereign power, and his constant affirmations of the need to *balance* the claims of the private and public domains. This authoritarian reading shows—rightly enough—that for Rousseau individual identity must be shaped in accord with the needs of social institutions, but it neglects to add that social institutions must be shaped in accord with the needs of individual citizens. Such interpretations exaggerate the authoritarian appearance of Rousseau's theory not only by omitting its essentials but also by subjecting it to an impossibly exacting standard of scrutiny. Crocker is especially guilty on this score: he argues that the techniques of social control utilized by Rousseau—the greatest offenses are deliberate manipulation of the people by elites and the attempt to establish social regimentation "through inevitable punishment and reward"—reveal the authoritarian character of his political theory (Crocker 1995, 250–53). Rousseau did indeed believe that these and other techniques were necessary, but his novelty consists not in his acknowledging the utility of subterranean methods of psychological control—in this he is like virtually every political philosopher who came before and many who came after him—but rather in his discovery that such practices are embedded in *all existing and all possible* forms of social control. This discovery, far from being intrinsically authoritarian, has instead been very useful for liberals seeking to protect freedom, for it points up both the fragility of human liberty and the cost of sustaining it in the face of social forces that seem determined to undermine it. So, too, does it show that the question of freedom cannot be resolved by simply eliminating social control in some defined sphere of individual action, for since freedom and social power emerge coterminously the effort to eliminate social control in some defined sphere of private action will prove only to be a reassertion of it. The very creation of privacy is itself a social act. To recognize this—which Rousseau surely did—is not to be an "authoritarian," which Rousseau surely was not.

Second, the tensions the self must face in the social and political world prevent the realization of the harmony it seeks. Rousseau's moral universe is an eternally disjointed place full of contradictory duties, desires, and expectations. We act and interact in all different kinds of capacities, and in the final analysis there is no way to reconcile the various responsibilities to which a complex social life gives rise. The unity the self requires would in principle be satisfied by the radical collectivism of Plato's *Republic*, but Rousseau's belief in the primacy of self-love leads him to reject this way of life as unnatural and endorse a mode of social organization that has (reasonably) distinct private and public spheres.

And yet the tension that inevitably emerges between these spheres violates the unity required by the self; its need for coherence is overcome by the perplexing multiplicity of social life. If this is right, then there can be no final synthesis of civic spirit and subjectivity, as Frederick Neuhouser has argued. There can be no stable solution to the tension between love of self and love of society, as Joshua Cohen and John Rawls have claimed. There can be no meaningful continuities between the public life of the just regime and the domestic life depicted in *Emile* and *Julie*, as Nicole Fermon and Elizabeth Wingrove have held. The tensions Rousseau thought into existence are held together not by their final complementarity but by their ultimate antagonism.

Epilogue

Rousseau, if he is anything, is polarizing. At once a revolutionary and a reactionary, a rationalist and a romantic, a liberal and a totalitarian, a solitary and a citizen, Rousseau has been blamed both for the excesses of the French Revolution and the conservative backlash it caused. He has been mocked for his Christianity and decried for his atheism. He has been attacked for his misogyny and chastised for his effeminacy. He has been extolled for his diagnosis of modern man's unfortunate condition and excoriated for his failure to alleviate it. Robespierre likened him to a deity and Edmund Burke to a beast.

It is no surprise that opinion on Rousseau is so divided or that we care so deeply about our disagreements, for in both his manner and his matter Rousseau invites controversy: questions of human happiness were his central preoccupation, and he speaks directly to his readers about these most personal affairs. He brings us into his most intimate confidences and makes us feel less like students than confidantes; he makes us believe that we understand him as well as he understands us. But if he speaks directly to all, he says different things to each: his intimate style makes us all feel as though we have special access to his intentions, but his studied indirection gives us very different ideas about what those intentions are. The heat of his prose warms the heart but blisters the mind.

In the previous eight chapters I have sought to bring into focus a vision of Rousseau which centers on the development of social relations and emphasizes the complications that attend that process. More specifically, I have sought to show that Rousseau's theory of human association is best understood to have two distinct but interlocking aims: first, to raise our hopes with respect to what may be hoped for from our associational life and, second, to subtly undermine the very hopes which he himself has encouraged us to entertain. These aims, understood together, show that full human redemption is on his accounting both necessary and impossible in the context of civil society, and do much to point up Rousseau's curious tendency to disclose the failure of his own projects. Insofar, however, as the "tragic" interpretation I have developed is a reasonable approximation of Rousseau's own view, serious questions remain—questions about what we, as readers, should take away from Rousseau's work, and about what kind of impact Rousseau, as author, sought to have on his audience. I would like to conclude by briefly taking these up.

| Living in the Light of the Silver Lining: The Consolations of Tragedy

Though the tragic interpretation developed above seems to be exegetically plausible, its ultimate meaning and significance remain somewhat unclear. How are we to understand a theory that subtly undermines the very possibilities that it encourages readers to explore? And, perhaps more important, what are we to *do* once confronted with the futility of our own social desires? One possibility, ultimately embodied by Rousseau himself, is to withdraw from society and seek to recapture natural wholeness through solitude and, by extension, philosophic reflection. This possibility is held out by Cooper (2008, 76) as Rousseau's final and most satisfactory resolution to the problem of human dividedness: the "most exalted life in Rousseau's corpus," he claims, "is not Emile's but rather his own, that is, the life of a philosopher, as depicted in the late autobiographical writings." Cooper's claim has considerable force, as Rousseau's own words suggest that solitude gave him not only peace and lucidity but also a purity of feeling and expansiveness of soul that eluded him in society. In the fifth walk of the *Reveries*, Rousseau reports that the time he spent floating aimlessly in a small boat on the "limpid waters" of Lake Bienne were the best of his life. Unlike the "short moments of delirium and passion" which dotted his social (and most especially his romantic) life and which caused him more pain than satisfaction, the time he spent in solitude on the banks of St. Peter's Island gave him the "simple and permanent" sentiment of enduring happiness that has no equal and "for which [his] heart longs" (*RSW* 45). Exiled from society, Rousseau found peace by becoming invisible to others: "I know that the only good which might henceforth be in my power is to abstain from acting, from fear of doing evil without wanting to and without knowing it" (50). Rousseau's own peculiar virtue, then, consists in inaction; the condition of his being good for himself is being nothing for others. In living thus, he satisfies the requirements of natural goodness, reconciles himself to himself and to the world, and makes himself an exemplar of his own thought. Reports like these do much to point up the choiceworthiness of the solitary life.

However, it is important to note that withdrawal from society and the concomitant embrace of philosophy is neither the only nor, perhaps, the most effective way of coping with the disappointments to which social life gives rise. Such a strategy is, in the first place, potentially more problematic than it at first seems, for when we ask whether the Rousseau of the *Reveries* can be said to be happy, the sense that that term acquires in the fifth walk is enough to give the careful reader concerned pause. There, he explains that complete absorption in the sole sentiment of one's own existence—a state completely undisturbed by thoughts of past or future or sensations of pain or pleasure—is the only feeling that carries with it a "sufficient, perfect, and full happiness which leaves in the soul no emptiness it might feel a need to fulfill" (*RSW* 46). In this state, fully realized only in solitude, we "are like God" and "enjoy nothing external to ourselves." But after having abstracted away from everything external to us, after having removed all those distractions that compromise the pure experience of oneself as himself, it is fair to ask: what, if anything, is left? The existence that Rousseau describes as most perfect is dangerously close to nonexistence; it appears closer to death than to life. Todorov (2001, 47) elaborates on this concern:

> After having eliminated everything, by a remarkable labor of subtraction and introspection, man plumbs his depths. But these depths are, strictly speaking, nothing; the subject coincides with the predicate in a perfect tautology. The self is precisely the very existence of the self—nothing more. We thereby attain repose and peace. Rousseau . . . ends up discovering that his nature consists precisely of searching for himself. The destination is the journey itself. So the quest becomes intransitive and is transformed into reverie; the self-sufficient

man is similar to God, but his existence is now equivalent to nonexistence, to radical repose. Now, nothing separates him from death.

I raise this concern less to demonstrate the unsatisfactoriness of solitude than to suggest that it, at least as embodied in Rousseau's self-presentation, is not an obviously unproblematic alternative to social life as a means of attaining wholeness. It remains unclear whether the path to wholeness that Rousseau himself walked actually led him there, or whether philosophy, as Rousseau wrote to his onetime friend Mme d'Epinay, leads instead to sorrow.

Even if it is conceded that the alternative embodied by Rousseau is sound on its own terms, the *Reveries* do not establish its absolute priority over social life quite as clearly as Cooper would have it. Rousseau says as much in the sixth walk, where he confesses that the pleasures of the solitary life lack the intensity and emotional expansiveness of the joy of togetherness. The feeling of making "another heart content," Rousseau explains, is "sweeter than any other," but it proved intolerable for him because of its fragility. Social life, he explains, carries with it obligations that destroy spontaneity and, over time, sour the pleasure of associating with others: recounting his interactions with a crippled boy to whom he would occasionally give alms, Rousseau—sounding much like Emile explaining why he had cooled toward Sophie—recalls that their daily interaction was initially "a pleasure" but eventually transformed into "a habit" and, finally, into an "annoying" duty (*RSW* 49–50). The pleasures of solitude are preferable not because they are deeper, more expansive, or more rewarding than those of social life—indeed, Rousseau suggests that they are *less* so—but rather because they are more durable. The fullness of feeling felt through social connectedness still seems to be the existential limit point with reference to which Rousseau interprets the wholeness of isolation. Solitude is for Rousseau a kind of consolation prize, a good to be enjoyed by a singular man singularly unable to sacrifice personal pleasure to duty and, thus, unable bear the commitments that human association entails.

Rousseau's singularity raises yet another concern about the satisfactoriness of the solution to the problem of dividedness that he himself embodied: can his experiment in living be replicated? Rousseau's belief in his own distinctiveness—expressed repeatedly throughout his autobiographical works—seems to belie the notion that any and all could strike out and discover repose in solitude. The problem is especially acute if we take philosophic activity to be solitary man's primary consolation, for since Rousseau consistently reserved the privilege of philosophizing to a select few and actively discouraged everyone else from its pursuit, it would seem that the very activity that makes solitude rewarding would also be inaccessible to virtually everyone who would seek it. Now, it must be admitted that Emile, an Everyman who lacks Rousseau's unique gifts, nonetheless appears capable of finding peace in solitude, for in *Emile and Sophie* he tells his tutor that he has found satisfaction despite being isolated. But if this is true, we are entitled to wonder why, first, Emile was educated for society at all and, second, why he felt the need to communicate his self-discovery with someone else; absent an answer, we may reasonably view his claim to have found peace in solitude to be rather unreliable—a form of protesting too much. It would certainly not be the only instance in which Emile proved to be self-deceived.

Insofar as the individualist, philosophic path to wholeness trod by Rousseau is not a viable alternative to social life—either because it replicates the failures of social life or because it is inaccessible to most people—we are obligated to return to society and search for consolations within it. But what, if any, consolations does Rousseau make available to us? We can begin to answer this question by noting from Rousseau's point of view that wrestling with the question of human relations *as* a question is part of what it means to be human. The development of self-consciousness and social feeling effect irreversible changes in the structure of human being—changes that lead us to seek the greater part of our happiness through social recognition—and insofar as we wish to live in accord with our nature we cannot remain in ignorance of the difficulties that attend such changes. One who concerns himself with the question of what may be hoped for from his associations, far from indulging the "vain curiosity" Rousseau so violently declaims in the *First Discourse*, instead follows Rousseau's own example in considering a matter that bears directly and immediately on the character of the human good.

Because our prospects for happiness are affected so powerfully by the way we are connected to others, it seems clear that we cannot afford *not* to think and feel through these connections. Indeed, to retreat from sustained and honest consideration of social possibility is to retreat from the burdens of genuinely human life; it is to leave our natural capacities for social feeling underdeveloped, to quit our estate as human beings and try futilely—with kings and beggars—to be something that we are not (*E* 446). With this in mind, we can see that the failure to seriously inquire after the character of human association would appear to magnify rather than ameliorate the difficulties to which social life gives rise, for such a failure precludes real engagement with the intransigently difficult question of self-knowledge, and leads to moral blindness, breakdowns of self-awareness, a diminished feeling of the sentiment of existence, and the very psychological dividedness Rousseau was so concerned to mend. Social beings that are unwilling or unable to think through the possibilities and limitations of their associational lives owe their obscure feelings of dissatisfaction, their "conflict and drifting," to their incuriosity. Salutary ignorance is not an option.

If social beings must reflect on their relations, and if (proper) reflection leads inevitably to an awareness of the limits of human connection, then what prevents this awareness from engendering despair and moral paralysis? I believe that Rousseau provides at least three consolations that compensate us for the disappointments inherent in social life and, thereby, also keep us from slipping into disillusioned drift. The first, most evident in chapter 6's analysis of friendship, is that connectedness of a less ambitious but perhaps no less comforting kind becomes possible once our divided condition is exposed for all to see. The public disclosure of our various failings—be they of mind, body, or soul—may weaken the esteem others feel for us, but it simultaneously creates a new emotional space in which social bonds, albeit of an aim-attenuated kind, are consummated and strengthened. Friends like Bomston and St. Preux, to say nothing of well-educated persons like Emile, find in their failures and imperfections a ground for community, for they know the sting of disappointment and that no one is exempt from humiliation. Emile's example, and its effect on the reader, is especially instructive in this regard, for though Emile is ultimately unsuccessful in his quest to find wholeness through marriage, we do not begrudge him his failure but rather admire his effort. It is, in fact, his very failure that allows readers to identify with him: in the end, we no longer see a "model of perfection" whose excellence we could never hope to approximate, but rather a victim of fate whose difficulties we have lived out. His grizzled reflections on the trials of life, won by hard experience, excite our sympathy without inspiring our disgust. They also command our moral attention: the courage that he and Sophie exhibit through their hardships attracts us in spite—or *because*—of the fact that it does not shrink from but rather partakes in the imperfections of the world. The shared awareness that such imperfections attach to everything, that the human condition is one of weakness and travail, that life is too strong, too great, and too confounding for even the best and brightest, creates a ground for sympathetic community among all human beings and allows us to identify with—and, importantly, to approach—the everyday heroism of figures like Emile and his beloved.

The second, borne out most fully in chapters 2 and 3, has to do with how the development of social sentiment activates and sharpens the sentiment of existence. The experience of this sentiment is not only a vindication of life itself (and hence an answer to Camus, who histrionically wondered two hundred years after Rousseau whether death was preferable to life) but also a standard for determining the choiceworthiness of our own lives. To live a good life, Rousseau avers, "is not to breathe; it is to act; it is to make use of our organs, our senses, our faculties, of all the parts of ourselves that give us the sentiment of our existence." He goes on: "The man who has lived most is not he who has counted the most years but he who has most felt life" (*E* 42). The mere absence of pain is thus not the appropriate standard for a final assessment of human life (cf. *DI* 132); that standard is supplied, rather, by the quotient of felt life that we are able to enjoy, by the richness of experience and range of emotional and intellectual sensitivity through which we are able to make use of all our capacities, to press the boundaries of being, and to acquire knowledge of ourselves by acquiring knowledge of our limitations. Even with all its disappointments, then, a genuinely human—that is to say, social—life is, on Rousseau's accounting, far preferable to the delusively grandiose aspirations of a tyrant or the petty, mechanical pleasures of an honest bourgeois because it gives expression to the full range of human powers while providing consolations when those powers, as they are so often, are insufficient for their task.

The third and final consolation that emerges from Rousseau's tragic theory of social relations is the acquisition of virtue. This acquisition is significant, for Rousseau himself heaped so much praise on virtue that many commentators have ultimately concluded, with Reisert (2003, 10), that virtue is the "central lesson of Rousseau's constructive works." While this "lesson" has hardly been our central preoccupation, we have nonetheless seen how it figures into Rousseau's mission: he has shown us how public and domestic forms of virtue emerge from different kinds of social arrangements and, in many cases, endure beyond the social structures that help to produce them. Emile's example most clearly illustrates not only how the desire to be virtuous grows out of the eroticized desire to be social but also how the consolations of virtue help to soothe the wounds inflicted by frustrated eros. After the breakdown of his marriage to Sophie, Emile finds solace in his resolve to be virtuous and in "finding his daily duties" around him. Though he had abandoned the hope of exclusive and enduring sexual love, he kept the moral discipline that that hope had cultivated in his youth. Trying to discourage his pupil from marrying Sophie simply because cold weather will make it more difficult to travel to see her, Jean-Jacques tells Emile that the marriage will outlive the snow (*E* 447). He leaves it for Emile to discover that virtue would remain after the marriage disappeared.

| Reforming the Reader: Rousseau's Mission as a Writer

We have now seen that Rousseau's veiled social tragedy holds out important consolations for readers who might otherwise become disillusioned by his skepticism concerning human relations. But in continuing to tease out the implications of the "tragic" interpretation it is necessary to shift our gaze from reader to *author*, and to seek to understand a bit more about the kind of writer that would develop a teaching like the one I have found in Rousseau. It is worth mentioning at the outset that throughout the twentieth century Rousseau has been often interpreted, both by his defenders and his detractors, as a preeminently political thinker who wrote in order to effect practical political change. The criticisms of Karl Popper, Robert Nisbet, and J. L. Talmon all presuppose that Rousseau wrote the *Social Contract* animated by the hope that the regime depicted there would one day be realized, and John Rawls (2007, 207–8)—seeking to save Rousseau from those very criticisms—characterizes him as a reasonable optimist seeking social progress through institutional reform. If, as I have argued above, Rousseau is too circumspect about the limits of social connection to believe that the possibilities he explores could be fully realized in the world—especially in the modern world—then this "practical" interpretation of his work will not do. Why, then, did he write? What *did* he hope to achieve, if not practical political reform?

The question is a good one, and for guidance I turn to an eminently qualified, albeit somewhat unsympathetic, source: Voltaire. Writing to Genevan pastor Jacob Vernes, the arch philosophe complained of Rousseau's obscurantism and unwillingness to address himself directly to the concrete problems of his day. "Jean-Jacques writes only in order to write," sneered the lord of Ferney, "and I write in order to act" (Adams 1991, 162n46). Though wrong to dismiss Rousseau's work as mere armchair speculation, Voltaire's frustration with his onetime friend is nonetheless instructive, for it reveals important differences in the two thinkers' respective conceptions of how philosophic writers ought to engage with their readers and, more broadly, with world they inhabit. For Voltaire and his fellow philosophes, to be engaged in philosophy is to seek to bring the world into conformity with reason; it is, therefore, to be necessarily engaged in a political program of reform. And since philosophy qua philosophy is a tool of social change, philosophers themselves have an obligation to improve society by bringing both its design and its customs into accord with reason. Assuming this obligation meant, among other things, taking strong stances on a variety of concrete social questions: Voltaire had his Calas affair, Diderot his *Encyclopedia*, and D'Alembert the vaccination debate. They united under the slogan *Ecrasez l'infâme!* and univocally cried for toleration, liberation from superstition, and rational institutional design.

Rousseau, by contrast, could never find harmony with the heavenly chorus or bring himself to fully endorse its understanding of the philosopher's role in society. To the degree that he felt compelled to address current events or the questions of the day, the views he expressed were, because of their complexity, far less amenable to policy prescription than were those of his contemporaries: he supported toleration but defended a well-educated fanaticism; he depicted a virtuous atheist but insisted that religion was necessary to a healthy political society; he inveighed against medicine but had very little to say about vaccination; he pioneered a new educational theory but discouraged efforts to institutionalize it. This, of course, is not to deny that Rousseau contributed meaningfully to the debates that surrounded him (see, e.g., Hulliung 1994; Mostefai and Scott 2009), but rather to say that his intellectual mission was not *defined* by his contribution to those debates. To the contrary, when Rousseau raised the questions of his day, he did so not to resolve but rather to *problematize* them, and in so doing he invited his readers to think about them more deeply and more productively. This more nuanced and individualistic authorial mission emerged most clearly in the aftermath of the publication of the *Second Discourse*: by the spring of 1756 Rousseau had grown so weary of the philosophes' intrigues, and so skeptical of their radical activism, that he found it necessary to leave the bustle of Paris for the quiet of Montmorency. There he would dispense with efforts to reform society and focus instead on reforming himself—he sought the country in order to escape the distractions of the capital and embark on a personal program of moral "reform" that would coincide with a period of astounding literary productivity (Cranston 1991, 100). Thus it would seem that Rousseau's decision to leave Paris was not motivated simply by a need for a change of scenery; it was, rather, an essential condition for living out his distinctive vision of what it meant to be a philosopher. In order to live and philosophize as he thought appropriate, it was as necessary for Rousseau to leave Paris as it was for the philosophes to stay there.

Rousseau's extreme inwardness and attendant need to distance himself from the other "opinion makers" of his day point, I think, to the distinctive way he viewed his mission as an author. In this respect, he shared a great deal more with the French moralists of the seventeenth century than with the social reformers of the Enlightenment era, for it was not the reform of large-scale social institutions—but the moral improvement and transformation of individual readers—that Rousseau sought to effect through his writing. He wanted first and foremost to produce a revolution in the understanding, and it was in the service of this goal that his efforts as an author, including his occasional forays into practical politics, were largely devoted. Indeed, it is in light of this goal that we can understand Rousseau's "tragic" theory of human relations, for insofar as the romantic, fraternal, and political ideals he evokes may be understood not as templates or blueprints to be replicated in the world but rather as pedagogic tools intended to help readers better understand themselves, their aspirations, and their condition, we have a sense of why he would invite us to explore possibilities that he himself ultimately finds it necessary to undermine. These possibilities, however unrealizable, are themselves part of the structure of social life, and it is only in their light that a properly human happiness may be approached and approximated.

Rousseau's concern for the salvation of individual readers is evident even before his symbolic move from Paris, for he begins the preface to the *Discourse on Inequality* (91) by invoking the famous inscription at the temple of the oracle at Delphi and claiming that "the most useful and least advanced of all human sciences seems to me to be that of man." Modern man's complete lack of self-knowledge becomes the principle theme in the *Discourse*'s preface and exordium, with Rousseau taking up the actual question asked by the Academy at Dijon only insofar as he thought it might help his fellows better understand themselves and one another. The *Second Discourse* was, of course, only the first of many efforts to get readers to view themselves in a new way and in light of new possibilities. Thus we find Shklar (1969, 2) claiming that Rousseau wrote not to alter government policy but rather to "induce moral recognition in the reader," to shake him out of his dogmatic slumber and awaken in him an "outraged awareness" at his condition. "The object of [Rousseau's] models," she avers, "was not to set up the perfect community, but simply to bring moral judgment to bear on the social misery to which men have so unnecessarily reduced themselves."

Lest we think this goal too modest for a writer of Rousseau's range and power, Scott (2012; 2014, 533) has shown how difficult it is to get readers to view the world with new eyes. He identifies a series of rhetorical techniques that Rousseau utilized in order to persuade others of his new and radically different interpretation of human experience, and on that basis argues that "Rousseau's mission as an author . . . is to make his readers see what he saw" and, in so doing, to "transform [their] perspective." This reading of Rousseau's intention both underscores the Shklarian view that Rousseau was more interested in helping individual readers with their personal salvation than with institutional or policy change, and it shows Rousseau to be an *intentionally* difficult writer rather than, as has so often been claimed, a muddleheaded obscurantist. Scott deftly reveals how Rousseau strategically and deliberately utilizes obscurity, indirection, and paradox as ways of helping readers see the limitations of their own understandings of reality and envisage social possibilities previously blocked from view by the ossified telos of Aristotle, the antisocial hypocrisy of Christianity, and the reductive bilge of Hobbes. Insofar, then, as we can understand Rousseau as deliberately sowing confusion for the pedagogic purpose of helping readers interpret their experiences more productively, we may conclude with Zaretsky and Scott (2009, 100) that in Rousseau, "paradoxes were not mere extravagances; they were critical to his philosophical enterprise."

Both the style and substance of Rousseau's work tend, I think, to support the view that he wrote less to effect programmatic social change than to show individual readers the limitations of their old ideas and conceptions. Rousseau's tone, for one, is not that of a reformer but of a confidante. It is intimate, confessional, immediate, and highly personal; he directly addresses his reader with great frequency and spends an unusual amount of time anticipating their criticisms, undermining their presuppositions, disclosing his own sincerity, and ingratiating himself into their confidences. Even when he addresses the entire species, as he does in the *Discourse on Inequality*, he manages to speak in an immediate way to each member of his audience. Thus we find Reisert (2003, ix) saying what so many readers of Rousseau have felt: "Whenever I read Rousseau, I feel that he is speaking directly to me—not in the way that all great thinkers who address universal human concerns necessarily speak to each reader because they speak to all—but in a more personal way." The "personal" tone to which Reisert refers has an important effect: it helps soften the skeptical reader and prepare him to accept Rousseau's authority as a knower and a teacher. To be sure, the tone that Rousseau adopts does not preclude a separate intention to reform society's basic institutions, but surely it is better suited to an individualized pedagogic intention than a reformist, "political" one.

It is, however, not just the intimacy but also the indirection of Rousseau's style that distinguishes his work from that of a more practically minded reformer. Rousseau combines his highly intimate and confessional tone with a love for jarring paradoxes, and his distinctive blend of emotional immediacy and philosophic ambiguity is designed to generate deep uncertainty in individual readers—uncertainty not only about Rousseau's meaning but also about the reader's own interpretation of reality. The paradoxical and somewhat obscure nature of Rousseau's work has, of course, been noted by many, but the response it elicited from one his earliest and most distinguished readers—David Hume—is particularly instructive. Writing to a mutual friend of his and Rousseau's, Hume noted that though Rousseau's works were "admirable, particularly on the head of eloquence," so, too, were they inevitably "intermingled [with] some degree of extravagance." To this he added that even a reader as attentive as he did not quite know what to make of Rousseau: his writings were less texts than "performances" that, it seemed to Hume, had been undertaken not to demonstrate truth but rather "from the pleasure of showing his invention and surprising the reader with his paradoxes" (in Zaretsky and Scott 2009, 100). A writer as practical as Hume saw that Rousseau's peculiar, aporia-inducing manner was ill suited to the task of concrete political reform. What he failed to see, however, is that Rousseau had a different understanding of how a writer ought to engage in the world, and that the paradoxes he deployed were essential to this alternative vision. At least part of the reason Hume failed in this regard is that he made very different assumptions about his reading public than did Rousseau: serving in his self-appointed role of ambassador between the learned and the layman, Hume wrote to and for a world that he believed to be fundamentally sensible or, at the very least, not in need of complete moral and intellectual transformation. Rousseau, on the other hand, believed his readers so corrupt, and the world they inhabited so rotten and irredeemable, that nothing short of complete moral transformation would be at all useful. Hume could be content with informing and edifying his public, but Rousseau had to fundamentally *reorient* his, and his ingratiatingly indirect style was one of the many ways he got readers invested in his reformation project.

None of this, of course, is to deny that Rousseau believed the modern world could be better than it was, or to say that he was simply uninterested in the realm of practical politics. *Poland*, the *Constitution Project for Corsica*, and the *Letter to D'Alembert* all suggest otherwise: they address themselves to concrete political problems, make reasonably specific suggestions for reform, and, on the whole, suggest that more sensibly designed institutions could play an important role in ameliorating human misery. It is, however, to say that Rousseau's significance as an author does not lie in his having made this or that policy prescription, but rather in the novel way that he interrogates—and thereby *remakes*—his readers. It is in light of this aim, and no other, that both his tragic theory of human relations and his success or failure as a writer must be judged.

NOTES

CHAPTER 1

1. For expositional convenience I occasionally use the gender-specific "man" instead of "human beings" or "humanity."
2. *DI* page numbers refer to Rousseau (1964).
3. This martyrdom is underscored by the date of the tenth walk, which Rousseau records as Palm Sunday. Rousseau makes himself the Christ figure in his own passion play: his metaphorical return to Les Charmettes, the only place where he was loved for who he was, evokes Jesus's return to Jerusalem. And much like Jesus, Rousseau's love of others was rewarded with betrayal: having set out to save Mme de Warens, he was promptly sacrificed by his enemies.
4. *Lev.* refers to Hobbes (1994).
5. *2 Tr.* refers to Locke (1980).
6. *ECHU* refers to Locke (1975).
7. Page numbers for *DSA* refer to Rousseau (1964).
8. Rousseau is very particular about the use of the term *citoyen*, and he chastised his contemporaries as well as Bodin for failing to understand the significance of the word. Besides D'Alembert, Rousseau claims in a footnote to the *Social Contract* that "no other French author, to my knowledge, has understood the true meaning of the word *citizen*" (*SC* Vn54).
9. *GM* refers to the *Geneva Manuscript*. All passages quoted from Rousseau (1978).

CHAPTER 2

1. Compare with *Lev.* X, 51: "The *value* or WORTH of a man is, as of all other things, his prices, that is to say, so much as would be given for the use of his power; and therefore is not absolute, but a thing dependent on the need and judgment of another."
2. Rousseau, like many sentimentalists, expressed a belief that facial features revealed the disposition of the soul: "It is believed that the face is only a simple development of features already drawn by nature. I, however, think that beyond this development the features of a man's visage are imperceptibly formed and take on a typical cast as a result of the frequent and habitual impression of certain affections of the soul" (*E* 230).
3. *ML* refers to the *Moral Letters*. All citations from Rousseau (2007).

4. Rousseau is aware that pity for the rich and for the poor can quickly degenerate into contempt. He thus recommends that Emile be publicly humiliated as a way of staying in touch with his own vulnerability (*E* 245). See also *E* 172–75, where Rousseau provides an example of how this might be done.

CHAPTER 3

1. Translator Judith Masters somewhat misleadingly renders *amour-propre* as the pejorative term "vanity."
2. Rousseau also replaces his judges, claiming that Plato and Xenocrates are better able to assess his work than are the readers at the Academy of Dijon. His explicit disregard of the Academy's ability to properly judge his *Discourse* is likely among the reasons why the milquetoast Abbé Talbert won the essay competition instead of Rousseau.
3. All *Preface to Narcisse* citations refer to Rousseau (2007).
4. *BGE* refers to Nietzsche (2002).
5. Cranston (1991, 36) reports that Diderot was displeased with Deleyre's initial entry and made him extensively revise it before agreeing to publish it in the *Encyclopedia*.
6. See Neuhouser (2008, 376n) for a different account of the relationship of *amour-propre* to the principle of reciprocity. Rawls (2007, 198n) endorses Neuhouser's account.
7. On the distinctness of love and friendship, see Reisert (2003, chap. 4). Per usual, however, Rousseau is himself the exception to his own rule, for he reports in the *Confessions* that his relationship to Mme de Warens was something between love and friendship.

CHAPTER 5

1. It is unclear exactly how much time has passed between letters I and VIII, but Rousseau indicates in an editorial note placed at the beginning of letter VIII that there is a "lacuna" between it and the previous letters.
2. This letter is never posted; instead, it is delivered by hand to an unsuspecting St. Preux, who was given a brief note that informed him to meet Julie and Claire at the bower.
3. Some attention to context is necessary. St. Preux is not thinking clearly at all as he writes letter XXXVIII: he is anticipating his tryst with Julie and is overcome by his illusions. This would tend to militate against taking seriously the passage I have cited above, but it should be noted that St. Preux's mental stability as he writes letter XXIII is questionable as well: he is insecure and even hysterical in the Valais country, believing himself to be forgotten by Julie and then threatening suicide in order to bring an end to his exile.

CHAPTER 6

1. Cicero and Montaigne were very influential in Rousseau's age and known to Rousseau himself. Thus I treat their theories of friendship as important parts of the intellectual context Rousseau seeks to reshape. On Cicero see Wood (1988, 3); and Garsten (2006, 60). On Montaigne see Marchi (1994); and Fontana (2008, 24–25).
2. *DI* 95. How critical Rousseau's engagement is, though, is a matter of some debate. Sorenson (1990) occupies a middle ground between Plattner (1979), who views Rousseau as breaking radically with traditional teleology, and Lemos (1977), who believes that Rousseau's providentialist language moors him to a broadly teleological view of the world.
3. Though the tutor calls Emile "friend" several times, Emile responds in kind only once, preferring the hierarchical "father" or "master." The disproportion here suggests either that the two are cogniz-

ing their relationship in very different ways or, more likely, that Jean-Jacques is calling the pubescent Emile his "friend" as part of a pedagogic strategy designed to win his pupil's consent. More on this below. Cf. Reisert (2003, 104–5).

CHAPTER 7

1. *RRF* refers to Burke (1993).
2. Rousseau's French reads, "On pourrait, sur ce qui précède, ajouter a l'acquis a l'état civil la liberté morale qui seul rend l'homme vraiment maître de lui."
3. *CGP* refers to Rousseau (1997c).
4. *DPE* refers to Rousseau (1997a).
5. Rousseau's *Final Reply* refers to Rousseau (1992).
6. I cannot find this hypothesis in Aristotle, and it would—as Rousseau knew—have been a very odd position to take for a philosopher who insisted on the distinctness of all animal species. Though Rousseau, too, affirms the eternality of species, it is he and not Aristotle who provides many of the resources for thinking through the question of whether human beings evolved from some quadrupedal species (e.g., *DI* 183–86).

CHAPTER 8

1. For an excellent, and nontechnical, introduction, see Riker (1988).
2. Condorcet actually presupposed a relatively high degree of voter competence: the probability of each individual voter reaching a correct independent decision must be at least 0.5 in order for the law of large numbers to work. If the probability of a correct evaluation is less than 0.5 then average voter competence actually *decreases*. See, for example, Waldron, in Estlund et al. (1989, 1322–23).
3. Rousseau singles out as his opponent William Warburton, bishop of Gloucester (1668–1779), who penned *The Alliance between Church and State* and *Divine Legation of Moses*.
4. *LCT* refers to Locke (2010).

BIBLIOGRAPHY

Adams, Geoffrey. 1991. *The Huguenots and French Opinion, 1685–1787: The Enlightenment Debate on Toleration*. Waterloo, Ont.: Wilfrid Laurier University Press.

Arendt, Hannah. 1998. *The Human Condition*. Introduction by Margaret Canovan. Chicago: University of Chicago Press.

Aristotle. 1984. *The Politics*. Translated by Carnes Lord. Chicago: University of Chicago Press.

———. 1998. *Nicomachean Ethics*. Translated by David Ross, revised by J. L. Ackrill and J. O. Urmson. New York: Oxford University Press.

Bellah, Robert, Richard Marsden, William M. Sullivan, Ann Swidler, and Steven M. Tipton. 1985. *Habits of the Heart: Individualism and Commitment in American Life*. Berkeley: University of California Press.

Berlin, Isaiah. 1990. *Four Essays on Liberty*. Oxford, U.K.: Oxford University Press.

Bloom, Allan. 1979. "Introduction." In *Emile*, by Jean-Jacques Rousseau. New York: Basic Books.

———. 1993. *Love and Friendship*. New York: Simon and Schuster.

Boyd, Richard. 2004. "Pity's Pathologies Portrayed: Rousseau and the Limits of Democratic Compassion." *Political Theory* 32 (4): 519–46.

Bronfenbrenner, Urie. 1981. *The Ecology of Human Development*. Cambridge, Mass.: Harvard University Press.

Burke, Edmund. 1993. *Reflections on the Revolution in France*. Introduction and notes by L. G. Mitchell. Oxford, U.K.: Oxford University Press.

Camus, Albert. 1991. *The Myth of Sisyphus, and Other Essays*. Translated by Justin O'Brien. New York: Vintage.

Cassirer, Ernst. 1989. *The Question of Jean-Jacques Rousseau*. New Haven, Conn.: Yale University Press.

Charvet, John. 1973. *The Social Problem in the Philosophy of Rousseau*. Cambridge, U.K.: Cambridge University Press.

Cicero. 1923. *On Old Age. On Friendship. On Divination*. Translated by

W. A. Falconer. Cambridge, Mass.: Harvard University Press.

Cohen, Joshua. 1986. "Reflections on Rousseau: Autonomy and Democracy." *Philosophy and Public Affairs* 15 (3): 275–97.

———. 2010. *Rousseau: A Free Community of Equals*. Oxford, U.K.: Oxford University Press.

Cooper, Laurence. 1999. *Rousseau, Nature, and the Problem of the Good Life*. University Park: Pennsylvania State University Press.

———. 2004. "Between Eros and the Will to Power: Rousseau and 'The Desire to Extend Our Being.'" *American Political Science Review* 98 (1): 105–19.

———. 2008. *Eros in Plato, Rousseau, and Nietzsche: The Politics of Infinity*. University Park: Pennsylvania State University Press.

Cranston, Maurice. 1991. *The Noble Savage: Jean-Jacques Rousseau, 1754–1762*. Chicago: University of Chicago Press.

Crocker, Lester. 1995. "Rousseau's Soi-Disant Liberty." In *Rousseau and Liberty*, edited by Robert Wokler, 244–66. Manchester, U.K.: Manchester University Press.

Cullen, Daniel. 1993. *Freedom in Rousseau's Political Philosophy*. DeKalb: Northern Illinois University Press.

Dagger, Richard. 1997. *Civic Virtues: Rights, Citizenship, and Republican Liberalism*. New York: Oxford University Press.

DeMan, Paul. 1979. *Allegories of Reading: Figural Language in Rousseau, Nietzsche, Rilke, and Proust*. New Haven, Conn.: Yale University Press.

Dent, N. J. H. 1988. *Rousseau: An Introduction to His Psychological, Social, and Political Theory*. Oxford, U.K.: Blackwell Press.

Diderot, Denis. 1956. *Rameau's Nephew, and Other Works*. Edited by Ralph Bowen, translated by Ralph Bowen and Jacques Barzun. Indianapolis: Hackett.

———. 1967. *Encyclopédie ou Dictionnaire raisonné des sciences, des arts et des métiers, Tome Sixieme (Et–Fn)*. Stuttgart: Bad Cannstatt.

Disch, Lisa. 1994. "Claire Loves Julie: Reading the Story of Women's Friendship in *La Nouvelle Héloïse*." *Hypatia* 9 (3): 19–45.

Estlund, David, Jeremy Waldron, Bernard Grofman, and Scott L. Feld. 1989. "Democratic Theory and the Public Interest: Condorcet and Rousseau Revisited." *American Political Science Review* 83 (4): 1317–40.

Fermon, Nicole. 1997. *Domesticating Passions: Rousseau, Woman, and the Nation*. Hanover, N.H.: Wesleyan University Press.

Fontana, Biancamaria. 2008. *Montaigne's Politics: Authority and Governance in the "Essais."* Princeton, N.J.: Princeton University Press.

Forster, E. M. 2007. *Howards End*. New York: Bantam Dell.

Freedman, Jonathan A., Steven E. Butler, and David H. Wahl. 2012. "Impacts of Invasive Asian Carps on Native Food Webs." Available online at http://www.iisgcp.org/research/reports/Wahl_final report_2012.pdf.

Garsten, Bryan. 2006. *Saving Persuasion: A Defense of Rhetoric and Judgment*. Cambridge, Mass.: Harvard University Press.

Garver, Eugene. 1994. *Aristotle's Rhetoric: An Art of Character*. Chicago: University of Chicago Press.

Gauthier, David. 2006. *Rousseau: The Sentiment of Existence*. New York: Cambridge University Press.

Gildin, Hilail. 1983. *Rousseau's Social Contract: The Design of the Argument*. Chicago: University of Chicago Press.

Grofman, Bernard, and Scott Feld. 1988. "Rousseau's General Will: A Condorcetian Perspective." *American Political Science Review* 82 (2): 567–76.

Hickman, Jonathan, Shiliang Wu, Loretta J. Mickley, and Manuel T. Lerdau. 2010. "Kudzu (*Pueraria montana*) Invasion Doubles Emissions of Nitric Oxide and Increases Ozone Pollution." *Proceedings of the National Academy of Sciences* 107 (22): 10115–19.

Hobbes, Thomas. 1994. *Leviathan*. Edited by Edwin Curley. Indianapolis: Hackett.

———. 1998. *On the Citizen*. Edited by Richard Tuck and Michael Silverthorne. Cambridge, U.K.: Cambridge University Press.

Hulliung, Mark. 1994. *The Autocritique of Enlightenment: Rousseau and the Philosophes*. Cambridge, Mass.: Harvard University Press.

Johnston, Steven. 1999. *Encountering Tragedy: Rousseau and the Project of Democratic Order*. Ithaca, N.Y.: Cornell University Press.

Kateb, George. 1961. "Rousseau's Political Thought." *Political Science Quarterly* 76 (4): 519–43.

Kelly, Christopher. 1999. "Taking Readers as They Are: Rousseau's Turn from Discourses to Novels." *Eighteenth Century Studies* 33 (1): 85–101.

———. 2003. *Rousseau as Author: Consecrating One's Life to the Truth*. Chicago: University of Chicago Press.

Lemos, Ramon M. 1977. *Rousseau's Political Philosophy: An Exposition and Interpretation*. Athens: University of Georgia Press.

Levine, Alan. 1976. *The Politics of Autonomy: A Kantian Reading of Rousseau's Social Contract*. Amherst: University of Massachusetts Press.

Locke, John. 1975. *An Essay concerning Human Understanding*. Edited by Peter Nidditch. Oxford, U.K.: Clarendon Press.

———. 1980. *Second Treatise of Civil Government*. Edited by C. B. MacPherson. Indianapolis: Hackett.

———. 1996. *Some Thoughts concerning Education*. Edited by Ruth Weissbourd Grant and Nathan Tarcov. Indianapolis: Hackett.

———. 2010. *A Letter concerning Toleration, and Other Writings*. Edited by Mark Goldie. Indianapolis: Liberty Fund.

Machiavelli, Niccolo. 1981. *La Mandragola*. Translated by Mera Flaumenhaft. Prospect Heights, Ill.: Waveland Press.

Macpherson, C. B. 1964. *The Political Theory of Possessive Individualism: Hobbes to Locke*. Oxford, U.K.: Clarendon Press.

Marchi, Dudley M. 1994. *Montaigne among the Moderns: Receptions of the "Essais."* Providence, R.I.: Berghahn Books.

Marks, Jonathan. 2007. "Rousseau's Discriminating Defense of Compassion." *American Political Science Review* 101 (4): 727–40.

Marshall, David. 2005. *The Frame of Art: Fictions of Aesthetic Experience, 1750–1815*. Baltimore: Johns Hopkins University Press.

Melzer, Arthur M. 1983. "Rousseau's Moral Realism: Replacing Natural Law with the General Will." *American Political Science Review* 77 (3): 633–51.

———. 1990. *The Natural Goodness of Man: On the System of Rousseau's Thought*. Chicago: University of Chicago Press.

Montaigne, Michel de. 1958. *The Complete Essays*. Translated by Donald Frame. Stanford, Calif.: Stanford University Press.

Mostefai, Ourida, and John T. Scott. 2009. *Rousseau and l'Infâme: Religion, Toleration, and Fanaticism in the Age of Enlightenment*. Leiden: Rodopi Press.

Neuhouser, Frederick. 2008. *Rousseau's Theodicy of Self-Love: Evil, Rationality, and the Drive for Recognition*. New York: Oxford University Press.

Nichols, Mary. 1985. "Rousseau's Novel Education in Emile." *Political Theory* 13 (4): 535–58.

Nietzsche, Friedrich. 2002. *Beyond Good and Evil*. Edited by Rolf-Peter Horstmann and Judith Norman, translated by Judith Norman. New York: Cambridge University Press.

Nisbet, Robert. 1943. "Rousseau and Totalitarianism." *Journal of Politics* 5 (2): 93–114.

Nussbaum, Martha. 2001. *Upheavals of Thought*. Cambridge, U.K.: Cambridge University Press.

O'Hagan, Timothy. 1999. *Rousseau*. London: Routledge.

Okin, Susan Moller. 1979. "The Education of Rousseau's Natural Woman." *Journal of Politics* 41 (2): 393–416.

Orwin, Clifford. 1997a. "Moist Eyes: From Rousseau to Clinton." *Public Interest* 128 (Summer): 3–20.

———. 1997b. "Rousseau and the Discovery of Political Compassion." In *The Legacy of Rousseau*, edited by Clifford Orwin and Nathan Tarcov, 296–320. Chicago: University of Chicago Press.

Parry, Gereint. 1995. "Thinking One's Own Thoughts: Autonomy and the Citizen." In *Rousseau and Liberty*, edited by Robert Wokler, 99–120. Manchester, U.K.: Manchester University Press.

Plato. 1968. *Republic*. Translated by Allan David Bloom. New York: Basic Books.

———. 2001. *Plato's "Symposium."* Translated by Seth Benardete, with commentaries by Allan Bloom and Seth Benardete. Chicago: University of Chicago Press.

Plattner, Marc F. 1979. *Rousseau's State of Nature: An Interpretation of the Discourse on Inequality*. DeKalb: Northern Illinois University Press.

Rawls, John. 2007. *Lectures on the History of Political Philosophy*. Edited by Samuel Freeman. Cambridge, Mass.: Belknap Press.

Reisert, Joseph R. 2003. *Jean-Jacques Rousseau: A Friend of Virtue*. Ithaca, N.Y.: Cornell University Press.

Riker, William. 1988. *Liberalism against Populism: A Confrontation between the Theory of Democracy and the Theory of Social Choice*. Prospect Heights, Ill.: Waveland Press.

Rousseau, Jean-Jacques. 1960. *Politics and the Arts: The Letter to M. D'Alembert on the Theatre*. Edited and translated by Allan Bloom. Glencoe, Ill.: Free Press.

———. 1964. *The First and Second Discourses*. Translated by Roger and Judith Masters. New York: St. Martin's Press.

———. 1978. *On the Social Contract, with Geneva Manuscript and Political Economy*. Translated by Roger and Judith Masters. New York: St. Martin's Press.

———. 1979. *Emile: or, On Education*. Translated by Allan Bloom. New York: Basic Books.

———. 1992. *Discourse on the Sciences and Arts (First Discourse) and Polemics*. Edited by Christopher Kelly and Roger D. Masters, translated by Judith D. Bush, Christopher Kelly, and Roger D. Masters. Hanover, N.H.: University Press of New England.

———. 1995. *The Confessions and Correspondence, Including the Letters to Malesherbes*. Edited by Christopher Kelly, Roger D. Masters, and Peter G. Stillman, translated by Christopher Kelly. Hanover, N.H.: University Press of New England.

———. 1996. "Emile et Sophie, ou Les Solitaires." In *Finding a New Feminism: Rethinking the Woman Question for Liberal Democracy*, edited by Pamela Grande Jensen. Lanham, Md.: Rowman & Littlefield.

———. 1997a. *The Discourses, and Other Political Writings*. Edited and translated by Victor Gourevitch. New York: Cambridge University Press.

———. 1997b. *Julie; or, The New Heloise: Letters of Two Lovers Who Live in a Small Town at the Foot of the Alps*. Translated by Phillip Stewart and Jean Vaché, edited by Roger D. Masters and Christopher Kelly. Hanover, N.H.: University Press of New England.

———. 1997c. *The Social Contract, and Other Later Political Writings*. Edited and translated by Victor Gourevitch. New York: Cambridge University Press.

———. 2000. *The Reveries of the Solitary Walker, Botanical Writings, and Letter to Franquières*. Edited by Christopher Kelly, translated and annotated by Charles Butterworth, Alexandra Clark, and Terence E. Marshall. Hanover, N.H.: University Press of New England.

———. 2007. *On Philosophy, Morality, and Religion*. Edited and translated by Christopher Kelly. Hanover, N.H.: University Press of New England.

Schaeffer, Denise. 1998. "Reconsidering the Role of Sophie in Rousseau's 'Emile.'" *Polity* 30 (4): 607–26.

Schiller, Friedrich. 1979. *Naive and Sentimental Poetry*. New York: Frederick Unger.

Schwartz, Joel. 1984. *The Sexual Politics of Jean-Jacques Rousseau*. Chicago: University of Chicago Press.

Scott, John T. 2002. "Re-presenting Achilles in Rousseau's *Emile*." Presented at UCLA Clark Memorial Library, Los Angeles.

———. 2012. "Do You See What I See? The Education of the Reader in Rousseau's *Emile*." *Review of Politics* 74 (3): 443–64.

———. 2014. "The Illustrative Education of Rousseau's *Emile*." *American Political Science Review* 108 (August): 533–46.

Shklar, Judith N. 1969. *Men and Citizens: A Study of Rousseau's Social Theory*. London: Cambridge University Press.

Simpson, Matthew. 2006. *Rousseau's Theory of Freedom*. New York: Continuum.

Sorenson, Leonard. 1990. "Natural Inequality and Rousseau's Political Philosophy in His *Discourse on Inequality*." *Western Political Quarterly* 43 (4): 763–88.

Starobinski, Jean. 1988. *Jean-Jacques Rousseau, Transparency, and Obstruction*. Chicago: University of Chicago Press.

Strauss, Leo. 1953. *Natural Right and History*. Chicago: University of Chicago Press.

Strong, Tracy B. 1994. *Jean-Jacques Rousseau: The Politics of the Ordinary*. Thousand Oaks, Calif.: Sage.

Talmon, J. L. 1952. *The Origins of Totalitarian Democracy*. New York: Norton.

Tanner, Tony. 1982. "Julie and 'La Maison Paternelle': Another Look at Rousseau's *La Nouvelle Héloïse*." In *The Family in Political Thought*, edited by Jean Bethke Elshtain, 96–124. Amherst: University of Massachusetts Press.

Todorov, Tzvetan. 2001. *Frail Happiness: An Essay on Rousseau*. University Park: Pennsylvania State University Press.

Trachtenberg, Zev. 2009. "Civic Fanaticism and the Dynamics of Pity." In *Rousseau and l'Infâme: Religion, Toleration, and Fanaticism in the Age of Enlightenment*, edited by Ourida Mostefai and John T. Scott, 203–26. Leiden: Rodopi Press.

Velkley, Richard L. 2002. *Being after Rousseau: Philosophy and Culture in Question*. Chicago: University of Chicago Press.

Voltaire, François. 1972. *Philosophical Dictionary*. Edited and translated by Theodore Besterman. New York: Penguin.

Williams, David. 2007. *Rousseau's Platonic Enlightenment*. University Park: Pennsylvania State University Press.

Wingrove, Elizabeth Rose. 2000. *Rousseau's Republican Romance*. Princeton, N.J.: Princeton University Press.

Wittgenstein, Ludwig. 1958. *Philosophical Investigations: The English Text of the Third Edition*. Translated by G. E. M. Anscombe. New York: Prentice Hall.

Wood, Neal. 1988. *Cicero's Social and Political Thought*. Berkeley: University of California Press.

Yenor, Scott. 2011. *Family Politics: The Idea of Marriage in Modern Political Thought*. Waco, Tex.: Baylor University Press.

Zaretsky, Robert, and John Scott. 2009. *The Philosophers' Quarrel: Rousseau, Hume, and the Limit of Human Understanding*. New Haven, Conn.: Yale University Press.

Index

adolescents. *See also* children
   awakening of sexuality in, 52–55
   compassion in, 141
   desires of (*Emile*), 42–43
   in *Emile*, 53
   friendship versus sexual desire in, 56–57
   processing willfulness of others by, 48
aesthetics
   criteria for moral love, 24, 51, 136
   in friendship context, 144
   influence of, 43, 53
affection, 6, 12
alienation. *See also* dividedness
   of bourgeois, 207
   in civil society, 7
   dividedness and, 178
   in *Emile*, 13
   Hobbes on, 178
   between husband and wife, 25
   in *Julie*, 114
   of politicized man, 183
   of rights of humanity, 182–83
   Rousseau's, 6
   self-centered, 28, 178
   in the social compact, 182
   in *Social Contract*, 28
   total, 183
allegiances, divided, 178, 205, 207–8

ambition, 43–52, 63, 192
amour-propre
   confusion caused by, 35
   corrupt, 76–77
   destructiveness of, 44, 47
   development of, 85
   in *Emile*, 20, 91
   expressions of, 58–59
   healthy forms of, 161
   interaction between sexual desire and, 24
   longings of, 53
   love versus friendship, 55–59
   malignant form of, 21, 31, 46–47, 72–73, 144, 192
   materialization of anger with, 46–47
   moral ambition and, 43–52, 63
   moralized, 78–79
   pity and ordered development of, 72–76
   politicized, 138–39
   problems of malignant, 47–48
   reciprocity principle and, 230 n. 6 (ch. 3)
   in romantic situations, 95–96
   Rousseau's theory of, 19–23, 58
   self-assessment and, 72
   and sexuality in *Emile*, 96–97
   sexual passion as expression of, 24–26

stimulation of, by social compact, 193
understanding, 22
vanity versus, 230 n. 1 (ch. 3)
anger
    causes of, 47
    materialization of, 46–47
    pity as counteraction to, 3–4
    Seneca on, 45–46
    solving danger of, 49
animal desires and instincts, 22–23
antisocial tendencies, 47–48, 72
anxiety, 38, 59
approval, desire for, 48–49
argument, structure and character of, 2–4
Aristotle
    on complete friendship, 143–44
    mentioned, 14, 137, 182, 231 n. 6 (ch. 7)
    on natural sociability, 60
    Nichomachean Ethics, 139–40
    on relation between friends, 141
assemblies, public, 190–92, 201–2
associational life/associations. *See also* societal good
    capture of unity through, 13
    dependence and, 181
    embeddedness in, 22, 32–34, 58, 162
    Hobbes on, 15, 35
    in *Julie,* 148–49
    Locke on, 15, 38
    partial societies, 193–94
    political (*See* political association[s])
    possibilities and limitations of, 221
    private associations, 31, 188, 199–200, 210
    purpose and functions of, 9–10
    role of pity and sexual passion in, 63–64
    Rousseau's forms of, 4
    Rousseau's theory of, 217
    sub-political, 199
    sympathetic associations, 26, 71, 148–49
    understanding of, 37
    wholeness in context of, 137
attachment(s), 57–58, 71
attraction(s)
    causes of, 37–38
    destructive, 155
    in friendship, 143
    mutual, 101
    sexual/erotic, 51, 95–96, 119, 128
    subjective, 14
authoritarianism, 164–65, 169, 194, 209, 214
authority, 178, 189, 205–8
autonomy, 166–67, 169–70

behavior(s)
    ambiguity of impulses, 42–43
    habits of thought and action, 50
    Hobbes on sources of, 34
    moral, 36–37
    moral and social, 36–37
    motivations for, 47
    unsociable, 76
beliefs, 78, 209, 227–28
benevolence, 26, 47–48, 60–61
Berlin, Isaiah, "Two Concepts of Liberty," 165
betrayal, 106–7, 150–51
Beyond Good and Evil (Nietzsche), 75
biological equipment, operation of our, 23
body politic metaphor, 180
boundaries, 12–13, 82
bourgeois
    dividedness of, 14–19, 173–74
    domestic community of emerging, 130
    in *Emile,* 41, 173
    sociability of, 95
    social recognition, 36–39
    state of being of, 18
Brutus, Junius, 175–76

C. See Confessions, The (Rousseau)
cercles (social groups), 199–201
CGP. See Considerations on the Government of Poland (Rousseau)
character deficiencies, 158–59
children, 45–47. *See also* adolescents
Christianity. *See also* religion
    Christian allusions in *Julie,* 114
    citizenship and, 108
    as civil religion, 208–9

Christianity *(continued)*
    effect on civic engagement of, 206–7
    martyrdom in, 229 n. 3
    political influence of the Church, 178
    priests as distinct from, 205–6
    requirements of political freedom and, 187
    scrutiny of Christian sect in *Emile*, 78
    in *The Social Contract*, 205
    transcendental individuals of, 207
    vulnerability of Christian societies, 207
church and state, 178, 181, 206
Church authority and influence, 178, 205–6. *See also* religion
Cicero, *De Amicitia*, 137, 139, 230 n. 1 (ch. 6)
Citizen, The (Hobbes), 37
citizens
    of Clarens (in *Julie*), 129–34
    conception of, in *Emile*, 134
    connection between good institutions and good, 191
    creation of, 90
    desubjectivized, 92–93
    embeddedness of, 108
    Emile in contrast to, 93
    ennoblement of, 192–93
    fallen, 102–3
    freedoms of, 167, 170
    harmonious existence for, 181
    individual identification as, 191
    individuality of, 165
    men versus, 88–89, 174
    private business, 194–95
    relationship between State and, 168–69
    roles of, 190, 200
    young, 202–3
citizenship
    in *Emile*, 30–31, 90–94, 107
    in *Geneva Manuscript and Political Economy*, 30–31
    ideal of classical, 175–76
    patriotism and, 92, 106–7, 135, 193
    requirements of, 94
    Rousseau's definition of, 29–30, 92–93
    Rousseau's model of domestic society and, 187–88
    sexual union as preparation for, 89
    Spartan woman story on, 176–77
    universalism in, 108
citoyen, 229 n. 8
civic education. *See* education
civic identity, 188
civic spirit, 215
civil connectedness, 9
civil freedom, 166–67, 183
civil man, 65, 73
civil society, 180–81
    conflicts of interest in, 16–17
    embeddedness in, 22, 32–34, 58, 162
    motivations for formation of, 15–16
    requirements for, 37
Clarens community (in *Julie*), 129–34
class prejudice, in *Julie* (Rousseau), 117
commiseration, 63, 74–75
common good. *See* societal good
community, 14–16, 84. *See also* sociability/social relations
compassion, 3, 76–82
competition, 48, 160–61
Condorcet jury theorem, 194–95, 231 n. 2 (ch. 8)
Confessions, The (Rousseau), 12–13, 15, 145
conflict. *See also* tension
    between discreteness of self and embeddedness, 213
    between duty and love, 116
    between institutions and citizens, 187–88
    internal/external, 7–8
    motivations for, 34–35
    political, 14
    between private passion and public good, 172–73, 198
    psychological and social, 48–49
    religious, 14
    resolving, 90
conflict/tension
    conflict between public good and private passions, 172–73
    political conflict, 14
    religious conflict, 14
conjugal society, 15–16
connectedness, 6. *See also* associational life/associations

as consolation for disappointment, 221
forms of, 91–92
in human relations theory, 11–13
of love, 98
Rousseau's teachings on, 10
to the state, 167
through political associations, 9
conscience, 116, 123, 209
Considerations on the Government of Poland (Rousseau), 168–69, 211–12, 228
consolations, 10, 151–52
Constitution Project for Corsica (Rousseau), 228
contexts, for self-understanding, 8
corrupting forces, 162–63

DA. See *De Amicitia* (Cicero)
D'Alembert, Jean Le Rond, 199–200. See also *Letter to D'Alembert on the Theater* (Rousseau)
L'Encyclopédie, 76
De Amicitia (Cicero), 139–40
death, 114, 122–23, 144, 176–77, 201, 218, 234
Deleyre, Alexandre, 77–78
dependence
of civil association, 181
dangers of personal, 91
forms of, 170
freedom from, 169
on moral environment, 182
transformative consequences of, 170–71
desire(s). See also longing(s); love (eros); sexual passion/desire
ambiguity in, 38
to be lovable, 49
to be loved, 47
causes versus consequences of, 8
companionship, 57
dependence on things and, 41–42
extended being, 36
fanatical, 81
Hobbes's phenomenology of, 38
intimate society, 97
Locke on, 38–39
love and esteem, 35

possession of goods, 47
private, 8, 13, 24
recognition, 9
reinforcement of, 37–38
Rousseau's, 13
satisfaction of, 10
self-preservation, 60
social approval, 21
DI. See *Discourse on Inequality (Second Discourse)* (Rousseau)
disappointments, 221–23
Discourse on Inequality (Second Discourse) (Rousseau), 16–17, 224
amour-propre, 7, 9
amour-propre in, 75
animal desires and instincts in, 22–23
applied science on disease/health in, 67–68
changes in environment and man, 182
connection to others through pity, 25–26
dangers of moral love in, 96
desire for social approval in, 21
dividedness in, 172
ecosystem metaphor in, 179–82
emergence of friendship in, 144
friendship as product of pity in, 84, 140, 149
grounding of friendship in pity in, 143
identity creation in, 23
individualism in, 105
interdependence in, 170
merit and beauty in, 51
model of human community in, 16
moral and social possibility in, 62
natural man in, 180–81
natural versus civil man in, 65, 73
personal tone of, 226–27
pity in, 61
preface to, 225–26
savage man, 68–69
self-preservation in, 60
sexual desire and love in, 24, 50
social motivations in, 34–35
state of nature and account of pity in, 65–66
Voltaire on, 44

Discourse on Political Economy (Rousseau), 108, 168–69
Discourse on the Origin and Basis of Inequality Among Men. See *Discourse on Inequality (Second Discourse)* (Rousseau)
Discourse on the Sciences and Arts (First Discourse) (Rousseau)
    critics of, 175
    friendship in, 137
    hopes for associations in, 220
    Junius Brutus example in, 175–76
    model of human community in, 16
    vain curiosity in, 220
disease/illness, 66–68
disengagement, 206, 209
disgust, moral, 76–82
disrespect, 79, 167
distrust/trust, 16, 83, 111, 129, 151, 158, 163, 189–90
divided allegiance(s), 178, 205, 207–8
dividedness, 2
    accepting and managing, 18–19
    alienation and, 178
    bourgeois, 14–19
    of bourgeois, 17–18
    condition of, 18
    destructiveness of, 171–77
    domestic solution to, 135
    healing of, 7
    Hobbes on, 178
    language of, 17, 172
    in *The Letter to D'Alembert on the Theater*, 204–5
    of personality, 6–7
    Rousseau's account of, 178
    of social life, 28
    solutions to problem of, 219–20
domestic healing strategy, in *Emile* and *Julie*, 163
domestic relations. *See* family; household(s); marriage
domestic theory, 188–89
double object, 90–94, 135
DPE. See *Discourse on the Sciences and Arts (First Discourse)* (Rousseau)
duck-rabbit image, 82–83

E. See *Emile* (Rousseau)
ECHU. See *Essay Concerning Human Understanding, An* (Locke)
ecological systems theory, 163–64
ecology metaphor, 178–84
economic issues, 189
education
    creating a man through, 88–89
    debates over civic, 28–29
    in *Emile* (See *Emile* (Rousseau))
    within friendship, 140–41
    in *Julie*, 156
    moral learning, 137–38, 151–54, 184–85
    moral learning and friendship, 151–54
    political, 28–29
    public, 28–31, 135, 204–5
    Rousseau's theory of, 224
    through friendship, 137–38
embeddedness, 179
    in associational contexts, 22, 32–34, 58, 162
    in environment, 28, 61, 163, 177, 179–82
    tension between discreteness of self and, 213
    of the true citizen, 108, 190
embodied love, 119–27
Emile (Rousseau), 4, 20, 22, 76–77
    adolescence in, 42–43
    amour-propre in, 73–74, 78–79
    analysis of pity in, 84–85
    bourgeois in, 173
    characterizing human nature in, 70
    citizenship in, 30–31, 94, 191
    comparing self to others, 49–50
    compassion in, 143
    creation of passion in, 45
    dependence on things in, 41–42
    depiction of household in, 188
    dividedness in, 171–72
    education issues in, 28–30, 74, 88–89, 92, 108, 135, 168, 204–5
    emergence of friendship in, 144
    Emile's psychology, 41
    eros in, 135
    exclusive romantic attachment in, 24

the fallen man in, 102–3
family structure in, 129–30, 201
fatherland in, 29–30, 93, 106–8, 131, 168–69, 197, 203–5
friendship versus sex in, 55
harmony and dissatisfaction in, 13
household concept in, 197
human struggle in, 69–70
idea of love dying in, 118
importance of friendship in, 137
on Julie in, 80
just regime in, 191
lives of citizens in, 197
loss of love in, 219
man's estate in, 21
marriage in, 87–88, 223
meaning of friendship in, 156–57
pity in, 72
political instability and friendship in, 140
political interpretations of, 92–93
politics in, 134–35
protection of children in, 46
psychic forces in, 36
psychological mechanics of liberality in, 40–41
psycho-sexual character of education of, 89
puberty and *amour-propre* in, 73
reason for tragic veil in, 104–5
retreat from social possibility in, 220–21
role of nascent sexuality in, 52–55
romantic love in, 25, 97–102
Rousseau on usefulness of, 96
Rousseau's domestic and political visions in, 27
Rousseau's psychological theory in, 110–11
scholarly interpretations of man and citizen in, 90–91
scrutiny of Christian sect in, 78
second birth metaphor in, 21
seeing our own errors in, 80
self-understanding in, 41
sex education in, 95–97
sexual desire and love in, 99–100
sexual maturity in, 56–57
sociability in, 105
social approval in, 49
Spartan woman story in, 176–77
study of politics by, 93–94
teacher/pupil relationship in, 157–58
theory of love in, 123
true love in, 51–52
understanding of love in, 89–90
unity in, 172–73
values conflicts in, 175
worthiness of life in, 222
Emile and Sophie (Rousseau), 102–3, 107–8, 110–11, 140, 220
L'Encyclopédie, D'Alembert, Jean Le Rond, 77
entertainment, 160–61, 197–98, 210–12
environment
  citizen's ability to create, 167
  effects on passion with change in, 180
  embeddedness in, 28, 61, 163, 177, 179–82
  harmony between man and, 163–64, 171
  moral, 182
  social, 188
equality. See *Discourse on Inequality (Second Discourse)* (Rousseau)
equilibrium, 210–11, 214
eros. See love (eros)
ES. See *Emile and Sophie* (Rousseau)
Essay Concerning Human Understanding, An (Locke), 16, 38–39
esteem, self-. See *amour-propre*
ethical disgust, 80
ethical impulses, 63, 79
ethical learning, 154–59
ethics, 51, 139
evil, sources of, 47–48

false pride, 64, 72, 74, 76
family. *See also* household(s); marriage
  development of modern, 7
  in *Emile,* 129–30, 201
  in *Julie,* 129–30, 134–35, 201
  in *Letter to D'Alembert on the Theater,* 201–2
  nuclear, 201

family *(continued)*
- role of, 129–30
- roles within, 212–13
- Socratic view of, 130, 201

fanaticism, 15, 64, 76–82, 208, 224

fatherland
- in *Emile*, 29–30, 93, 107–8, 131, 197, 203–4
- love of, 168
- relationship between citizens and, 168–69

felicity, 37–38

Final Reply to critics of *First Discourse* (Rousseau), 175–76

Finis Ultimus, 15

First Discourse. See *Discourse on the Sciences and Arts (First Discourse)* (Rousseau)

fragility, 184–85

frail happiness, 63, 71, 184

freedom (liberty)
- Burke's denunciation of radical, 165
- claims of individual, 211
- dividedness and unity in, 171–77
- exchange of natural for moral, 165–66
- within the just regime, 167
- moral, 167
- negative, 170–71
- political, 202
- republican, 201–2
- Rousseau's conception of, 165, 169
- as self-mastery, 165
- in *Social Contract*, 164–71
- unity in, 170–77

friendship, 3
- activity characteristic of, 83
- of adolescents, 56
- character of, 141
- classical tradition of, 139–47
- connection between moral learning and, 137–38
- connection between suffering and, 145
- as consolation for disappointment, 221
- defenders of Rousseauan, 140–41
- definition/description of, 156–57
- distancing of pity from, 143–44
- enmity and hate and, 48
- forms of, 7, 9
- Hobbes's interpretation of, 15
- ideal of, 140
- initial conditions for, 144
- instability of, 188–89
- language of silence in, 8, 145, 147, 149–51
- limitations and dangers of, 161
- loss of, 16
- love versus, 42, 55–59, 230 n. 7 (ch. 3)
- moralizing functions of, 138
- moral learning and, 151–54
- pity as basis for, 60–61
- political effectiveness of, 160
- in political thought, 137
- as private phenomenon, 15, 26
- as product of pity, 26
- recognition attached to, 49
- role of, 4
- Rousseau's portraits of, 10, 26
- Rousseau's theory of, 86, 138, 141–42, 145–49, 159–61
- transition from love to, 82, 101, 113, 124, 127–29

generosity, 40–41, 80

Geneva
- church of, 204
- citizens/society of, 131, 160, 189, 197–99, 203
- daily life of citizens in, 210
- family structure in, 202
- in *The Letter to D'Alembert on the Theater*, 203–4
- republican, 160, 199
- social order in, 211–12
- Socinianism in, 203–4

Geneva Manuscript and Political Economy (Rousseau), 30–31, 193–203

GM. See *Geneva Manuscript and Political Economy* (Rousseau)

Golden Age, 7

good, societal. *See* societal good

happiness, 7
- common, 191

controversy over Rousseau's questions
of, 216
frail, 63, 71, 184
gaining access to, 96–97
of household, 129–30
inspiring, 49
Locke on, 38
with love, 120
obstacles to, in *Julie,* 114–16
prospects for, 220–21
restructuring of social forces for,
26–27
security of, 104
and suffering of others, 76
unhappiness, 72, 83
harmony
among humans, 163, 189
between church and state, 181
between desire and power, 7
in dynamic unity, 180
lack of, 18
between man and environment, 4,
163–64
of natural man, 65
psychological and social, 28
resolution of tensions for, 189
for Rousseau, 224
within the self, 13, 179–82, 188, 214
social, 13, 28, 211
of social institutions, 185–86
of the soul and environment, 171
of state of nature, 185
hate, 16, 45, 48–49, 80
health/illness, 66–68
healthy form of *amour-propre,* 31–32, 35,
48, 161
Hobbes, Thomas
on ambiguity in human desire, 38
The Citizen, 37
definition of felicity, 37–38
on disputes about science, 14
empiricism of, 23
establishment of sovereignty, 182–83
on human behavior and self-interest,
60–61
on human desire, 37–38
Leviathan, 15, 34, 38, 183
mentioned, 95

philosophy of dividedness of, 178
on political life and human association, 15
on rational self-interest, 14–15
Rousseau's radicalization of, 20
on selfishness and private interest,
188
self versus other, 20
serving of interests, 17
on social and political order, 19
theories of, 36, 39
view of relations with Locke of, 8
household(s)
creation of, 203
domestic and political, 196–97
in *Emile,* 89, 108–9
function in just regime of, 188–89
idea of happy, 129–30
institution of the, 26–27
as metaphor for political life, 109
private, 108
relation of state and, 129–30
romantic rituals of, 129
Howard's End (Forster), 5–6
human community model, 15–16, 41, 64,
105
human condition. *See also* man
fragility of, 184–85
freedom as trait of, 171
friendship and social identification,
144
pity's place within the, 62–63
as prey species, 66–67
Rousseau's characterization of, 61–63
sociability of, 139
sympathy, society and the, 69–72
human development, 7, 56
humanity, 44, 62. *See also* rights of
humanity
human nature, 14–15, 34
human relations theory. *See also See also*
associational life/associations;
relationships
analysis of Rousseau's, 2
integrative impulse in, 11–13
judgment of, 228
the just regime in, 26–28
nature of Rousseau's, 8

human relations theory *(continued)*
    overview, 5–10
    political aspects of, 28–31
    questions of, 220
    rational performances, 14–19
    reimagining self-love and human relations in, 19–23
    understanding of, 225
human rights. *See* rights of humanity
Hume, David, 227

identification
    of desires, 39
    friendship and social, 144
    of individuals as citizens, 191
    with others, 71–72, 142
    political identification theory, 114, 160
    social, 61
    sympathetic, 71, 79–80
identity
    citizen, 190–91
    confusion about, 43
    creation of, 23
    human, 135
    individual, 214
    moral, 183
    in a unity, 172
illness/disease, 66–68
imperfections, 63, 79–80
inaction as virtue, 218
indecisiveness, 17–18
indeterminacy, social feeling and, 40–43
inequality. *See Discourse on Inequality (Second Discourse)* (Rousseau)
institutions. *See* social institutions
intentionality, 21, 45–47, 60
interdependence, 3, 13, 29, 91, 170, 179–80, 182
interdependent impulses, 63–64
interpretations of Rousseau, 213–14
intimacy, avoidance of, 6
invulnerability, 46
isolation, 6, 106–7, 220

J. *See Julie* (Rousseau)
Julie (Rousseau), 110–11
    bonds of pity in friendship in, 147
    as bridge between domestic and political spheres, 27
    Christian allusions/metaphors in, 114
    class prejudice in, 117
    compared to *Emile* on romantic love, 110–13
    connection between friendship and suffering in, 145
    consequences of mistakes in, 184
    context of letters in, 230 n. 3 (ch. 5)
    decision making by, 174–75
    depiction of household in, 188
    dialectical interpretations of, 114
    divided loyalties in, 113–18
    domestic community of Clarens in, 129–34
    eros in, 135
    family structure in, 129–30, 201
    fragility of humans in, 185
    friendship as product of pity in, 149
    household concept in, 197
    importance of friendship in, 137
    limits of embodied love in, 119–27
    lives of citizens in, 197
    love and friendship in, 82–83
    meaning of friendship in, 156–57
    memory of events in, 149–50
    moral development in, 152, 154
    nature of love in, 125–27
    need for romantic love in, 117–18
    parents in, 114, 116–17
    politics in, 134
    portraits of friendship in, 145–46
    relationships after sexual consummation in, 122–23
    resolution of problems in, 114–15
    sympathetic associations in, 148–49
    transition from love to friendship in, 127–29
    virtue in, 80–82
    wish for death in, 122–23
jury theorem, 194–95
just regime, 191
    demands of the, 131
    dependence required by the, 181
    in *Emile*, 191
    function of household in, 188–89
    in human relations theory, 26–28

in *Letter to D'Alembert,* 210
moral environment of, 182
particularized self in, 213
protection for freedom from the, 164
public versus private life in the, 215

Kantian autonomy, 166

La Nouvelle Heloise; or, Julie. See Julie (Rousseau)
lawfulness, 166–67, 189–90
lawmaking process, 192
LD. See *Letter to D'Alembert on the Theater* (Rousseau)
learning, moral, 137–38, 151–54, 184–85
legislation, self-, 166–67
Letter to D'Alembert on the Theater (Rousseau), 76, 160–61, 210, 228
associational life in, 199–200
concept of family in, 201
emotional responses of theater-goers, 197–98
gatherings of families in, 212–13
on Geneva, 131, 173
image of dance in, 212
law and morals in, 202
lives of citizens in, 197
martial discipline in Geneva in, 211
unity in, 173
Leviathan (Hobbes), 15, 34, 38, 183
liberality, 40–41, 140
liberty. *See* freedom (liberty)
life
balance in, 210, 214
enrichment of, 23
perfect existence, 218–19
sentiment of existence, 222
social (*See* social life)
use of, 96
worthlness of, 222
Locke, John
conjugal society, 15–16
on disputes about science, 14
An Essay Concerning Human Understanding, 16, 38
on human association, 38
mentioned, 76, 95, 183
model of human community of, 16

on political life and human association, 15
on psychological mechanics of liberality, 40–41
on rational self-interest, 14–15
Rousseau's radicalization of, 20
Second Treatise of Civil Government, 15–16
on selfishness and private interest, 188
serving of interests, 17
on social and political order, 19
on social life and development, 35
Some Thoughts concerning Education, 40
theories of, 36, 39
understanding of human community, 15–16
view of relations with Hobbes of, 8
longing(s). *See also* desire(s)
accounting for, 97
of *amour-propre,* 52–53
for communion, 15
confusion caused by, 43
dangerous and illusory, 15, 38
depth of, 8
erotic, 8 (*See also* sexual passion/desire)
experience of social, 53
moral, 3–4
for perfection, 44, 52
for self-protection, 42
social, 4, 57 (*See also* friendship)
for unity, 6
love (eros), 7, 36, 95, 135, 222
as abstract phenomenon, 100
demise of, 99, 120
embodied, 119–27
enmity and hate and, 48
failure of, 136–37
friendship versus, 42, 55–59, 230 n. 7 (ch. 3)
Hobbes's interpretation of, 15
imaginary/real, 97–98
instability of, 188–89
moral, 24, 51–52, 88, 96
physical dimensions of, 119
private and public acts of, 25
recognition attached to, 49

love (eros) *(continued)*
    romantic (*See* romantic love)
    Rousseau's views of, 18, 26, 97, 129
    self- (See *amour-propre;* self-love)
    sexual (*See* sexual passion/desire)
    tension between duty and, 116
    theory of, 123
    through marriage, in *Emile*, 89–90
    transition to friendship from, 82, 101, 124, 127–29
    true, 51–52
loyalties, divided, 113–18

M. See Moral Letters (Rousseau)
malignant form of *amour-propre*, 21, 31, 47, 72–73, 144, 192
man. *See also* human condition
    alienation of politicized, 183
    changes in environment and, 182
    characteristics and creation of, 29–30, 90
    civil, 73
    fallen, 102–3
    harmony between environment and, 4, 163–64, 171
    moral experience of modern, 18
    natural, 180–81
    natural versus civil, 65, 73
    political association of, 20
    savage, 68–70
    scholarly interpretations of man and citizen in, 90–91
    value/worth of, 229 n. 1 (ch. 2)
    visage of, 229 n. 2 (ch. 2)
man's estate, 21
marriage. *See also* family
    duties of men in, 199–200
    effects of social forces on, 26–27
    in *Emile*, 87–90, 110–11
    in *Julie*, 110–11, 128–29
    Locke on, 15–16
    mate selection for, 24–25
    romantic-marital relation, 105–6
    wholeness in, 221
martyrdom, 12, 229 n. 3
mate/partner selection, 24–25
materialism, 36
mate selection, 51

maturity, social, 36
meaning, crisis of, 14–19
memory(ies), 112–13, 126–27, 129, 149–50, 212
Men and Citizens (Shklar), 10
men versus citizens, 88–89, 174
mistakes, consequences of, 184
Molière, 76
Montaigne, Michel de, 137, 230 n. 1 (ch. 6)
    "Of Friendship," 139–40
moral ambition, *amour-propre* and, 43–52, 63
moral behavior, 36–37, 43
moral capacity, 15
moral character, 89
moral confusion, 152
moral disgust, 76–82
moral ecology, 26–28
moral energy, 83
moral experience, 18
moral forces, 44
moral freedom, 166–69
moral identity, 23, 172, 183–84
morality, universal, 106, 108
moral learning, 137–38, 151–54, 184–85
Moral Letters (Rousseau), 44
moral longings, 3
moral love, 24, 51–52, 88, 96
moral perfection, desire for, 52
moral personality, 6–7, 74
moral personhood, 23, 43–44
moral persons, 213
moral-psychological theory, 85–86
moral psychology, 36, 52, 101, 136
moral universe, Rousseau's, 2–3
mortality, 66–67, 78, 82
motivation(s)
    explanations of social, 8
    for harming others, 47
    human desire (*See* desire[s])
    for lawfulness, 166–67
    love, 37
    moral and social, 63
    passions as, 45
    pity as supplemental, 139
    social, 33–35
    utility-based, 35

mutually beneficial exchange system, 15, 158–59

narcissism, 142
natural freedom, 166–67, 171, 183
natural man, 65, 73, 180–81
nature. *See also* human nature
    laws of, 181
    right of, 183
    state of, 65, 166
NE. See *Nichomachean Ethics* (Aristotle)
needs. *See also* sexual passion/desire
    affection, 12
    attachment, 71
    natural, 180
    physical, 121–22
    psychological and social, 63
    recognition, 55, 63
    for romantic love in, 117–18
    satisfaction of, 8
    social relations, 35
    unity, 63
Nichomachean Ethics (Aristotle), 139–40
Nietzsche, Friedrich, 75–76
Nouvelle Heloise; or, Julie (Rousseau). See *Julie* (Rousseau)

obedience, 79, 166–67, 175, 177, 206
"Of Anger" (Seneca), 45–46
"Of Friendship" (Montaigne), 139–40
others
    affection for, 84–85
    awareness of, 58
    boundaries between self and, 12–13
    comparing self to, 49–50, 72–73
    conflicts between self and, 90
    connection to, 24–26
    demonization of, 79–80
    distress of, 60–61
    exploitation of, 39
    happiness and suffering of, 76
    hurting, 114–15
    identification with less fortunate, 71–72
    intentionality of, 46–47
    loving others as, 105
    motivations for harming, 47
    pity for unfortunate, 72
    recognizing otherness of, 63
    self versus, 20
    sense of superiority over, 75
    sensitivity to distress of, 60–61
    sympathetic/beneficent actions toward, 106
    value of company of, 42–43
    well-being of, 20, 40, 75
    willfulness of, 48–49

partial societies, 193–95
particularized self, 213
partner/mate selection, 24–25
passion(s)
    conflict between public good and private, 172–73
    development of social, 36
    fanatical, 208
    Locke on, 38
    moralized, 76
    natural, 40
    sexual (*See* sexual passion/desire)
patriotism, 92, 106–7, 135, 193
perfect existence, 218–19
perfection/perfectionism
    drive for, 10
    in *Emile*, 104, 221
    moral, 52
    in *Moral Letters* (Rousseau), 44
    mutual perfection, 15
    pity and, 76–82, 85
    in romantic love, 99–100
    Rousseau's commitment to mutual, 12
performances, 14–19, 160, 197–98, 202, 227. *See also* entertainment
persecution, religious, 14
person, conceptions of, 14
personality
    effects of *amour-propre* on, 21
    forces affecting, 185
    influences on, 50, 1170
    moral, 6–7, 74, 80, 167
    unity of parts of, 6
personhood, 43–44
philosophist party, 78
philosophy, point of, 97
physical sexuality. *See* sexual passion/desire

pity, 3–4
  amour-propre and, 72–76
  benevolence and, 60–61
  capacity for, 84
  as catalyst for togetherness, 63
  character of, 63
  communication of, 147
  conceptual opposites in, 148
  connection to others through, 24–26, 138
  contempt and, 230 n. 4 (ch. 2)
  development of, 85
  distancing of friendship from, 143–44
  effects of, 62
  ethos of, 138–39
  friendship as modified expression of, 140
  in human condition, 69–72
  lack of, 71
  mediation of difference and, 82–85
  moral force of, 63–64
  naturalness of, 68
  negative character of, 63
  for others' ills, 74
  perversity in, 75
  perversity in experience of, 75
  role of, 144
  in romantic love, 101
  Rousseau's view of, 65
  for semblables, 142
  sexual passion and, 86
  tension between love and, 116–17
  through sympathetic identification, 79–80
Plato, 230 n. 2 (ch. 3)
  eros, 52
  perfect justice, 130
  Republic, 18
  Symposium, 95
Poland. See *Considerations on the Government of Poland* (Rousseau)
polarities, experience of, 5–6
political association(s), 4
  community, 14
  connectedness, 9
  in *Emile*, 92
  family relation to, 129–30
  as natural to man, 20
  privileging of, 9–10
political conflict, 14
political freedom, 202
political identification theory, 114, 160
political life
  character of, 28
  Hobbes on, 15, 34
  hybrid character of, 28
  Rousseau's portrayals of, 210–12
  unity in, 210
political order, 19
political philosophy and principles, 20, 161, 163
political society(ies)
  aim of, 15
  cross-pressures of, 27–28
  obstacles to stability of, 190
  problems of, 103
  psychic forces of individuals in, 213–14
political theory, 2, 114
  concern for freedom in, 165
  dynamics of Rousseau's, 213–15
  identity-constitutive element in, 169–70
  Rousseau on, 14, 28–31
political unity, 178–85, 188–90
political visions, 27, 108
politicizing functions of Rousseau's works, *Emile* and *Social Contract*, 27
positive freedom, 170–71
Preface to Narcisse (Rousseau), 62, 160
prey/predator condition, 66–67
pride, false, 64, 72, 74, 76
private affairs, 193, 195, 202, 212, 214
private associations, 31, 188, 199–200, 210
private beliefs, 78
private conscience, 209
private desires, 8, 13, 24, 183
private life, 130–33, 197
private purposes, 40–41
private self, 4, 28, 37, 174–76
private spaces, 129–30
privilege, 9–10, 167
problem resolution, in *Julie* (Rousseau), 114–15

psychic economies, 3
psychic forces, 36, 44
psychological control, 214
psychological unity, 13, 20–21
puberty, 43, 45, 73
public assemblies, 190–92
public good, 172–73
public instruction, 28–29. *See also* education

rationality, 78–79
rational performances, 14–19
rational self-interest, 14–15
reality versus expectations, 124
reason, 5
    age of, 15
    consolation through, 208
    distractions of, 128
    in *Emile*, 157, 204
    Locke on, 40–41
    love and, 100
    as master, 17
    pity and, 141
    role of, 146
    self-love and, 25
    shared, 139
    societal, 224
    Socrates' error of, 108
    understanding of, 40–41
recognition
    dangers of seeking, 49
    denial of, 47
    desire for, 9, 47
    erotic, 95
    indiscriminate seeking for, 48
    kinds of, 22
    and need for unity, 63
    sexual form of seeking, 51–52
reflection, self-, 182
Reflections on the Revolution in France (Burke), 165
relationships
    associational contexts of, 32
    boundaries in, 82
    changing the nature of, 127–29
    decay of romantic, 100
    in *Emile*, 230–31 n. 3 (ch. 6)
    expectations for, 33–34
    influence of, 43
    intrinsic value of, 35
    modern view of, 8
    natural bases for, 24–26
    purposes of kinds of, 58
    reimagining, 19–23
    in Rousseau's oeuvre, 9
religion. *See also* Christianity; church and state; Church authority and influence
    civil, 208–9
    political control over beliefs in, 209
    in *The Social Contract*, 78, 189
    social unity and, 203–9
religious conflict, 14
Republic (Plato), 18
republican societies
    Christian, 208
    freedom in, 201–2
    moral tastes and values in, 202
    politics of, 30–31, 165–66, 200
    religion in, 207
republics, character of, 198–99
respect, 49, 79, 158, 165
Reveries of a Solitary Walker, The (Rousseau), 11, 13, 217–19
rights of humanity, 94
    freedom and, 165
    public/private, 182
    of social compact, 166
    social compact and alienation of, 182–83
romantic love, 2–3, 9, 88. *See also* love (eros)
    character of, 121
    corporeal character of, 121
    dissatisfaction with, 123–24
    dynamics of, 97–102
    in *Emile* (See *Emile* [Rousseau])
    exclusive attachment in, 24
    individuation in, 101
    insufficiencies of, 125
    in *Julie* (See *Julie* [Rousseau])
    marital relation aspect of, 105–6
    nature of, 125–27
    psychology of, 25, 97, 117, 126–27
    sexuality and, 92
    tragic aspects of, 105

Index | 251

Rousseau, Jean-Jacques. *See also specific works by name*
   alienation of, 6
   amour-propre theory of, 19–23, 58
   beliefs of, about his readers, 227–28
   conception of unity, 19
   critics of, 18, 175, 223
   desires of, 13
   interpretations of, 217
   mission of, as a writer, 223–28
   paintings by, 8
   patriotism of, 193
   pessimism of, 10
   philosophic life and exile of, 11–12
   private meditations of, 61
   quest for unity by, 209–10
   radicalization of Hobbes and Locke by, 20
   on self-love, 19–26, 214
   significance of, as an author, 228
   social vision of, 10
   as thinker, 1
   understanding of psyche by, 35–36
   views of love, 18, 26, 97, 129
   worldview of, 230 n. 2 (ch. 6)
RSW. See *Reveries of a Solitary Walker, The* (Rousseau)

satisfaction
   of desires, 10
   of needs, 8
   optimizing net, 18–19
   resistance to, 10
savage man, 68–70
SC. See *Social Contract, The* (Rousseau)
"Schlegel, Margaret," 5–6
Second Discourse. See *Discourse on Inequality (Second Discourse)* (Rousseau)
Second Treatise of Civil Government (Locke), 15–16
self
   comparing others to, 49–50, 72–73
   divisions within the, 7
self-creation, 147–48
self-esteem. See *amour-propre*
self-growth, 72–76

self-interest, 8, 14–15, 19–20
selfishness, 14–15, 37–38
self-knowledge, 42–43
self-legislation, 166–67
self-loathing, 81
self-love, 192–93. See also *amour-propre*
   centrality of, 40, 210
   development of, by Hobbes and Locke, 78
   extending our, 73
   fostering of, in children, 45
   healthy, 31–32, 35, 48, 161
   importance of, 44–45
   malignant, 31–32
   pity's function in, 63, 198
   Rousseau's reimagining of, 19–26, 214
self-mastery, 165
self-preservation, 18, 22, 60
self-reflection, 182
self-respect, 49, 165
self-transcendence, 13
self-tyranny, 75
self-understanding, 8, 80–81
semblables, 142–43
Seneca, "Of Anger," 45–46
sensory experience, 23
sentiment of existence, 222
sexual identity, 55
sexual passion/desire, 3–4. *See also* love (eros)
   abstinence and, 119–21
   as connection to others, 24
   development of, 85
   discriminatory factors in, 51
   in *Emile* (See *Emile* [Rousseau])
   influence on personality of, 50
   male versus female, 118–19, 123–24
   moralized, 52
   moral love and *amour-propre* related to, 51
   as motivation in human connections, 35
   natural structure of, 56
   onset of, 96
   pity as coequal role with, 63–64, 86
   role of nascent, 52–55
   Rousseau's views of, 202

sexual/erotic attraction, 51, 95–96, 119, 128
    waning of, 102–3
sharing, 51, 105, 197
shelter, 93
silence, 8, 145, 147, 149–51
similarity of character, 139, 147–48
skeptical (tragic) characterization of argument, 2–3
slavery, 166, 208
sociability/social relations, 13
    Christianity and, 207
    desire for meaningful, 6
    development of, 217
    effect on human ends of, 8
    halfway, 14
    as natural to man, 20
    reasons for needs for, 35
    Rousseau's understanding of, 37
    sexuality and, 52–55
    value of company of others, 42–43
social change, 226
social compact, 166, 169–70, 182–83, 185, 192–93
Social Contract, The (Rousseau), 29, 89, 108, 210
    alienated self-centeredness in, 28, 178
    analysis of civil religion in, 189
    Christianity in, 205, 207–9
    citizenship in, 177
    civil religion in, 78
    dividedness in, 171–72
    equal distribution of rights and obligations in, 192
    freedom in, 166, 169
    interpretations of, 194–95
    limits of sovereign power in, 182–83
    marriage and friendship models in, 197
    moral teachers in, 184–85
    political life in, 170
    political program of, 92, 134
    principles of political right in, 164–65
    private desire/common good in, 193–94
    public assemblies in, 190–91
    Rousseau's domestic and political visions in, 27
    social and moral conditions for humans in, 182–84
    union of church and state in, 178
social institutions, 214
    assessing, 163
    character of, 182
    connection between good citizens and good, 191
    harmony of, 185–86
    identity-constitutive character of, 182
social issues
    autonomy, 167, 169–70
    connectedness, 40
    development of social passions, 36
    harmony, 13, 28
    indeterminacy and feeling, 40–43
    interdependence, 13
    motivation, 24, 64
    need for recognition, 36–39, 55
    perils of social incorporation, 30, 102–3
    protection from destructive forces, 170
    restructuring of social forces, 26–27
    Rousseau on social organization, 6–7
    social anxiety, 59
    social consciousness in *Emile*, 29–30
    social phenomena, 1
    social sentiment, 35, 53
    solution to problems of, 8
    stability, 190–91
socialization, effects of, 7
social life, 2–3, 9, 20, 76–77
social mixing of genders, 200
social order, 19
social sentiment, 222
social theory
    aims and motivations of, 19
    character of, 10
    concern for freedom in, 165
    pessimistic character of, 10
social unity, 203–9, 211
societal good, 14, 136, 198
    conflict between private passion and, 172–73
    devotion to, 193
    harmful, 207
    in *Julie* and *Emile*, 162

societies, partial, 193–95
society, 14–16, 69–72, 217–18
Socinianism, 203–4
Socrates, 108, 188, 210
solitude/solitary life, 37, 217–19
Some Thoughts concerning Education (Locke), 40
soul, development of, 72–73
sovereignty
    allegiance to/authority of, 178, 206
    citizens' autonomous self and, 165, 195
    citizen's role in, 181
    control over religion by, 206–7
    description of, 169
    imposition on subjects by, 177
    limits of, 181–83, 213–14
    purpose and capacity of, 188
    religious forms of social control under, 208–9
    role in society of, 189–90
    Rousseau's theory of, 213
Sparta, as model for assembly, 199
spiritual authority/power, 186, 206
state of nature, 65–69, 166, 180–81
state of weakness, 65–69
submission to the state, 165–66
suffering
    commiseration for, 74
    connection between friendship and, 145
    from frustration of desires, 63
    identification with others', 142
    of parents, in *Julie*, 116–17
    Rousseauan pity for, 76
Summun Bonum, 15–16
sympathetic associations, 26, 71, 148–49
sympathetic identification, 79–80
sympathy
    attenuated, 82–85
    in friendship, 26
    importance of, 61
    lack of, 83
    reinforcement of, 49
Symposium (Plato), 95

temporal powers, 186
tension. *See also* conflict
    between duty and love, 116
    between love and pity, 116–17
    between private passion and public good, 172–73, 198
    sexual, 118
    between social and political worlds, 214–15
    between social passions, 4
theater performances, 160–61, 197–98, 210–11
theories
    associational life, 217
    domestic theory, 188–89
    ecological systems theory, 163–64
    education, 224
    friendship theory, 86, 138, 141–42, 145–49, 159–61
    Hobbes's, 34, 36, 39
    human relations (*See* human relations theory)
    of love, 123
    moral-psychological, 85–86
    political identification theory, 114, 160
    psychological, 110–11
    Rousseau's theory of *amour-propre*, 21–22, 58
    social (*See* social theory)
    of sovereignty, 213
tragedy, 102–3, 217–23
tragic (skeptical) characterization of argument, 2–3
tragic interpretations of Rousseau, 217, 223–28
transcendence, over humanity, 44
trust/distrust, 16, 83, 111, 129, 151, 158, 163, 190
"Two Concepts of Liberty" (Berlin), 165
two minds concept, 17

unhappiness, 72, 83
unity, 2–3, 12–13
    of church and state, 178, 181, 206
    feelings of, 75
    in freedom, 170–77
    identity in, 172
    longing for, 6
    of the moral person, 175

natural, 4
political, 178–85, 188–90
in political society, 185
as precondition for healthy life, 19
psychological, 13, 20–21
Rousseau's conception of, 19
Rousseau's quest for, 209–10
social, 203–9
through associational life, 13
through citizenship, 92
wholeness versus, 170–71
universal morality, 106, 108
utopian visions, 3, 19

values conflicts, 175
vanity. See *amour-propre*
Vernes, Jacob, 223–24
virtue(s), 7
acquisition of, 89
basis for social, 25–26, 60–61
capacity for civic, 15
as consolation for disappointment, 222–23
cruel, 176
energy that produces, 78–79
for erotic recognition and attraction, 95
friendship, 151–54
in *Letter to D'Alembert on the Theater*, 198
pity's effect on, 80
pursuit of, 139
Rousseau's disregard or, 18
search for, 155
sources of, 63
Voltaire, François, 40, 44, 77, 211, 223–24
vulnerability. See also weakness
awareness of, 69–70, 72
of Christian societies, 207
effects of, 62, 64

in *Emile*, 230 n. 4 (ch. 2)
forms of, 66
invulnerability, 46
in *Julie*, 81, 153
to nature's dangers, 68
Rousseau's characterization of, 85
sense of pity as, 85
shared, 71, 142

wants. See desire(s)
Warburton, William, 231 n. 3 (ch. 8)
Warens, Mme de, 12
weakness. See also vulnerability
in *Emile*, 70–72
in *Julie*, 81–82
sense of pity as, 85
signs of, 66
state of, 65–69
well-being
attraction to factors in, 45
conditions destructive to, 172
Hobbes on, 60
of members of society, 131
of others, 20, 40, 75
wholeness. See also unity
as alternative to social life, 220
in associational contexts, 137
development of, 88
Emile's quest for, 221
freedom as, 170–71
in human relations theory, 11–13
individual, 6, 179
Rousseau's clarification of, 136
social conflicts that damage, 187–88
unity versus, 170–71
will, 45–46, 190
willfulness of others, 47–49
Will to action, 39

Xenocrates, 230 n. 2 (ch. 3)

www.ingramcontent.com/pod-product-compliance
Lightning Source LLC
Chambersburg PA
CBHW021940290426
44108CB00012B/905